The editor said
"If you don't
write sex scenes
then you're
through."

I said,
"Okay, then
I'm through."

For over 21 years, author Al Lacy wrote for leading publishers Bantam, Dell and Doubleday, using his gifts as a storyteller to write books that would financially support his greatest passion: traveling around the country as an evangelist, leading people to salvation in Christ.

With 47 best-selling novels written under pseudonyms, Al's success as an author was clear. But when faced with pressure to add sex and violence to his books, he refused—choosing instead to take a stand for his beliefs.

That decision led one of the country's best Western and historical fiction authors to the Christian bookseller's market, where he has launched the exciting new *Battles of Destiny* Civil War series and *The Journeys of the Stranger* with Multnomah Books.

Here is Al Lacy's incredible story, told in his own inspiring words.

Q: How did you get started as an author?

AL: It all goes back to my call to preach. I pastored for several years before I went into full-time evangelism. The church I pastored had fantastic growth, and I didn't want to leave it. But it's hard to explain how God works. It's like being in love…you can't really explain it, but you know it's there.

I didn't want to be gone for weeks on end like an evangelist has to do. But God made it so plain. I've been doing preaching in churches around the country for 21 years now.

The problem is, there are a lot of expenses in evangelism that I never dreamed of. Some of the small churches can't pay anything, but I go anyway.

> It's hard to explain how God works. It's like being in love… you can't really explain it, but you know it's there.

I feel that I should do that—help the young ones get on their feet and go. But that means I wasn't putting anything away for retirement.

I thought,

"What else can I do and travel at the same time?" Then I was inspired by my wife. She said, "Well, you've read Westerns and historical books all of your life. You've talked about writing. Why don't you try writing one?" So I sat down and I wrote a Western novel called *Dead Man's Noose*.

Q: How did you first get published?

AL: I sent *Dead Man's Noose* to a few publishers. Most didn't even answer me. But one wrote back and said, "You're going about this all wrong. You have to have an agent."

So I prayed about that. I said, "Lord, I need the right agent." Then one day when I was flying, I read in the back of a magazine about an agent who was trying to find new writers. I contacted him, he read *Dead Man's Noose*, and he loved it. We signed a contract, and six weeks later, the book was sold.

I wrote several books for that publisher. Then my first editor left, and the new editor said, "I love your work. Your stories are exciting and captivat-ing. But I want some sex scenes in here."

I told him that I don't write sex scenes. He said, "If you don't, then you're through. I said, "Okay, then I'm through."

He probably thought I would give in. But I will not give in. I have standards. They are based on the Bible, and I won't break them.

After that, I worked for other publishers. But the problem continued over the years. I would get a new editor, and my book would come out with a few cuss words in it. I would call them and say, "Hey, I didn't put those words in there. I don't want that kind of language in there." Several books would go by, and everything would be fine. And then a new editor would come along, and—ZAP—out would come another.

I will not give in. I have standards. They are based on the Bible, and I won't break them.

It broke my heart that my publishing career seemed to be coming to an end, but I wasn't going to bend. God blessed me in that. Just a year ago, a pastor friend asked me, "Have you ever thought about writing for a Christian publisher?" He introduced me to Questar Publishers and Multnomah Books. And so the story goes…

Q: How do you find the time to write?

AL: The fiction series, traveling, preparing for sermons…it just takes a lot of discipline. And I don't watch a lot of television. Football season is rough on me. I love football. Writing takes a little midnight oil some times. But when you love it like I do, it's easy. I love to create stories, almost as much as I love to preach. I am amazed that I get paid to do the two things I love to do the most: preach and write. What a blessing!

> # Football season is rough on me. I love football.

Al Lacy *is the author of over fifty titles with over 2.8 million copies in print. He lives in Littleton, Colorado, with his wife JoAnna when he's not on the road "winning souls."*

BELOVED ENEMY

AL LACY

BELOVED ENEMY
© 1994 by Al Lacy
published by Multnomah Books
a part of the Questar publishing family

Edited by Rodney L. Morris
Cover design by David Uttley
Cover illustration by Phil Boatwright

International Standard Book Number: 0-88070-626-0

Printed in the United States of America.

For information:

Questar Publishers, Inc.
Post Office Box 1720
Sisters, Oregon 97759

94 95 96 97 98 99 00 01 02—10 9 8 7 6 5 4 3 2 1

PREFACE

As a long-time Civil War buff, I have read volume after volume on this dynamic period in American history. The more I read, the more fascinated I become with its human drama.

Over the years I have read with interest about the other wars our country has been involved in—the Revolutionary War, the Mexican-American War, World Wars I and II, Korea, Vietnam, and Desert Storm. World War II is of special interest because I was a young (*very* young, you understand) and impressionable child during those four years, and it touched me deeply. But the Civil War is most captivating to me, I believe, because it was different than all the others in one striking way. Instead of United States servicemen in mortal combat against foreign foes, it was *Americans* fighting *Americans*.

The blood shed in villages and hamlets, cities and towns, in forests and fields, pastures and meadows, rivers and seas flowed from the veins of men, women, and children same homeland. It was a nation divided under two flags—the United States of America and the Confederate States of America.

Since 1980 I have written and sold an even fifty historical novels. You hold number fifty in your hands. As I am ever alert for sermon ideas and illustrations that will keep my preaching fresh, interesting, and productive for the glory of my Saviour. As a novelist, I am ever alert for story ideas that will keep my writing in demand by my publisher and my readers. In reading the historical accounts of the Civil War battles, campaigns, and combat encounters, my mind is stimulated with ideas for stories that will make for pleasurable, exciting, and educational reading.

As in the first two books of this "Battles of Destiny" series, I have endeavored to weave the story in such a manner as to bring a smile once in a while, put a lump in your throat periodically, and push you to the edge of your seat at times. If I am successful in even two out of three, it will have been worth the effort.

PROLOGUE

✦

In the wake of the Confederate assault against Fort Sumter on April 12, 1861, both the North and the South rushed to prepare for war. When President Abraham Lincoln called for volunteers to put down the "rebellion" on April 15, the act propelled the wavering Southern states of Virginia, North Carolina, and Tennessee into the new Confederacy.

A distinctive self-confidence inspired both sides as their hale and hearty citizens-turned-soldiers began their military training. In the South, the Rebels convinced themselves that the Yankees would never go to war. Having been soundly beaten at Fort Sumter, they would not have the courage for real battle. The Rebels believed that they were physically, mentally, and spiritually superior to the Northerners, and that success in establishing a new and free nation was foreordained for them by God Himself.

Meanwhile, north of the Mason-Dixon line, Yankee soldiers felt a keen resolve to avenge the attack on Fort Sumter, and at the same time an absolute conviction that the Rebels were nothing more than blustering, blundering "sod-buster" soldiers. With one swift campaign the Southern rebellion against the Union would be put down for good.

For fifty years the problems of states' rights and slavery had been fomenting sectional hostility between Northern and Southern states. At long last, the waiting was over. The war had finally come.

Yet the war that began with such impact at Charleston Harbor proceeded only by fits and starts during the weeks that followed. There were a couple of small engagements or skirmishes, mostly of a tentative nature. The first was at Philippi, Virginia (now West Virginia), on June 3, and the second was at Big Bethel, Virginia, on June 10. The first real battle took place at Rich Mountain in western Virginia, also now in West Virginia, on July 11 (see *A Promise Unbroken* from the "Battles of Destiny" series).

The Confederates had been put on the run at Philippi, and had been beaten at Rich Mountain, but having defeated the Yankees at Big Bethel, they were still confident they could drive the Northerners across the Mason-Dixon line for good if they engaged them in a full-scale battle.

The Yankees, however, exultant over their victories at Philippi and Rich Mountain, were gearing up to make a big thrust on the Confederate capital at Richmond, Virginia, and end the whole thing in a hurry. On Sunday, June 30, 1861, the *New York Daily Tribune* came out with bold headlines that screamed:

THE NATION'S WAR CRY!

Forward to Richmond! Forward to Richmond!
The Rebel Congress must not be allowed to meet there on
the 20th of July! BY THAT DATE THE PLACE MUST
BE HELD BY THE NATIONAL ARMY!

In response to this threat, President Jefferson Davis sent twenty thousand Confederate troops to Manassas Junction where the Orange and Alexandria Railroads met. To Davis, this appeared to be the best route for the Federal army to approach Richmond. The Confederates were commanded by their national hero, who had captured Fort

Sumter in April. He was Brigadier General Pierre G.T. Beauregard. The general and his troops were camped along a meandering stream known as Bull Run Creek.

Meanwhile, in Washington, D.C., the Federals made preparations for their Richmond offensive under Major General Irvin McDowell. President Lincoln would give him thirty-five thousand men to do the job. The rest of the Union army would camp around Washington to protect it in case of some sneak attack by the Rebels. Lincoln and McDowell, however, were unknowingly at a disadvantage. When the split came between the North and the South, certain individuals employed in strategic offices in the U.S. capitol building kept their jobs though secretly they were loyal to the South.

These spies became a crack intelligence unit, gathering classified military information that would prove invaluable to the Confederacy. The information was carried to the Confederates in Virginia by a network of young female spies under the direction of widow Rose O'Neal Greenhow, an attractive forty-year-old Washington socialite whose loyalty was with the Confederacy.

From the young women who charmed their way past Union lines on various pretenses for entering Virginia, General Beauregard learned the size of the Union army and on what date the assault was planned. Quickly he dispatched a message to President Jefferson in Richmond and received 12,500 additional troops prior to the Union attack.

Since the Union army had proven itself formidable over their enemies at Rich Mountain, the Northerners had no doubt that the battle at Bull Run Creek would result in victory over the Rebels. Certain that the men-in-blue would quickly vanquish the gray-clad Southerners, several Washington politicians took their families to the hills overlooking Manassas Junction to watch the show. Many other Washingtonians went along, taking their children and carrying picnic baskets. It was to be a day of rejoicing and celebration as General McDowell and his army vanquished what the civilians *and* the military thought was a much smaller army of "blundering plow-boys." The Civil War would be over almost before it got started.

There is nothing in military history quite like the story of the first conflict at Bull Run. It was the battle where some things went wrong for the Rebels and *everything* went wrong for the Yankees. The absolute rout of the Union army by the Southern "plow-boys" jolted Northerners into reality. The Northern dream of a short and glorious end to the war was shattered in one day. After Bull Run, the Federal government and its people knew the Civil War was going to be a long haul.

Here is my version of the Battle of First Bull Run.

CHAPTER ONE

★

A cool and quiet resolve filled him as he descended the stairs of Springfield's Illinois Hotel, shouldering into his overcoat. Feeling the weight of the two revolvers in his shoulder holsters, he approached the desk, hat-in-hand.

The slender, middle-aged clerk looked down at the small uniformed man, smiled and said, "Good morning, Colonel."

Laying his hat on the counter and pulling his wallet from his hip pocket, Colonel Elmer Ellsworth smiled in return. "Good morning."

"So this is the day, eh?" remarked the clerk.

Ellsworth's dark eyes ran to the calendar that hung on the wall behind the desk. Bold letters displayed the date: February 11, 1861.

Nodding, he said, "This is the day. If you'll tally up my bill, I'll be on my way."

"There's nothing to tally, Colonel."

"Pardon me?"

His smile broadening, the clerk replied, "You met our manager, Mr. Spalding, last week, I believe."

"Yes. Very cordial man, I might say."

"Well, Mr. Spalding left Springfield for Chicago on business yesterday, but before he left, he told me that your bill was on the house. There'll be no charge."

"But I've been here for nearly two weeks. It really isn't right that I should—"

"Mr. Spalding said to tell you that what you're doing to protect Mr. Lincoln is pay enough to more than cover your bill, Colonel. We love Congressman Lincoln—or I should say *President-elect* Lincoln. With all the threats that have been voiced against him, we are most grateful that he has someone like you looking out for him."

"I appreciate that, sir," smiled Ellsworth. "I assure you, and you can assure Mr. Spalding, that I am determined to get Mr. Lincoln to Washington safely. I've hired Allan Pinkerton and a host of his detectives to provide additional protection along the way, and I've laid out a plan in coalition with General Winfield Scott for military protection in addition to the Pinkerton men on Inauguration Day. We are not taking the Secessionists' threats of assassination lightly."

"I'm glad," nodded the clerk. "I understand, though, from what I've read in the newspapers, that Mr. Lincoln has not taken the threats seriously. Is this true?"

"I'm afraid so."

"Has he approved of all this protection you are providing?"

"He balked when I first told him what I had in mind, but Mrs. Lincoln put the pressure on him. That's all it took. When he saw the tears in her eyes, he gave in."

"God bless Mrs. Lincoln," said the clerk.

Ellsworth returned his wallet to its place and picked up his hat. "You be sure to thank Mr. Spalding for me."

"I will do that, Colonel. God speed. We need Mr. Lincoln in the White House to pull this nation together."

"Yes, we do," agreed Ellsworth. "I believe when the Secessionists hear his Inauguration Address and understand his intentions for this country's future, they just might take another look at the situation."

"I certainly hope so," said the clerk.

"And even if they don't, Mr. Lincoln is the man to lead us if civil war comes."

The clerk shook his head sadly. "Oh, I hope that doesn't happen, Colonel. I hope that doesn't happen."

"So do I. But if it does, I'm glad Mr. Lincoln will be at the helm."

Donning his hat, Ellsworth nodded toward the clerk and headed for the door. When he stepped outside, the cold wind knifed through his coat all the way to his bones. He pulled up his collar and walked toward the carriage that awaited him.

It was dawn, but the heavy gray clouds that covered the sky allowed little light. Snow was falling and the driving wind gusted it along the street. Bending his head against the wind, Ellsworth looked up at the driver, wrapped in a blanket, and asked, "You haven't been waiting long, have you, Charles?"

"No, sir. Just a few minutes."

"I assume the bell boy brought my luggage to you."

"Yes, sir. You'll find it inside."

Climbing in behind the driver's seat, Ellsworth said, "Let's go. I have to have the Lincolns at the depot by seven thirty."

As the carriage pulled away from the hotel and headed down the snow-covered street, Ellsworth brushed snow from his hat and coat and settled back for the ride across the city to the Lincoln home.

Colonel Elmer Ellsworth, who stood barely over five-feet-five and weighed 135 pounds, had earned his rank two years previously at the unheard-of age of twenty-two. His name was a synonym for patriotism to millions of Northerners. In a time when virtually every town in the northeast sponsored its own volunteer militia, the diminutive colonel was America's foremost parade-ground soldier and, in the popular imagination, the army's most promising military talent.

Stationed in Utica, New York, Ellsworth gained popularity as commander of the U.S. Zouave Cadets, whom he had transformed from a lackadaisical group of Northern soldiers into the national-champion drill team. He modeled his unit after the French Zouaves of Crimean War fame, dressing his men in bright-colored baggy-trousered uniforms. He developed his own variations of the Zouave drill, featuring hundreds of maneuvers with musket and bayonet.

In the summer of 1860—with the threat of civil war in the air—Ellsworth toured twenty cities in the northeast, challenging men to sign up in the U.S. army. He became a celebrity overnight. Newspaper and magazine writers lionized him, women idolized him, and politicians sought his friendship.

Ellsworth had followed Abe Lincoln's political career from a distance and became a great admirer. It was while demonstrating his drill team at Springfield in June of 1860 that they met. Lincoln took an instant liking to the brilliant young colonel and invited him to his home. Mrs. Lincoln and their two sons, Willie and Tad—ten and eight at that time—also were drawn to Ellsworth's warm and bright personality. When summer was over and the drilling demonstrations ceased, the youthful Zouave leader was invited back to the Lincoln home.

He returned on several occasions and was always welcomed, especially by the Lincoln boys because he would never fail to play "war" with them. Ellsworth was so close to Willie and Tad that he caught the measles from them. He was especially drawn to bright-eyed Tad, whom he called, "Mr. Personality."

Because of his love for Abraham Lincoln, Ellsworth campaigned for him in the 1860 election. Lincoln acknowledged that the "little colonel" had a great deal to do with his winning the election.

When the president-elect gave in to Ellsworth's protection plan, the young colonel also announced that he would be Lincoln's personal bodyguard on the trip from Springfield to Washington. Knowing that argument would be useless, Lincoln had quietly accepted.

The icy wind had eased some as the carriage pulled up in front of the huge two-story house, but snow was still falling. Two larger carriages were there, which would carry the six Pinkerton men and the Lincoln family's luggage to the depot.

It was a comfort to Ellsworth to see the grim-faced detectives huddled on the front porch. Heads turtled into their coat collars, they nodded at the young colonel as he mounted the snow-crusted steps. Even as Ellsworth, each man wore two revolvers in shoulder holsters.

"Good morning, gentlemen," Ellsworth said. "Are they about ready?"

"Yes, sir," answered the detective in charge. "Miss Winters just stuck her head out to say that it would be about ten minutes."

Before Ellsworth could knock, the door came open and a happy, childish voice exclaimed, "Uncle Elmer!"

"Hello, Tad!" laughed Ellsworth as the boy wrapped his arms around his neck.

Moving inside with the nine-year-old in his arms, Ellsworth closed the door just in time to brace himself for eleven-year-old Willie, who dashed up and hugged him.

Mary Todd Lincoln entered the vestibule, smiled and said, "Elmer, those boys will rub the hide off you."

The small man laughed. "Can't happen, ma'am. I'm a tough-hided Zouave, remember?"

Mrs. Lincoln laughed also, then said, "Boys, get your coats on."

Letting go of their adopted uncle, Willie and Tad hurried to a nearby closet.

The boys' governess, Patricia Winters, appeared at the top of the staircase, carrying her coat and hat. At twenty-two, Patricia was yet unattached. She liked the handsome colonel, but because she stood an inch taller, had never shown anything more than friendship. Leaning against the railing, she smiled, "Good morning, Colonel."

"And good morning to you," Ellsworth responded, sweeping off his hat and making a bow.

"Mrs. Lincoln, is there anything up here you were planning to take along?" Patricia asked.

Smiling up at the governess, Mary said, "No, honey. Everything I wanted to take is already in the suitcases and trunks."

"How about our toys?" Tad butted in while slipping into his coat.

"They're all packed," replied Mary.

"Don't worry about that, Tad," spoke up Ellsworth. "I brought something that'll keep you boys busy on the train."

"What is it?" Tad asked, eyes wide.

"You'll see," chuckled the colonel.

At the same time Patricia reached the bottom of the staircase, the president-elect appeared, carrying a valise, and started down the stairs.

"Good morning, sir," said Ellsworth.

A smile broke on Lincoln's craggy face. "Good morning, Elmer. I saw from my window that you've got your army here."

"That's right, sir. Can't be too careful with all the threats that have been made."

"Just political claptrap, my boy."

Lincoln had a warmth about him that made it a pleasure to be in his presence. His dark eyes glowed and sparkled, and though he was anything but handsome, the fire of his genius played on every feature. He had a keen sense of humor and a humble sincerity about him, yet he was obviously a man of rare power and magnetic influence. He was a man of deep moral convictions and possessed the backbone to stick by them. He had a deep resonant voice and eloquent command of the

English language. His speech was edged with a slight Kentucky-Southern accent, and whether hearing him in personal conversation or from a speaker's platform, people found him captivating.

Ellsworth made no reply to Lincoln's "political claptrap" comment. They had been over the subject many times. Elmer was just glad Mrs. Lincoln had won out.

As the tall Kentuckian was putting on his overcoat and top hat, he said, "Patricia, I assume all the luggage is in the carriages."

"Yes, sir," replied the governess, tying a scarf around Tad's neck. "Everything is ready."

Mary had her hat on and her husband helped her into her coat. Bending down, he kissed her cheek and said, "Well, Mrs. Lincoln, I guess we're ready to go."

Mary ran her gaze over the house and, fighting tears, replied, "Yes, Mr. Lincoln, I guess we are."

Leaving her Springfield, Illinois, house was not easy for Mary Lincoln. She was a sentimental person and had a close attachment to the place. Her husband had hired a caretaker to watch over their home until the Lincoln family returned, whenever that might be. Mary was proud of her husband and looked forward to living in the White House. But she knew her stay there would not be permanent; she would keep a close attachment to her home in Springfield.

Patricia placed stockingcaps on both boys and pulled them down over their ears. Elmer helped her into her coat.

Tad moved close and said, "You got *two* guns on, don't you, Uncle Elmer. I felt 'em when we hugged."

"Yes, I do. I'm making sure your daddy gets to Washington safely."

When they stepped out onto the porch, both boys eyed the Pinkerton detectives. It was impetuous Tad who looked them over and said, "How many guns you guys carryin? Uncle Elmer's got two under his coat!"

"Tad!" came his father's sharp voice. "That's enough."

The boy knew when his father spoke, he was to obey. He looked up at Ellsworth and asked, "Can Willie and me ride with you, Uncle Elmer?"

"That's the way I planned it," grinned the colonel. "You and Willie head for that smaller carriage."

Snow was still falling as the train chugged out of Springfield at eight o'clock. Lincoln's private coach was furnished with overstuffed chairs and sofas, leaving an open area in the center. The six Pinkerton men placed themselves strategically with two by the doors at each end, and a man at the windows midway on both sides. When porters brought breakfast trays, they were not allowed inside. Pinkerton agents took the trays at the door.

When breakfast was over and the trays and dishes were stacked on a counter in one corner, Tad said to Ellsworth, "Uncle Elmer, you said you brought something with you to keep me and Willie busy on the train. It must be somethin' to play with. Can we see it, now?"

"Tad," came the level voice of the governess, who sat next to Ellsworth on a sofa. "It's *Willie* and *me*."

"I know," he sighed. "I jus' forgot. But I said it right on the porch this morning when I asked Uncle Elmer if Willie and me could ride with him in the carriage."

The Lincolns were sitting together on another sofa, looking on with pleasure. They appreciated the effort Patricia took to teach the boys correct English.

"Willie and *I*," said Patricia, trying to look stern.

"Huh?" said Tad, releasing an infectious smile. "*You* didn't ride with Uncle Elmer. Willie and *I* did!"

Patricia could hold it no longer. She broke into a laugh and said, "You little scamp! You know how to say it. You're just giving me a hard time, aren't you?"

"Me?" said Tad innocently, pointing to his chest.

The governess laughed again, left her seat, and threw her arms around the boy. While Tad hugged her back, he said, "I love you, Miss Patricia."

"I love you, too, you little scamp."

A Pinkerton agent seated at a window grinned at the Lincolns and said, "Quite a charmer, isn't he?"

The president-elect chuckled, rubbed his stubbled chin, and said, "Yes, he is. He could charm his way into Buckingham Palace and talk Queen Victoria out of her crown. He's especially successful with the ladies."

"It's because he's such a deceiver," spoke up Willie, who stood nearby. "Mom let's him get away with all kinds of things, and so does Miss Patricia."

"No, sir!" retorted Tad defensively. "I ain't no deceiver!"

"Tad!" cut in Patricia. "*Ain't* isn't in the dictionary."

"It will be when I write one."

"It'll be *dumb* if you write one," said Willie.

"Oh, yeah?" snapped the younger brother. "Well, if you wrote one—"

"Wait a minute!" blurted Ellsworth. "Before we get a fight started, let me show you what I brought."

Rising from the sofa, the colonel picked up a satchel he had carried aboard and opened it. He pulled out a cloth sack and handed it to Willie. "There you go, boys. Take a look inside."

Willie loosened the draw string on the sack's neck and said, "Oh, boy! Soldiers!"

As Willie spilled the wooden soldiers onto the floor, Tad said excitedly, "C'mon, Uncle Elmer! Play war with us!"

The hours passed as Abraham Lincoln worked on his inaugural speech at a small desk near the rear of the car. Mary and Patricia sat on a sofa together talking. The Pinkerton men stayed ready and alert for any sign of trouble. And Elmer Ellsworth played war on the floor of the rocking, swaying coach with his favorite "nephews."

When the train pulled in and rolled to a stop at the Philadelphia railroad station that evening, Allan Pinkerton himself boarded the train with twenty-two more of his men. Pinkerton chatted with Lincoln, explaining that he was leaving nothing to chance. He had planted agents along the rail bed all the way to Washington. He had arranged a series of lantern signals to be used by these agents against the possibility of track sabotage. There were more men waiting at the station in the nation's capital. In all, Pinkerton had employed over two hundred agents to see that the president-elect arrived safely in Washington.

Arriving without incident in Washington at six o'clock on the morning of February 12, the Lincolns, along with Patricia Winters and Colonel Elmer Ellsworth, were accompanied to the Willard Hotel by Allan Pinkerton and an army of his agents. Pinkerton and a number of his staff would stay in Washington and be a part of Lincoln's phalanx of protection until Inauguration Day was over.

At breakfast in the presidential suite, Lincoln eyed his boys with admiration, thinking how much they looked alike. Their facial features were very similar, as were their ears, which were overly large like his own. Both boys had mouse-brown hair and hazel eyes.

In personality, the brothers were vastly different. Where Willie was quiet, reserved, and laid back, Tad was high-spirited, boisterous, and aggressive. There was often a fun-loving devil-may-care look in Tad's eyes that had never appeared in those of his brother. Abraham Lincoln loved them both.

As Lincoln mopped gravy across his plate with a biscuit, he set his quiet eyes on Ellsworth and said, "Elmer, I want to thank you for everything you've done to see me safely here. It has taken valuable time from your work with the Zouaves. I really think you should return to

New York, now, and catch up on lost time."

"I can't argue with you, sir. My work with the Zouaves is important in view of what's boiling in the South. We need to be ready for combat if war comes. I'd like to be here for the inauguration, but taking all things into consideration, I think I should get back to camp. As far as protection is concerned, you'll have plenty of that."

In view of the secession by the Southern states and the strong possibility of civil war, Ellsworth had gone to New York City a few weeks earlier and recruited a regiment of tough volunteers from the New York City Fire Department. He had set up a training camp near Utica, upstate some 250 miles. The colonel called his new regiment the New York Fire Zouaves.

"Thanks to you, I'll have plenty of protection," smiled Lincoln. He took a sip of steaming coffee, then said, "I'm going to work hard to avoid war, Elmer, and I hope I'll be successful. But just in case I'm not, the North must be prepared to fight. I appreciate what you're doing toward that most vital preparation."

After breakfast, Colonel Ellsworth hugged his "nephews," bid the Lincolns and Patricia good-bye, and took a carriage to the railroad station where he caught a train for New York.

Abraham Lincoln spent the next several days receiving an almost uninterrupted stream of visitors, newspaper reporters, and friends in his hotel suite. His most important visitor was President James Buchanan, who came by during the last week of February to work out plans for the day of inauguration.

In the precious private moments allotted him, Lincoln worked hard writing and revising his inaugural speech.

On the cloudy and brisk morning of March 4, the president-elect rode with President Buchanan in an open barouche from his hotel to the Capitol. Mary, the boys, and Patricia followed in a second carriage. Allan Pinkerton's agents and U.S. troops were everywhere along the route. Squads of sharpshooters were stationed on the roofs along Pennsylvania Avenue. Lincoln, his family, the governess, and Buchanan entered the Capitol through hedges of U.S. marines, alert and armed to the teeth.

A crowd, much larger than expected, was gathering on the east side of the Capitol where a platform had been built out from the steps to the eastern portico, with benches for distinguished guests on three sides.

At precisely one o'clock, Mrs. Lincoln, her sons, and their governess were ushered out of the Capitol onto the platform and seated on a bench near the lectern. U.S. Marines and Pinkerton men surrounded the platform, eyes scanning the crowd for would-be assassins.

Moments later, President James Buchanan appeared with the president-elect at his side. Buchanan, a large, heavy, awkward man, short compared to Lincoln, had to take two steps for one of Lincoln's to keep up.

Lincoln wore his black top hat, a three-piece black suit, and carried a huge ebony cane with a gold head the size of an egg. Cheers arose from the crowd as he reached the platform. He was a bit pale, but the only discomfort he showed was when he couldn't decide what to do with his hat and cane.

For a moment, he stood there holding cane in one hand and hat in the other, looking around. Finally, he stood the cane in a corner of the railing, but could not find a place for the hat. Senator Stephen A. Douglas, who had defeated Lincoln in his bid for a senate seat in 1858, was on the platform. Douglas stepped up and offered to take the hat. Lincoln smiled and handed it to him. Douglas returned to his seat and held the hat in his lap.

Chief Justice Roger B. Taney approached Lincoln, showed him a seat, then stepped to the lectern. Lincoln glanced at his family. Mary gave him a teary smile and the boys waved.

After a few introductory words, Taney called for the president-elect to come to the podium. Lincoln stood, nodded at Mary, and she hurried to him, taking his arm. When Lincoln moved onto the podium, Mary stayed close, lifting her adoring eyes to his craggy face.

While the crowd watched and listened intently, Abraham Lincoln laid his left hand on a large Bible, raised his right, and took the oath of office. After a prayer by the congressional chaplain, Mary Todd Lincoln returned to her seat. Chief Justice Taney introduced the country's new president to the crowd and sat down.

As Lincoln stepped up to the lectern and laid out his notes, there were loud cheers, mixed with a few boos and hisses. The eyes of the Marines and Pinkerton agents noted the areas of adversity and watched them carefully.

As the nation's sixteenth president began speaking, his nerves were taut and his voice slightly constricted. It took only a few minutes for him to overcome the tension, and soon he was waxing eloquent. In his moving address, Lincoln insisted that the Union was perpetual and that the secession by the Southern states was unconstitutional. He made it clear that the Federal government was determined to maintain its authority and would not bend to the whims or demands of the law-breaking Confederacy. After pointing out the physical impossibility of separation between Americans who occupied the same land, he urged the Southern people to return to their place in the American household.

Pointedly addressing the people of the South, he said, "If it were admitted that you who are dissatisfied hold the right side in the dispute, there is still no single good reason for precipitate action. Intelligence, patriotism, Christianity, and a firm reliance on Him who has never yet forsaken this favored land, are still competent to adjust in the best way all our present difficulty."

Still directing his words to the Southerners, Lincoln said, "In your hands, my dissatisfied fellow countrymen, and not in mine, is the momentous issue of civil war. The government will not assail you. You can have no conflict without being yourselves the aggressors. You have no oath registered in heaven to destroy the government, while I have the most solemn one to preserve, protect, and defend it.

"I am loathe to close. We are not enemies, but friends. We must not be enemies. Though passion may have strained, it must not break our bonds of affection. The mystic cords of memory, stretching from every battlefield and patriot grave to every living heart and hearthstone all over this broad land, will yet swell the chorus of the Union when again touched, as surely they will be, by the better angels of our nature."

Lincoln picked up his notes and took two steps backward. There was some applause, but it lacked enthusiasm, and quickly faded.

Amid a few cheers and some well-wishers shouting encouragement to the new president, Abraham Lincoln, his family, and the governess were escorted from the Capitol grounds by James Buchanan and a host of bodyguards. A short while later, Buchanan led them into the White House, gave them a tour, then climbed in a private carriage and bid them a polite farewell.

The Lincoln family and governess stood on the front steps and watched Buchanan's carriage drive away. When it reached the street and disappeared, Tad ran his gaze over the White House lawn and said, "Look at all that yard! I hope Uncle Elmer will visit us soon so Willie and me can play war with him."

Silently the president wondered if it would not be long until instead of playing war, Colonel Ellsworth would actually be fighting in one.

Patricia broke the silence by saying, "Willie and I, Tad."

Little devils danced in the lad's eyes as he grinned and said, "You can play war with Willie and Uncle Elmer too if you want, Miss Patricia."

The president and Mrs. Lincoln laughed as Patricia seized their youngest son by the ear and led him giggling and squealing inside the White House.

That night Mary Todd Lincoln awakened somewhere in the wee hours to find that her husband had left their bed. Worried, she arose, slipped into her robe, and went into the hall. Lanterns burned at both ends of the hall and near the top of the stairs. Moving toward the staircase, she heard a voice coming from one of the bedrooms along the way.

She paused in front of the partially open door and peered inside. In the vague light, she could see her husband on his knees beside a chair. He was weeping as she heard him say, "Dear God, the people of this nation have elected me their president. They trust me to lead them and make the right decisions in this darkest of hours. Oh, I cannot do it without Thy guidance. We are teetering on the verge of what could be the bloodiest civil conflict ever seen on this earth, dear God. Please, hear my cry."

Mary suddenly felt that she was standing on holy ground and had no right to be there. She could hear her husband's voice continuing in agonizing prayer as she returned swiftly down the hall.

CHAPTER TWO

✦

I n early February of 1861, the seven states that had seceded from the Union—South Carolina, Mississippi, Alabama, Georgia, Florida, Louisiana, and Texas—had held a convention at Montgomery, Alabama, and organized the government of the Confederacy. The convention drew up a provisional constitution (to be replaced in due time by a permanent document), chose Jefferson Davis of Mississippi as president and Alexander Stephens of Georgia as vice-president, and acted as a legislature pending the election of a regular Congress.

During March, both Lincoln and Davis chose their cabinets and set up their administrations under the gathering clouds of pending conflict. Lincoln clung tenaciously to the hope that war could be avoided. The Confederate nation had been born, but its creation might simply be a means of forcing concessions from the Union. No shots had been fired. The seven states that had left the Union might return if a compromise could be reached.

Leaders in Congress worked hard the last few days of March to perfect a last-minute compromise, and a committee led by Senator John Crittendon of Kentucky put one together. It would establish the old line of the Missouri Compromise, banning slavery in territories north of the line and protecting it south of the line. It would let future states enter the Union on a popular sovereignty basis, and it called for enforcement of the fugitive slave law, with Federal funds to compensate slave owners whose slaves got away. It also provided that the Constitution could never be amended in such a way as to give Congress power over slavery in any of the states.

Because of his conviction that slavery was wrong, Lincoln rejected the inclusion of slavery in the territories as provided by Crittendon's Compromise. His firm words were, "I refuse to entertain any proposition for a compromise in regard to the extension of slavery."

The Compromise collapsed.

Now Abraham Lincoln and Jefferson Davis faced each other across an ever-widening gulf. What happened in the minds of those two national leaders would determine whether a nation already divided by mutual hatred and antagonism would be torn apart by bloody conflict.

In his inaugural address, Lincoln had stated that the Federal government would not be the aggressor in a civil war; there would be no conflict unless the Confederates were the aggressors. Realizing the strong possibility of that aggression, Lincoln set up a Senate Military Committee on April 2. The Committee consisted of seven senators.

Meeting with the Committee on April 3 to set up a war strategy, the president and the senators soon realized they lacked a member with military experience. The seven senators agreed that the Committee was necessary—Congress had to have control over the Union's military leaders should war come. But the Committee that represented Congress would need advice from a qualified, well-experienced military man.

"How about General Winfield Scott?" spoke up one of the senators.

Lincoln rubbed his temples and replied slowly, "We can't spare him. His experience in the Mexican War is invaluable. He must be out there to lead the army."

"Then how about Major Irvin McDowell, Mr. President?" asked

another. "He's a graduate of West Point and served under General Scott in the Mexican War...with distinction, I might add."

"I know," nodded Lincoln. "I already have him in mind for leading our forces if war comes. I must leave him available for that. We all know that General Scott cannot actually go on the battlefield. He's too old for that, and besides, he's not in good health."

There was a long silence, then Senator Henry Wilson, whom Lincoln had appointed chairman of the Committee, said, "Mr. President, I have just the man—Lieutenant Colonel Jeffrey Jordan."

The name brought nods from the rest of the Committee.

Continuing, Wilson said, "I know Colonel Jordan quite well, Mr. President. I believe you've heard of the widow Rose O'Neal Greenhow."

"Yes," smiled Lincoln. "The doyenne of Washington society."

"Well, my colleagues all know that my wife died three years ago, and for the past year or so, I have been seeing Mrs. Greenhow. She and Colonel Jordan are good friends. It was through Mrs. Greenhow that I met Colonel Jordan, and he and I have become good friends, ourselves."

"I assume you are well acquainted with his military record?"

"Yes, sir. Since I've come to know him, I have done some checking in the Mexican War records. As with Major McDowell, he also fought under General Scott in the Mexican War and proved himself time and again as a military leader. His military record is impeccable, and I'm sure General Scott and Major McDowell will both tell you that few army officers have more knowledge of military theory. He'd be the perfect man to serve as military adviser to this committee."

Lincoln was taking the suggestion in with interest when another committee member said, "I'm not against Colonel Jordan, gentlemen, but I should point out that he is a Southerner...Virginia born and bred. Will he stay with the Union if war comes?"

"Virginia is still in the Union, Senator," spoke up another member.

"But she is in sympathy with the new Confederacy," came the quick retort. "If war comes, Virginia will secede."

"I'm afraid you're right about Virginia," said Lincoln. "However, there are many leaders in our army who are Southerners, but I don't think we'll lose them all to the South if war comes. I know a little of Colonel Jordan's background in the Mexican War. He's recognized as a hero for courage on the battlefield. If none of you object, I will talk to him about becoming this committee's military adviser."

The senators agreed that the president should offer Colonel Jordan the position.

The next day President Lincoln was at his desk in his special capitol building office, pouring over some papers, when there was a tap on the door. Looking up, he said, "Yes?"

The door came open, showing the face of Lincoln's private secretary, twenty-seven-year-old John Hay.

"What is it, John?"

"Colonel Jeffrey Jordan is here for his appointment, sir. Should I have him wait, or—"

"Oh, no!" said Lincoln, rising to his feet. "Show him in."

Hay widened the opening, looked behind him, and said, "Mr. Lincoln will see you now, Colonel."

"Thank you," came a pleasant voice, and Lt. Colonel Jeffrey Jordan appeared, smiling at the president as he moved into the office.

Hay closed the door, leaving the two men alone. Lincoln reached across the desk, shook Jordan's hand, and said, "I'm honored to meet you, Colonel."

Amazed at the strength of the president's grip, Jordan said, "The honor is mine, sir."

Jeffrey Jordan was slender, straight-backed, and stood just under six feet tall. At forty-three, his ash-blond hair was thinning and his sideburns and thick mustache were flecked with gray. There was a kind of seasoned completeness about him that Lincoln liked immediately.

"Have a seat, Colonel," said the president, gesturing toward a chair that sat in front of the desk.

There was an inquisitive look in Jordan's eyes as he placed his hat on an adjacent chair and sat down. Lincoln eased into his own chair, laid his elbows on the desk top, and leaned forward. "I'll get right to the point, Colonel. I need a man of your caliber for an important job."

"Yes, sir?"

"I have known of your war record for some time. Before calling you here, I had my secretary bring me your file so I could learn some more details. Very impressive, I might say. I guess you know you're considered a hero."

Jordan's face tinted. "To some people, sir," he said, his words showing a slight Southern drawl.

"Certainly to Colonel George McClellan. From the report I read, you risked your life to save his in the Mexican War."

"Well, sir," said Jordan, clearing his throat, "it wasn't exactly like that. You see—"

Throwing up a palm, Lincoln cut in, "I know how you heroes are. You never like to take any credit for your deeds. Let's get down to business."

The president explained that he had formed the Senate Military Committee because of the threat of war, and that the Committee needed a competent, experienced military man as adviser. Senator Wilson had brought up Jordan's name, and the Committee had agreed that he was the man for the job.

The colonel was both pleased and flattered, and consented to take the job, adding that he thought there were men available more qualified than he.

Lincoln sat back in his chair, fixed his dark eyes on Jordan, and said, "There is one thing I have to ask you, Colonel."

"Yes, sir?"

"You're a native Virginian."

A slight smile curved the colonel's mouth. "And you're wondering where my loyalty will lie if civil war comes and Virginia secedes."

Lincoln nodded.

"I love my home state, Mr. President, but if Virginia secedes, my loyalty stays with the Union. Like you, I'm against slavery."

"Fine, Colonel," Lincoln said, rising to his feet. "We'll set you up an office here in the Capitol right away. I've set a meeting for the Committee and its new adviser for tomorrow morning at eight. My secretary, Mr. Hay, will show you where the conference room is...and he'll be the one to see that you have everything you need for your office. You will learn exactly what we want of you in the morning."

"Thank you, sir," smiled Jordan, who was now standing. Picking up his hat, he said, "It will be a pleasure to work with you and the Committee. I'll get with Mr. Hay, and I'll see you at eight tomorrow morning."

Rounding the desk, the president walked Jordan to the door. "One other thing, Colonel."

"Yes, sir?"

"Mrs. Lincoln and I are hosting a dinner party at the White House Saturday night for the Committee members and their wives. Since you are now part of the Committee, I'd like for you to come. I know you are a widower, but if you have a lady friend you'd like to bring along, she'd be more than welcome. Senator Wilson is bringing Mrs. Greenhow."

Jordan rubbed the back of his neck and said, "I'm really not seeing any ladies, sir, but I have a twenty-year-old daughter. Would it be all right if I bring her?"

"Of course. What's the young lady's name?"

"Jenny Marie, sir. Only she doesn't like the way Southerners call everybody by both names, so she's just Jenny."

"I'll try to remember that," grinned the president. "Dinner is at eight."

"Thank you. Jenny and I will look forward to it, Mr. President."

It was late in the afternoon on Saturday, April 6. Mary Todd Lincoln was overseeing the decorating of the table in the White House dining room. The servants found Mary a warm and congenial First Lady and enjoyed working with her.

After having changed the flower arrangement in the table's centerpiece for the third time, Mary stepped back to scrutinize it. Nodding, she said to the two maids who stood close by, "Yes, that's it! Perfect! Now, you young ladies can go ahead with the place settings. Be sure to fold the napkins like I showed you. I'll be back shortly."

Mary then had to look in on the male servants, who were rearranging the furniture in the nearby drawing room where her guests would gather both before and after dinner. As she turned about, she found her two sons standing at the dining room door. She knew by the look on their faces, they were wanting something. "Yes, boys?" she said, smiling.

"Mama," spoke up Willie. "Uh...Tad wants to ask you something."

Because of his younger brother's persuasive ways with adults, Willie knew their objective had a much better chance of being realized if the request came from Tad.

Mary's eyes settled on her youngest. "Yes?"

Tad grinned broadly, glanced at the centerpiece, and said, "You sure fixed those flowers pretty, Mama."

"Thank you," she replied dryly, folding her arms over her bosom. "Now, what is it that you want?"

"Well, uh, me an' Willie...I know you said we can't eat supper in here tonight because we're just kids, but...we'd really like to meet Lieutenant Colonel Jeffrey Jordan. He's a hero, Mama. A *real* hero! Miss Patricia has been teachin' us about the Mexican War, an' she read to us out of some old newspapers about some of the things he did in the war. Me an' Willie would really like to meet him. Could we sit by him at the table and ask him to tell us some war stories? Please?"

Shaking her head, Mary said firmly, "No, Tad. This is strictly an adult occasion. You and Willie will get the same food, but as I told you before, you will eat it in the kitchen with Miss Patricia. Now, that's final."

Tad had told his parents that he planned to go to West Point when he grew up. His only dream was to be a soldier. He thought about using that angle to point out to his mother how beneficial it would be to his military career if he could spend some time with a great war hero, but the look in her eyes told him he'd best drop the subject. He made no attempt to veil his disappointment as he said, "Yes, ma'am. C'mon, Willie."

Mary smiled to herself as she watched Tad lead his brother away.

By seven-thirty that evening, all the guests were collected in the drawing room, waiting only for Jeffrey Jordan and his daughter to arrive. President and Mrs. Lincoln were moving among the guests together, spending a few moments with each couple. Mary Lincoln had heard much of Rose Greenhow and had been eager to meet her. The young widow proved to be lovely and amiable.

At seven-forty, Lieutenant Colonel Jordan and his daughter were announced. When they entered the room with Jenny on her father's arm, all eyes went immediately to the strikingly beautiful young woman.

Jenny Jordan stood four inches over five feet. Her long, raven-black hair lay in graceful swirls on her shoulders. She wore a deep-crimson floor-length dress fitted tightly at the neck and waist. Her figure was the envy of every woman in the room. At the neck and at the ends of her sleeves, Jenny wore white lace. Two pearl eardrops danced when she turned her head, and a long triple-string of pearls adorned her neck.

Jenny's eyes were dark-brown and direct. Her skin was smooth and fair, and her face had strong and pleasant contours. She glowed with personality and her warmth attracted people to her...men and women alike.

The Lincolns moved quickly to greet the colonel and his daughter. When introductions had been completed, Jenny—who indicated no intimidation in the presence of the president and the First Lady— smiled at the president and said, "May I say, Mr. President, that I agree in total with the young lady who wrote and suggested that you grow the beard. It most certainly adds to your dignity."

"Why, thank you, Miss Jordan," said Lincoln, returning the smile.

"I mean it most sincerely, sir," she added.

"I'm sure you do, and I appreciate it."

"And I would like to express my deep gratitude, sir, for the honor you have bestowed on my father by making him military adviser to the Committee."

Charmed by her slight Southern accent and congeniality, Lincoln responded, "The honor is actually mine, Miss Jordan. Your father is the perfect man for the job."

Jeffrey Jordan was about to speak when his daughter unwittingly cut him off by saying, "Mr. President, you may call me Jenny if you wish."

Lincoln smiled, winked at the colonel, and replied, "Just so I don't call you Jenny Marie, right?"

Jenny blushed. Looking at her father, she said, "Daddy, did you have to tell him that?"

Jordan chuckled, "Yes. I did."

Jenny turned to the First Lady and said, "Mrs. Lincoln, I love your dress. And your brooch. It's beautiful."

"Thank you, dear," Mary smiled, herself captivated by Jenny's charm. "The brooch was my mother's. I had the dress made in Springfield right after my husband won the election."

Mary and Jenny chatted for another minute, then the colonel took his daughter around the room, introducing her to the senators and meeting their wives for the first time. When they came to Senator Henry Wilson and Mrs. Greenhow, the senator greeted Jenny, saying he was happy to finally meet her. Then the Washington socialite embraced Jenny and said, "It's good to see you again, honey."

"You too, Rose," Jenny smiled, hugging her a second time.

"Isn't it just marvelous that your daddy will be working with the Committee?"

"Yes. I'm so proud of him."

"Let's just hope his job nor the Committee have to last very long," Senator Wilson interjected.

Rose turned to him and said, "None of us want a war, Henry, but as far as I can see, it looks inevitable."

"I know it does, but I'll hang onto the thread of hope until the Confederates jerk it out of my hand."

At that moment, the First Lady called her guests to the dining room. The Lincolns sat together at the head of the table. Mary was so taken with young Jenny that she arranged for her to sit at the corner to her left, automatically placing the colonel on the corner at the president's right.

As the meal progressed, Jenny was the spark of the evening. Committee members and their wives all along the table engaged her in conversation from time to time. Captured by her loveliness and fresh spirit, Abraham Lincoln looked at her at a quiet moment and joked,

"Jenny, if I were tall, dark, handsome, young, and free, I'd be a-courtin' you."

Mary's eyes twinkled as she mildly retorted, "Abe, dear...tall, dark, and handsome you are. But young and free you're not. Jenny will just have to find herself another man!"

Everyone laughed, then one of the senators said, "I have an idea Colonel Jordan has already had to build a high fence and employ attack dogs to keep the young men away from Miss Jenny."

Jordan chuckled and said, "My daughter has many young hopefuls hanging around, but so far she hasn't been serious with any of them."

Mary took Jenny by the hand and said, "Don't you worry about it. When that right young man walks into your life, you'll know him...just like I did when this tall, handsome man walked into my life."

The president snickered, and the guests showed their amusement as Jenny quipped, "If I can do half as well as you did, Mrs. Lincoln, I will be very happy."

In the White House kitchen, the Lincoln boys and their governess ate their meal. Noting the sour look on Tad's face, Patricia said, "Tad, if your face gets any longer, it's going to be in your plate."

The boy gave her a pitiful look and said around his food, "All I wanted to do was meet a war hero."

"I know, dear," Patricia said softly, "but it just isn't possible this time."

One of Willie Lincoln's chief occupations was watching his little brother charm his way into just about anything he wanted. He observed as Tad said with a break in his voice, "I don't really care if me an' Willie can't eat in there, but wouldn't it be all right if we just went in an' *met* Colonel Jordan?"

"I'm afraid your father would consider your entrance a serious interruption, Tad. Those senators are very important men. It just isn't the time or place for children."

Willie knew his little brother had a special set of strings attached to the governess's heart. He smiled to himself as he watched Tad begin to tug on those strings. Willie had often thought Tad would make a better actor than a soldier.

Tad looked up at Patricia, showing misty disappointment in his eyes, his lower lip quivering. "But if that war starts, Colonel Jordan'll be too busy for me *ever* to meet him. I only want to see him for a minute, just so's I can say I met him. My daddy wouldn't get mad if *you* took us in and told him we just wanted to see Colonel Jordan for a minute."

Willie knew Patricia would give in. It was all over her face.

She held out a little longer by saying, "Tad, your father may not get angry at me, but I don't want even his slightest disfavor. Can't you see that—"

"He really likes you, Miss Patricia. He wouldn't even show— what'd you call it?"

"The slightest disfavor."

"Yeah, that."

Patricia looked at Willie, who pulled his mouth tight and shrugged his shoulders. With a long sigh, she said, "All right, Mr. Lincoln. I'll lay my neck on the chopping block and take you in there. But remember...it's only so you can meet Colonel Jordan, and that's all. It'll be real quick. Understand?"

Jumping from his chair, the nine-year-old charmer wrapped his arms around her neck, exclaiming, "Oh, thank you, Miss Patricia, thank you! I love you!"

In the dining room, the natural course for conversation was toward the threat of civil war. The senators expressed their fear that if war came, many of the good officers in the army who were Southerners would forsake the Union and join up with the Confederacy.

"We will no doubt lose some," conceded Lincoln, "but as I told you gentlemen before, I believe the majority of men from the Southern states will stay with the Union."

"There are a couple of officers that I'm concerned about, Mr. President," said Senator Wilson. Rose glanced furtively at Jeffrey Jordan, then looked intently at Wilson. "I speak of two well-known educators from Virginia—Colonel Robert E. Lee and Colonel Thomas Jackson."

Everyone there knew that for years Lee had been superintendent at West Point, and that Jackson was the best-loved instructor who had ever taught at Virginia Military Institute. Both were now active officers in the Regular Army.

Lincoln seemed a bit uncomfortable at the mention of their names. Adjusting himself on his chair, he said, "Since the subject has gone this far, we will take it a little further. But I will tell you ladies that what you hear at this table is to be kept under your hats unless and until Colonels Lee and Jackson abdicate their commissions in the Regular Army and join the Confederacy."

Each woman nodded her assent.

Continuing, Lincoln said to Wilson, "We have many officers who are Southerners, Senator. Why do you question the loyalty of these two men?"

"I question Colonel Jackson, sir, because he is so outspoken about being a Southerner. I find it hard to believe that if war comes, he could do anything *but* join the Confederacy."

"Even if Virginia should surprise us and stay with the Union?" queried one of the other senators.

Wilson grinned at him. "Once the first shot is fired, my friend, *everybody* will have to declare themselves. I'd lay my right arm down in a bet that Virginia will go Confederate the instant it happens, or short-ly thereafter."

The rest of the Committee agreed.

"And as for Colonel Lee," proceeded Wilson, "we all know that General Scott has approached Lee about assuming principal command of all the Union forces in his place if war comes...and Lee keeps delaying giving him an answer. Why the delay unless Lee is figuring to join the Confederacy if Virginia secedes?"

"Good question," nodded Lincoln. He paused, drew in a deep breath, and said, "Only time will tell. If we go into war and Lee and Jackson stay with the Union, we'll owe them an apology."

"I go on record right here," said Wilson. "I'll be the first to apologize if I'm wrong."

One of the senators' wives looked at Jordan and asked, "What do you think, Colonel? You're a Virginian."

"I can't rightly speak for Lee and Jackson, ma'am," Jordan replied softly.

"But Colonel Jordan has spoken for himself," put in Lincoln. "He has pledged his loyalty to the Union."

"Amen!" laughed another senator. "If he hadn't, we wouldn't have made him military adviser of the Committee!"

While laughter made its rounds, Jenny stole a quick glance at her father. He met it, then looked away.

At that moment, the dining room door came open and governess Patricia Winters appeared. Everyone looked her direction as she smiled and said, "Excuse me, Mr. Lincoln. I have two young men here who have asked me to make a request for them."

When the president's eyes settled sternly on the governess, she spoke quickly. "Tad is very eager to meet Lieutenant Colonel Jordan, sir, and so is Willie. Just...just recently I was teaching the boys about the Mexican War, and we spent some time on Colonel Jordan's heroic deeds in battle. As you know, sir, Tad plans on one day being a soldier. He...he asked me if he and Willie could come in and meet the colonel. I told them we would have to make it very quick...just a minute or so."

There was pleading in Patricia's eyes as she spoke. Mary looked at her husband, who was rubbing his chin.

Abraham Lincoln was fully aware of Patricia's soft spot for Tad, and how very persuasive the lad could be. A smile parted his lips. "All right, Patricia. Bring the boys in."

The governess opened the door wider, allowing the Lincoln brothers to move past her into the dining room. The president left his chair, put an arm around the shoulder of each son, and said, "Well, boys, since you're in here, I think it would be appropriate for you to meet all these ladies and gentlemen."

Lincoln took his sons around the table, introducing them to the senators and their wives, purposely saving Lieutenant Colonel Jordan and his daughter till last. Willie and Tad politely shook hands with the men and did a slight bow before the ladies.

While the introductions were in progress, Patricia found Mrs. Lincoln looking at her. The nervous governess smiled weakly. Mary was too kind to show anger for what Patricia had done. Tad had worked his mother in the same way more times than she cared to think about. When Mary smiled back, Patricia felt relief. She opened her hands at waist level and mouthed, "I couldn't turn him down."

Mary mouthed back, "I understand."

Finally, Lincoln brought his sons to the beautiful lady in the deep-red dress and said, "Boys, this is Miss Jenny Jordan. She is the colonel's daughter."

Jenny warmed them with a smile and said, "Hello, Willie. Hello, Tad."

The Lincoln brothers were struck with the warmth Jenny showed toward them. They bowed extra low and said almost in unison, "Glad to meet you, Miss Jordan."

"You are fine looking young men," she responded. "Maybe someday one of you will be president like your father."

"That'll be Willie, ma'am," said Tad. "I'm gonna be a soldier like *your* father."

Everyone laughed. The president then turned his sons to the colonel and introduced them to him. Jordan shook hands with Willie first, then Tad. As soon as he let go of Tad's hand, the bright-eyed boy held the hand up and exclaimed, "Willie! I ain't never gonna wash this hand again!"

There was another round of laughter, then the colonel chatted with the Lincoln brothers for several minutes, answering questions they had about certain incidents in the Mexican War they remembered from Patricia's lessons.

"Colonel Jordan," Tad said, "tell me what it's really like on the battlefield. You know...what it's like to be out there with cannons firing an' muskets shooting an'...an' smoke all around, an' soldiers bein' shot."

Jordan looked to Mary for any signal to hold back. When she only smiled, he proceeded to answer Tad's inquiry. Tad's eyes danced with excitement as he heard first-hand from a veteran soldier about battlefield experience.

"All right, boys, it's bedtime," Mary said when Jordan was done.

The president instructed his sons to tell everyone goodnight. They thanked Colonel Jordan for talking to them, and told him goodnight first. Next they went to Jenny. She smiled and asked if she could have a hug. Everyone looked on with pleasure as the boys gladly embraced her. It took them only moments to tell the rest of the group goodnight.

When the governess and her charges were gone, the guests commented to the Lincolns about what fine boys they had. They noted especially Tad's forwardness and his interest in military matters.

The Lincolns and their guests moved to the drawing room where they were served coffee and sat down to chat. After a while, the president turned to Jenny and asked if she was working.

"Yes, sir. In addition to keeping house for my father, I work as a seamstress three days a week for Manley's Clothiers downtown."

"Oh, yes," Lincoln nodded. "I've seen their store." He paused a moment, then asked, "Do you work the same three days every week?"

"Usually Monday, Wednesday, and Friday, but sometimes I switch it around. Mr. Manley gives me a great deal of leeway."

"The reason I ask is that I am looking for a part-time receptionist for the Senate Chamber at the Capitol. I like the way you handle yourself with people, and I believe you'd make an excellent receptionist. The young lady who has been working at it full-time, wants to drop back to two days a week. I could give you a Monday-Wednesday-Friday job if you want it. And if once in a while you wanted to switch days, I'm sure that can be worked out. The starting salary would be twenty-five dollars a week."

Jenny's eyes widened. "Twenty-five dollars a week for *three days*?"

"Yes."

Turning to her father, she said, "Daddy, that's twice what I make at Manley's!"

"Sounds like Mr. Lincoln is making you a generous proposition, honey," Jordan smiled.

Looking back at the president, Jenny said, "I'll take it, sir!"

CHAPTER THREE

✦

When South Carolina seceded from the Union in late December, 1860, Major Robert Anderson, commander of the Federal forces in Charleston Harbor, secretly moved his garrison of less than seventy men from Fort Moultrie across the harbor to Fort Sumter. He knew Sumter would be easier to defend than Moultrie if war came.

The question whether Anderson's small force should be withdrawn from the South Carolina harbor, or reinforced, agitated the closing weeks of the Buchanan administration and the opening weeks of the Lincoln administration. Before he had set up the Senate Military Committee, Lincoln discussed the problem with his cabinet over a period of several days.

While the fate of Fort Sumter was under lengthy discussion in Washington, Confederate president Jefferson Davis contacted the flamboyant General Pierre G.T. Beauregard, who was commander of Rebel forces at Charleston. Orders were given to Beauregard to lay siege on Fort Sumter.

Finally, against the advice of some of his cabinet members, Lincoln had decided not to reinforce Sumter but to merely send provisions. He was still clinging to a faint hope that war could be averted. To send reinforcements would invite hostilities. For many long weeks, Major Anderson and his tiny garrison had waited behind Sumter's walls, facing the silent, menacing guns of the Confederates.

At 8:20 A.M. on Friday, April 12, Jenny Jordan was at her desk in the lobby just outside the door of the Senate Chamber. She observed the members of the Senate Military Committee as they topped the stairs at the end of the hall two and three at a time and moved down the hall toward her.

As they passed her desk and entered the Chamber door that led to their meeting room, Jenny picked up their words. The discussion was about the standoff between Anderson and Beauregard at Charleston Harbor.

It was 8:25 when the receptionist saw President Lincoln's tall, lanky form top the stairs, sided by her father. They talked as they came down the hall. When they arrived at Jenny's desk, they stopped to greet her.

The president's features were drawn and his dark eyes looked weary. She wondered if he had slept at all in the past few days. Mr. Lincoln had repeatedly sent supply boats into Charleston Harbor, knowing that Major Anderson and his men were running low on provisions, but the boats were turned back by the Confederates.

Lincoln set his tired eyes on Jenny, released a half-smile, and said, "Good morning."

"Good morning, Mr. President," she responded softly.

Lincoln proceeded into the Senate Chamber. Jeffrey Jordan leaned over, kissed his daughter on the cheek, and said, "Things are pretty tight, honey. The president and the Committee are at their wits' end over this Fort Sumter situation. I think things are about to pop in Charleston Harbor."

Jenny watched her father vanish through the door, then turned to her paper work. At ten minutes before nine, Jenny looked up to see a White House aide hit the top of the stairs and run down the hall toward her. He stopped at her desk, his face pallid. The troubled look in his eyes told her that something bad had happened.

The thirty-ish aide looked down at Jenny's name plate and gasped, "Miss Jordan...I must see the president...immediately."

Jenny wanted to ask what the emergency was about, but refrained. Rising, she said, "This way."

The breathless aide followed as Jenny led him into the Senate Chamber and down a narrow corridor. Stopping at a pair of closed double doors, she rapped loudly. Seconds later, one of the senators opened a door and said, "Yes, Jenny."

"One of Mr. Lincoln's aides is here, sir. He needs to see him immediately."

The aide was taken into the meeting room and Jenny returned to her desk. No more than two minutes had passed when the president came out with the aide at his side. They passed the desk talking rapidly back and forth, but Jenny was able to pick up that something dreadful had happened earlier that morning at Charleston Harbor.

Jenny bit her lower lip. Had the war begun?

Suddenly the Senate Military Committee came bowling through the Chamber door. Their voices were strained as they talked among themselves. Jenny was picking up bits and pieces when her father appeared and drew up. "The war's on," he said with emotion. "General Beauregard fired on Fort Sumter at dawn this morning. Major Anderson and his men are fighting back. Charleston Harbor will turn into a blood bath unless Anderson surrenders quickly."

Jenny's hands were trembling. "Daddy, what are you going to do, now? The very thing we dreaded has become a reality."

"I don't have time to talk about it now. The president is going to call an emergency meeting of Congress immediately. As military adviser to the Committee, I'm expected to be there. We'll talk this evening."

With that, he was gone.

Jenny's stomach was jittery. She returned to her work but had a hard time concentrating. April 12, 1861, was going to be a long day...and a black day on the calendar of American history.

That evening, Lieutenant Jordan entered his house and smelled the mouth-watering aroma of food cooking. Hanging his hat on a hook in the parlor, he moved into the kitchen to find his daughter adding a log to the cookstove. Replacing the circular lid to its place, she turned and said with a faint smile, "Hello, Daddy."

"Hi, sweetheart," he responded, and moved across the room toward her. Planting a kiss on her cheek, he asked, "What's for supper? Sure smells good."

"Your favorite," Jenny replied softly.

"Chicken and dumplings?"

"Mm-hmm."

"You really are a sweetheart!"

Turning back to the stove, Jenny said, "Better get washed up. Supper will be on the table in about five minutes."

Jenny set the food on the table while the colonel washed at a nearby basin. While moving back and forth between the cupboard and the table, she asked, "So can you tell me what happened in Congress's emergency meeting?"

"Sure. They agreed unanimously to declare war on the Confederacy. Mr. Lincoln is very angry at Jefferson Davis for giving the order for Beauregard to fire on Sumter. There will be retaliation. It'll take a little time, but Confederate blood will be shed."

"Neither side is really ready for war, are they?"

Drying his hands on a small towel, Jordan shook his head. "No. It will be a while before either side can wage full-scale war."

Jenny's face was pale. "Let's sit down," she said with a tremor in her voice.

They took their places at each end of the kitchen table. Jordan thanked the Lord for their food, but did not mention the war in his prayer.

As they began to eat, Jenny said, "Daddy, Virginia will secede, won't she?"

"I'm sure of it."

Jenny had been raised by her parents to love her native state of Virginia, and she felt a strong compulsion to remain true to it. President Lincoln's words at the White House dinner on Saturday night came back to her. "Daddy, Mr. Lincoln said the other night at the dinner that you had spoken for yourself...that you had pledged your loyalty to the Union."

"I noticed you looked at me when he said it. I had to assure him of my loyalty to the Union in order to get the military adviser position."

Cocking her head, she asked, "Am I understanding you correctly? You took the position with an ulterior motive?"

"I'm really not ready to discuss it with you, okay? Let's see what happens in the next few days."

"I hate the thought of civil war, Daddy. What a horrible thing...Americans killing Americans."

"Yes, it's horrible, all right. But you and I can't control what's coming. All we can do is react accordingly when it happens."

News came to Washington late Sunday afternoon, April 14, that Major Anderson and his small garrison had surrendered Fort Sumter to General Beauregard. Miraculously, with all the shelling that had gone on for nearly two full days, not one man had been killed on either side. Nonetheless, the divided nation was in the grip of civil war.

After meeting with his Senate Military Committee for a special session on Sunday evening, Abraham Lincoln issued a strong proclamation. Because the seven seceded states had opposed and obstructed the laws of the United States, Lincoln was calling for seventy-five thousand militiamen to follow his leadership in punishing them for their lawlessness.

The next day headlines on all the Northern newspapers announced Lincoln's proclamation in bold letters. Later in the day, the news reached President Davis in Montgomery. Davis bristled at the naked threat of Lincoln's call to arms against the South and, through a large number of Southern newspapers, asked for every loyal, able-bodied son of the South to prepare to meet the Union's militia head-on.

On Tuesday morning, Jenny had just arrived at her desk when John F. Calhoun, a native of South Carolina who worked as a recording and vital statistics secretary in the Senate Chamber, emerged from the inner offices and said, "Good morning, Jenny. I thought you didn't work on Tuesday."

"Ordinarily I don't, but Nelda sent word yesterday that she's not feeling well and asked if I'd fill in for her today."

"I see. Well...have you heard the latest news?"

Jenny placed her purse in a lower drawer. "Probably not, John. Has it something to do with the extra-early meeting my father is attending with the Committee at this very moment?"

"Yes. As you probably know, the president is in there with them."

"I assumed he would be," she said, shoving the drawer shut. "So what is it?"

"General Winfield Scott is in there, too. Seems when the president's proclamation hit the newspapers yesterday, several army officers from the South turned in their resignations and headed for home. Most notable among them was Colonel Thomas J. Jackson!"

Easing into her chair, Jenny said, "That probably didn't surprise anyone. Colonel Jackson is known to be an outspoken Southerner."

"Somebody said once that Jackson is such a strong Southerner that the blood in his body flows south. He's a good friend of your father's, isn't he?"

"Yes. Daddy attended VMI before going to West Point. Colonel Jackson was a professor there at the time. He and Daddy became very good friends." Jenny paused a few seconds, then asked, "What about Colonel Lee? Was he one of them?"

"No. At least he's not among the first bunch to go. The men on the Committee are calling them *traitors*. It's pretty hot in that meeting room right now."

"What about you, John? You're a real beans-and-sow-belly son of the South, yourself. What are you going to do?"

At that instant, the Chamber doors burst open and Committee members poured out, heading quickly down the corridor toward the stairs. Behind them came Jeffrey Jordan, the portly General Winfield Scott, and President Lincoln.

Jordan halted at Jenny's desk. Lincoln said, "See you as soon as you get back, Colonel."

"Yes, sir," nodded Jordan.

Lincoln and Scott moved away. When they were out of earshot, Jenny said to her father, "I didn't know you were going somewhere."

"Well, something came up," he replied, looking around to make sure no one was around.

Jenny noted that Calhoun had disappeared.

"I'm going to Lexington," said Jordan. "Be back as soon as I can."

"Lexington, *Virginia?*"

"Yes. I'm leaving right now. I told Mr. Lincoln your Uncle Elbert has become suddenly ill, and that I need to go to him."

"But Uncle Elbert's healthy as a plow horse, Daddy," she reasoned. "Besides...he lives in Leesburg."

"I know," the colonel said hurriedly and kissed her on the forehead. As he hastened away, he said over his shoulder, "Tell you all about it when I get back."

Jenny stared after him. Who was he going to see at Lexington?

Some old friend from his VMI days? Then she remembered...Colonel Jackson still maintained his home at Lexington. Jenny had heard her father say so not too long ago. What had Calhoun just said? *Several army officers from the South turned in their resignations and headed for home.* Jenny's father was going to see Colonel Jackson!

On Wednesday morning, April 17, Colonel Thomas J. Jackson stepped off the back porch of his house in Lexington, patting his stomach. His wife stood at the kitchen door, smiling. She had just fed him a good breakfast. He was home so little, she loved to pamper and spoil him good when she had the opportunity. She watched him enter the small barn behind the house, then turned away to clean up the table.

Jackson moved into the deep shadows of the barn, took a curry comb and a brush from hooks on the wall, and exited from a rear door into the small corral. His bay gelding was drinking at the water trough. As the colonel approached, the horse nickered and bobbed it's head.

"Good mornin', ol' boy," grinned Jackson. "How'd you like a good brushin'?" The gelding stood still as its master brushed its coat and combed out the mane and tail. "Well, ol' boy," Jackson said as he brushed the sleek coat, "it looks like you and I are gonna be goin' to war."

The gelding stomped a hoof and nickered as if it understood. Then it swung its head around and nickered again. Jackson looked up to see a lone rider trotting into the yard. The rider had spotted him and was heading for the corral. Leaving the gelding, Jackson walked toward the corral gate, raising the curry comb to wave a welcome. "Jeff, what brings you here?" Jackson asked as Colonel Jordan hauled up and slid from his saddle.

Pushing his hat off his forehead, Jordan stuck a hand over the gate, and as the two old friends shook hands, he said, "I need to talk to you, Tom."

"Sure. Let's go in the house."

Jordan greeted Mrs. Jackson, who asked if he had eaten break-fast. Jordan explained that he had stayed at a country inn the night before and had eaten just before dawn.

Jackson led his former student into his den where they sat in overstuffed chairs, facing each other. "I'll get right to the point, Tom," said Jordan. "I learned yesterday morning that you had resigned from the Regular Army and gone home. I assume you're signing up with the Confederate Army."

"Already have. I'll be assigned a regiment to lead shortly. No doubt it'll be with a Virginia military unit."

"I guess you know you've been labeled a traitor."

"Yes," sighed Jackson. Picking up a well-worn Bible from a small table next to his chair, he opened it and began flipping pages, saying, "Have you ever read the book of Exodus, Jeff?"

"Yes."

"You will remember, then, that when the book opens, the Israelites are in Egypt under the thumb of Pharaoh."

"Yes."

"In chapter one, Pharaoh tells the Hebrew midwives that when they deliver babies for Hebrew women, they are to kill all the males."

"I remember that."

"Okay, now listen to verse seventeen, 'But the midwives feared God, and did not as the king of Egypt commanded them, but saved the men children alive.' You will notice, they disobeyed the king because they feared God. What God said came first with them."

"That's as it should be."

Flipping back to the New Testament, Jackson said, "In the days of the apostles, the government told them not to preach the doctrine of Jesus Christ to the people. But the apostles refused to obey the govern-ment. Acts chapter five. Listen to this in verse twenty-nine. 'Then Peter and the other apostles answered and said, We ought to obey God rather than men.' "

"I know where you're headed," smiled Jordan.

"Of course, the apostles' battle with the government of their day was the most vital and valorous battle men could ever wage...but ours is still very important. Paul wrote in Romans thirteen about obeying your government. He said to render to everyone their dues. Tribute to whom tribute is due, custom to whom custom is due, fear to whom fear is due, and honor to whom honor is due. Jeff, I can't honor a government that steps on the rights of plantation owners, telling them they cannot own slaves. I'm not particularly fond of slavery, but I'm for states' rights, and it is my conviction that God is, too. So, on that premise and the fact that I'm a Southerner to the core, I had to resign. I'm going to fight for the South and for dear ol' Virginia. Being called a traitor by Northerners doesn't bother me one bit."

Jordan's mouth pulled into a thin line. "That's what I want to talk about, Tom. I'm battling this loyalty thing myself."

"You're a Virginian, Jeff. That ought to settle it. I guess you know what's going on over at Richmond as we talk."

"Yeah. I heard about it at the inn last night. An emergency state convention to pass an ordinance of secession."

"It's as good as done," said Jackson, laying the Bible back on the table. "After hearing of Lincoln's call to arms, Virginians are more than happy to get out of the Union. On the way home, I heard that our esteemed governor spoke yesterday of Lincoln's call for militiamen to punish the Confederates for breaking the laws of the United States. He said Virginians will not stand for such 'crass, arrogant threats' and will gladly fight with the other seceded states against the Union."

Jordan was quiet for a moment. He bent his head, rubbed the back of his neck, and said, "Tom, I've got to take my stand with the Confederacy."

"Good! I'll see that you get a commission as colonel in the Rebel army."

Easing back into his chair, Jordan said, "I've been doing a lot of thinking, and I've got something else in mind."

"Oh?"

"I'm in a perfect position to get my hands on all kinds of classified military information. Have you heard about my being appointed military adviser to the Senate Military Committee?"

"No. I knew about Lincoln setting up the Committee, but I didn't know about you being made military adviser. Your talking about being a spy?"

"Yes."

"Do you know what it means if you're caught?"

"Immediate execution, if the old spy rule holds firm with Lincoln and Winfield Scott."

"I'm sure it will. It's a real risk."

"Is it really any more risk than if I was out there on a battlefield with bullets and shrapnel flying around?"

"I guess not. How will you get the classified information into the hands of Confederate military leaders?"

"I have two close friends in key places in Washington who are loyal to the Confederacy. One is a secretary in the Senate Chamber. His name is John F. Calhoun, and he's from South Carolina."

"So as secretary in the Senate Chamber, you figure Calhoun can lay hold on information that might not be available to you?"

"Right. I haven't approached John on it yet, but I'm quite certain he'll go along with it."

"So who's going to carry the information to the Confederate military leaders for you?"

"Well, I haven't got it all worked out yet, but the second friend I mentioned is Rose O'Neal Greenhow."

"Ah, yes. The Washington socialite. Quite attractive, I understand—a widow and very wealthy. That's about all I know. I assume her husband left her a great deal of money?"

"That's right. He was Dr. Robert Greenhow, a successful attorney and State Department official. Dr. Greenhow left her quite a sizable sum. She'll never want for anything. She continually hosts parties and invites all the important people in Washington."

"So I understand."

"Rose has already declared her loyalty to the Confederacy to me, so I know I can depend on her for help. She has contact with many young socialite women. Many are Southerners, and Rose will know how to pick them. My idea is for the young women to carry the information to Confederate military leaders in Virginia. They'll be able to get past Union lines that will no doubt be set up. Men would be suspect. The girls can give all kinds of reasons as to why they're going back and forth between D.C. and Virginia."

Colonel Jackson pulled at his beard, nodding slowly. "That will work, Jeff. You've got a brain in your head."

"Rose is also my prime choice for this venture because she is romantically involved with Senator Henry Wilson of Massachusetts. Wilson is chairman of the Senate Committee. Her relationship with him will help keep her above suspicion."

Jackson's eyebrows arched. "You mean she'll stay romantically involved with Wilson and work as a spy right under his nose?"

"I feel confident she will. I know Rose's devotion to the Southern cause. The romance between her and the senator isn't that serious. At least on her part."

"You must know her well."

"Not romantically, professor," grinned Jordan. "She's not my type. But we are close friends."

"Well, like I said, this spy stuff is risky, Jeff. But if you can get this spy ring set up, let me know immediately. No doubt because of its proximity to Washington, Virginia will become the first theater of war. Whoever Jefferson Davis sets up as top commander of the Confederate forces will no doubt be situated in Virginia."

"Any idea who that might be?"

"I think it'll be Beauregard."

"He's certainly the big hero in Southern eyes since he captured Fort Sumter." Jordan paused, then asked, "What do you know about Colonel Robert E. Lee?"

A wide grin spread over Jackson's face. "He'll come over to our side. Mark my word. It'll happen real quick, now that Virginia is seceding. The man has Southern blood in his veins just like yours and mine."

"I'm sure you're right. With his reputation, he'll no doubt become a leader in the Confederate army."

"No doubt about it," agreed Jackson.

Jordan rose to his feet. "Well, I'd better be heading back for Washington, Tom. I just felt if I could talk to you, it'd give me the impetus to make my move. I'll get word to you as soon as possible so you'll know about the spy ring. You'll have to let me know where to send information once we get rolling."

Jackson clapped a hand on Jordan's shoulder and said, "Fine. I can't tell you right now when I'll get my assignment, or where I'll be stationed, but if you'll send the message here, my wife will see that it gets to me right away."

"Will do."

Colonel Jordan said good-bye to Mrs. Jackson and was escorted to his horse. As Jordan mounted, Jackson smiled up at him and said, "Jeff, if you make this spy ring work, it'll have a devastating effect on the Union's military progress and success in the war."

"That's what I'm counting on."

As he trotted away, Jackson called after him, "God bless you, Jeff!"

Word of Virginia's secession from the Union spread fast. While President Lincoln and General Scott were in serious discussion at the White House on April 17, a Virginia military unit under orders from General Beauregard moved swiftly to take the Federal arsenal at Harper's Ferry. The small Union garrison there found themselves hopelessly outnumbered and made a hasty retreat across the Potomac River to Hagerstown, Maryland, leaving behind some five thousand rifles and a large supply of ammunition.

At 10:00 A.M. the same day, Lieutenant Jordan arrived at the Capitol. Climbing the stairs that led from the rotunda to the second floor, he moved down the hall to find three Military Committee members in discussion with his daughter at her desk. Jenny greeted him as he drew near. Jordan excused himself to the Committee members while he bent down and kissed his daughter's cheek.

"How's uncle Elbert?" Jenny asked for the benefit of the others.

"He's a sick man right now, but with proper care, he'll be all right. Said to give you his love."

"He's such a sweetie," she smiled.

"We're glad you're back, Colonel," said one of the senators. "Mr. Lincoln has called for a big meeting with the Committee, the Cabinet, and General Scott first thing in the morning."

"I'll be there with bells on," replied Jordan.

"I don't suppose you've heard about Colonel Robert E. Lee," spoke up another.

"No."

"Resigned his commission at four o'clock yesterday afternoon. Announced proudly that he was joining the Confederate army. I figured he'd turn traitor, too."

The word *traitor* went all the way to Jordan's spine. Covering it, he remarked, "Didn't we all know he would?" Then turning to Jenny, he asked, "Is John Calhoun in?"

"Yes. He's back in his cubbyhole."

Jordan spent an hour with Calhoun. When the Chamber secretary heard Jordan's plan, he was immediately interest and volunteered to do his part. He was elated to know the plan had Colonel Jackson's approval and did not flinch when Jordan warned him of the consequences if he was caught as a Confederate spy. Calhoun's loyalty to the South was as strong as his love of life itself.

Late that afternoon, Jordan and Calhoun paid a visit to Rose Greenhow at her fashionable home on Washington's 16th Street. She welcomed them warmly and granted Jordan's request for a private talk. They went to the library, and the servants were told not to interrupt them for any reason.

When Jordan explained his plan, which had Colonel Jackson's approval and Calhoun's cooperation, she flashed her winsome smile and wholeheartedly agreed to become the go-between in the spy ring. She assured both men that she could produce young ladies loyal to the Southern cause who would find it adventuresome and patriotic to carry vital messages to the Confederate military authorities.

Then Rose looked at Jordan and asked, "Does Jenny know about all this?"

"No. I'm going to have to tell her, though. Jenny thinks a lot of Mr. Lincoln, and she loves her job...but her heart belongs to the South. She'll understand what I'm doing and keep mum about it, of course. The hardest part for her will be the risk I'm taking. She knows what happens to spies when they're caught."

"Well, that's part of war," sighed Rose. "She'll handle it all right, the same as she'd handle it if you were fighting on battlefields. I can't say that I cherish the thought of facing a firing squad myself, but if my contribution as a spy can bring a quick victory for the South, I'll be happy."

"What about your relationship with Senator Wilson?" queried Calhoun.

"I'll keep it intact, of course," smiled Rose. "What better way to cover my tracks? My loyalty to the Southern cause is stronger than my infatuation with Henry. Have I stated my position clearly?"

"Yes, quite," replied Calhoun, looking at Jordan. "Wouldn't you say so, Colonel?"

"Quite clearly," agreed Jordan.

CHAPTER FOUR

✦

On Saturday afternoon, April 13, eleven hundred Fire Zouaves marched in perfect ranks on the training field just outside of Utica, New York. Leading the drill was Sergeant Casper Lynch, a tough, thick-bodied man with a gravelly voice.

Several hundred Utica residents looked on with pride from the surrounding hills as the Eleventh New York Fire Zouaves went through their paces under the brilliant glare of sunlight. The sound of a dozen snare drums echoed across the grassy field while the well-disciplined soldiers moved with precision as if all were part of one body.

The Zouaves were a striking sight to behold in their bright-colored uniforms. Styled after the famous French Zouaves of Crimean War days, Colonel Elmer Ellsworth's troops wore bright-red fezzes, white shirts, short blue coats, baggy red breeches, black boots, and yellow sashes about their waists.

Marching just behind Sergeant Lynch, in front of the line of drummers, were two Zouaves who carried flag staffs. Whipping in the breeze was a black-and-white regimental flag on one staff, and the red-white-and-blue of Old Glory on the other.

The sun was lowering toward the west when Colonel Ellsworth

came riding at a gallop across the rolling hills from Utica, where he had been since late morning. Though the marching Zouaves saw their leader thundering toward them, they did not break rank nor even turn their heads. When Sergeant Lynch saw Ellsworth excitedly waving his hat, he called for the marchers to halt.

The colonel skidded his mount to a stop in front of the neatly formed ranks, and said to Lynch, "I've got news from Washington."

"Is it what we've been expecting, sir?"

"Yes." Because of his lack of height, Ellsworth remained in the saddle to address his men. Sitting as tall as he could, he lifted his voice and said, "Men, I have news from Washington! While I was in town this morning to send some telegrams, a message came to me from President Lincoln's secretary, John Hay. Yesterday morning at dawn, under orders from Jefferson Davis, General Beauregard opened fire on our garrison at Fort Sumter The Confederates have started the war! Right now, they are battling it out with Major Anderson and his men. Sumter is surrounded. There is little hope for survival of Major Anderson and his garrison aside from surrender."

There was a stirring amongst the Zouaves, and one of them near the rear of the ranks raised a hand. Ellsworth acknowledged him. "What is it, Private Zeller?"

"When do we get to retaliate, Colonel?"

"I can't tell you when yet, but I *can* tell you that you will get your chance!"

Suddenly the Zouaves went into a wild uproar, shouting fiery words of indignation and defiance against the Confederates. The colonel let them blow off steam for a few minutes, then raised his hand for silence.

"When I received Mr. Hay's wire," Ellsworth explained with raised voice, "I sent a message back right away, asking for orders from President Lincoln concerning us. Mr. Hay answered back that Mr. Lincoln was busy, but would get a message to us within two or three days. In the meantime, we will continue to drill, target practice, and work on our combat training."

"Yes, sir!" shouted a Zouave. "But with more exuberance, Colonel!" Muskets were raised in the air and men shouted their agreement.

Ellsworth called for silence again, and when it came, he shouted, "Let's knock off for the rest of the day, men. Get yourselves a good rest. We'll hit the training field at sunup in the morning!"

Sergeant Lynch formally dismissed the brightly clad soldiers. They broke ranks quickly and headed for their barracks. Vengeance against the Confederates was their only topic of discussion.

Colonel Ellsworth saw the civilians coming toward him, banded together. They had heard enough to know that Fort Sumter had been fired upon, and they wanted the details. Ellsworth took the time to tell them all he knew about it, adding that their local newspapers would no doubt have more information by morning.

The next morning at sunrise, eleven hundred Fire Zouaves charged onto the training field, adrenaline pumping. They were eager for battle. It showed in the vigor and intensity of their training exercises. While half of the Zouaves were doing target practice under the guidance of Sergeant Lynch, the rest were working on their hand-to-hand combat skills.

Colonel Ellsworth stood by the crowd of 550 men at the south end of the field and observed as his training specialist, Corporal Francis E. "Buck" Brownell, lectured them on physical fitness. Brownell, a native of Saratoga County, New York, was considered the most tenacious of the Eleventh Zouaves, and had the respect of the entire regiment.

Buck Brownell stood an even six feet in height and weighed 175 pounds. At twenty-six, he was intelligent, well-conditioned, agile, and rawboned. Handsome in a rugged way, he was dark complected and had lively black eyes that could warm a person or send an icy chill down their backbone. He wore a well-trimmed mustache that matched his thick crop of jet-black hair.

Brownell finished his lecture. "All right, gentlemen, we're going to take some more lessons at bayonet fighting. After a couple of you do a demonstration for us, I will point out the good moves and bad ones. As I have told you before, when you go up against an enemy in a face-to-face bayonet fight, one of the two combatants is going to die. You must have the proper mental attitude about it, or you're whipped before you start. You must have absolute confidence in yourself when you face the enemy. The only way you can have that confidence is by proving yourself here on the practice field. Once you have been successful in combat, your confidence will grow."

Running his gaze over the young and eager faces, Brownell said, "All right, I'm going to pick one man who has little experience and put him up against a man who is well-experienced. The newer man will learn quickly that way."

His black eyes settled on a young recruit who showed real promise. "Private Phil Harrison," he said crisply, "you come."

While Harrison was threading his way amongst the men, Brownell was trying to decide which experienced man to choose. Suddenly the little colonel stepped forward and said, "Corporal Brownell, let me go up against Harrison."

Buck's brow furrowed. "You, sir?"

"Sure," grinned Ellsworth. "Why not?"

"Well...you're our leader, sir. You're a colonel."

"So? I'm well experienced. Let's see what I can teach Harrison."

A soldier stepped up and offered Ellsworth his rifle. It was already fixed with a bayonet. The colonel thanked him, and under the eyes of every man in the crowd, he squared off with Private Harrison.

Though Harrison was a much larger man, he was intimidated by the little colonel. They parried with each other for several minutes, with Ellsworth giving verbal instructions at the same time. Harrison kept leaving himself vulnerable to the colonel's feinting thrusts. Ellsworth warned him of it, pointing out that such mistakes would cost him his life in actual battle.

Harrison also was leaving himself open for a rifle butt against his jaw. Ellsworth explained what the young recruit was doing, making sure he understood that if he was caught with a rifle butt, he would go down, and his enemy would drive his bayonet into his heart.

Private Harrison did better at countering Ellsworth's bayonet thrusts, but once again left his jaw unprotected. Ellsworth decided it was time to give Harrison a lesson. The rifle butt came swiftly against young Harrison's jaw, and he went down, dazed. Standing over him, the colonel raised his weapon, pointing the bayonet at Harrison's heart, and brought it down. Harrison's eyes bulged. Ellsworth drove the steel blade into the ground inches from the young recruit's arm. He then offered a hand and helped him up.

"I want all of you to think about what you just saw," Ellsworth said. "One wrong move in a bayonet fight, and it's over. You don't get a second chance. So you all can see exactly how it should be done— Corporal Brownell, grab your rifle. Let's show them."

Brownell had never done a demonstration with his superior officer, and would rather not, but he had to obey him. Picking up his rifle, he moved close to Ellsworth. Taking his stance, with bayonet ready to thrust, the colonel said, "All right, Corporal, come and get me."

Brownell held his weapon at ready and moved in. Ellsworth adeptly dodged his mock thrust and parried, but the quick-footed Brownell turned speedily and swung his rifle butt dangerously close to Ellsworth's chin. The heads of the bright-uniformed spectators bobbed at the close call.

Ellsworth laughed and said to the Zouaves, "See, men? I made an error. I should have prevented him from making that move." Then to Brownell, "Congratulations, Corporal. For playing around, that was perfect. All right, let's go again. This time, you won't out-maneuver me."

As the two men danced about and parried with each other, Ellsworth was quickly out-foxed again. Brownell had the opportunity to connect with the colonel's jaw once more, but purposely missed. This time, Ellsworth took advantage of it and cracked Buck's jaw hard, knocking him down. The colonel raised his bayonet as if to stab him, and said, "You made a mistake, Corporal! If I was the enemy, I would have killed you."

Rising, Brownell shook his head. "No, sir. You wouldn't have killed me. If you had been an enemy, I would've connected with your jaw and put you down. *You'd* be the dead man."

Ellsworth squinted at his opponent. "Are you saying, Corporal, that you missed me *that* time on purpose?"

"Yes, sir."

Disbelief showed in Ellsworth's eyes. "I don't think so. If you honestly had the advantage of me, you should have put me down. It appeared to me that you just flat missed."

"I didn't put you down, sir, because you're my commanding officer."

Ellsworth grinned at him, and in a cocky manner, took a fighting stance. "Forget my rank, Brownell. I'm coming after you."

Far be it from Corporal Francis E. Brownell to disobey his commanding officer. When Ellsworth came at him, the corporal side-stepped swiftly and cracked him solidly with his rifle butt. Ellsworth sprawled on the ground and lay still. He was out cold.

The Zouaves looked on wide-eyed and open-mouthed as Corporal Brownell called for a canteen of water and knelt beside Ellsworth. Quickly the canteen was supplied. Brownell uncorked it and splashed water in the colonel's face. The colonel slowly came around. Blinking his eyes, he looked up at Brownell and shook his head to clear it.

"Here sir," said Brownell, placing a hand at the back of Ellsworth's head, "let me help you sit up." Buck eased him into a sitting position.

"I'm sorry, Colonel," said Buck. "I—"

"Don't be sorry, Corporal. I told you to do it. You did. And yours truly found out he needs to sharpen up on his bayonet practice."

Brownell helped the colonel to his feet, then said to the Zouaves, "All right, men. Let's pair off. I want you more experienced men to choose partners with less experience. Time is of the essence, now. We'll be going into battle soon. While you practice, I'll move amongst you and give pointers where they're needed."

As Zouaves prepared to follow Brownell's instructions, Colonel Ellsworth said, "Corporal, I like your style. When we leave here and go to war, I want you as my personal aide. You will stay close to me at all times."

"Yes, sir. It will be my pleasure."

On Monday, Colonel Ellsworth received a special wire from President Lincoln, announcing his call to arms of seventy-five thousand militiamen and ordering the colonel to bring his Eleventh New York Zouaves regiment to Washington. War was being declared on the Confederacy, and Lincoln wanted the Zouaves in Washington, ready for battle. The wire also informed Ellsworth that the New York Central Railroad—by the president's order—would add several cars to bring the Zouaves to Washington. Other militia units from New York and New England would also be heading for the nation's capital.

When Ellsworth made the announcement to his men, they shouted with joy. They were eager to punish the Rebels for their insurrection against the U.S. government.

When Colonel Ellsworth presented his regiment at the Utica depot, on Wednesday morning, April 17, railroad officials explained that they would change trains in New York City and be on their way to Baltimore on Thursday. A third train would take them the thirty miles to Washington from there.

The Zouaves boarded the special cars, carrying what luggage was necessary, along with their weapons and ammunition. When the train rolled into the depot in New York, the Zouaves found that eight hundred men of the Sixth Massachusetts Infantry were there, also going to Washington. The Sixth Massachusetts was under the command of Colonel Edward F. Jones. They would be on the same train to Baltimore, along with a small regiment of soldiers from the Seventh New York Militia, led by Captain Alex Frame.

Word spread throughout New York City that Federal troops would be changing trains in New York on their way to Washington. On Thursday morning, thousands of New Yorkers gathered to see them off and wish them well. A band played and people waved American flags.

Colonel Ellsworth was standing on the platform, observing his Zouaves as they boarded their special cars, when he saw Colonel Jones and Captain Frame coming toward him in a hurry, threading their way through the enthusiastic crowd. As they drew up, Edwards shouted above the din while waving a telegram, "This message just came to me through the telegraph office here. It's from John Hay, Mr. Lincoln's secretary. Mr. Lincoln wants us to know that there was serious trouble yesterday in Baltimore. A militia unit from Pennsylvania was passing through there on their way to Washington and was assaulted by a jeering mob of pro-Confederate civilians! They pelted the soldiers with rocks and bricks."

"So we need to prepare ourselves, is that it?" said Ellsworth.

"Exactly. We'll need to distribute ammunition to our men and have them load their weapons."

Captain Frame asked, "Are we supposed to fire at will if we are threatened, Colonel?"

"Tell your men to hold fire if at all possible, but if they judge that their lives are in danger, they have the president's permission to use their weapons to protect themselves."

Once on the train, the three regiments were given the president's instructions by their officers. Ammunition was distributed, and the troops loaded their guns.

The train reached Baltimore's President Street station at noon on Friday, April 19. Arrangements had been made for horses to pull the military cars over a track through the city to the Camden Street station, where the Baltimore and Ohio Railroad line to Washington commenced.

As the cars were detached from the train and horses harnessed to them, a railroad official entered Colonel Jones's car and warned him that an angry pro-Confederate mob was waiting in the streets. The Baltimore police estimated there were over ten thousand in the mob, and it was still growing. There were too few policemen to even begin to control them.

Jones called Ellsworth and Frame out of their cars and passed the warning on to them. As they discussed the situation, Ellsworth said, "Colonel, we'll be sitting ducks in these cars. Shouldn't we put the men in close ranks and just march them over to the other station?"

"Then we have no protection at all," argued Jones. "At least inside the cars, we have some protection."

"I think we'd be better off outside, sir," said Ellsworth. "I'm afraid our men will be hampered by the close quarters of the cars. They'll have a hard time wielding their weapons. If they're outside, they'll have freedom of movement."

"But they'll also be clear targets," objected Jones. "I say we stay in the cars."

Ellsworth knew army regulations quite well. When there are two officers of the same rank, and a decision has to be made, the officer with seniority is automatically in charge. Jones was nine years older than Ellsworth and had been in the army that much longer.

"All right, Colonel," said the younger man. "My men and I will do as you say. However, if we see that our cramped situation puts us in mortal danger, I will give them orders to move outside and fight."

"If that becomes the case and I see that my judgment was wrong, we'll join you," said Jones.

"Same for us," put in Frame.

"All right, gentlemen," said Jones, "let's get aboard. They're about ready to move out."

Colonel Ellsworth passed the word to his men to be prepared to move out and fight if he gave the order. The Zouaves trusted their leader explicitly, and would follow his orders without question. As Ellsworth had requested, Corporal Brownell rode in his car and sat beside him.

As the horses began to pull the cars out of the depot, Buck said, "Colonel, if this thing turns ugly, I'd like for you to get down on the floor."

Ellsworth shook his head. "Can't do that, Corporal. I'm the leader, here. I can't expect these men to have respect for me if I duck out of the fight."

"But you're our commander, sir. We can't afford to lose you."

"Only when I become a general will I remain aloof from the action. Until then, I'll fight right along with my men."

"I respect that, sir, but you've asked me to be your personal aide. At least let me do what I can to protect you."

"I want you as my aide to help me get things done when I need them. I didn't mean you had to risk your life to protect mine."

Buck grinned. "Okay, but since you want me as your aide, I'm sticking as close as the hide on a cow."

As the car moved slowly out of the station, they heard the roar of the angry mob. They could hear the sound of breaking glass in the cars ahead, and the soldiers in them were shouting amongst themselves. Buck moved to the front of the car, opened the door, and moved out onto the platform. Turning back quickly, he said so that every man in the coach could hear, "Colonel, the mob has blockaded the track. There's no way we can get the cars through. They're throwing bricks and stones...and they're looking plenty mean."

Suddenly the windows of the car began to shatter as rocks and bricks crashed through them. The wild throng was shouting and swearing at the Union soldiers. One man was heard to scream, "Welcome to Southern graves, Yankee swine!"

Colonel Ellsworth raised an elbow to protect his face from flying glass and shouted, "Let's get out of here, men! Use your guns. Maybe if a few of them go down, the rest will back off."

All along the line, soldiers poured from the cars and began firing into the mob. The first volley brought screams and curses, and for a moment it appeared that the Southern sympathizers would withdraw. But they quickly regrouped and attacked the soldiers, brandishing clubs and makeshift weapons. They also found more bricks and rocks to throw.

Colonel Jones was leading his troops toward the Camden Street station. Their progress was slow because the street had become a virtual battleground. Soldiers and civilians were going down and being trampled underfoot as rifles barked and the mob swung clubs, crowbars, hammers, and fists. When soldiers fell, their comrades dragged them along while fighting off the crazed citizens of Baltimore. Soon pistols and muskets were being fired at the uniformed men from windows, doors, and roofs of stores and houses. Most of the bullets, however, were hitting rioters.

The Union troops were sorely outnumbered, but fought back gallantly. Rioters wrestled with many of them, wrenching the muskets from their hands and using the bayonets on them. One Zouave took dead aim at a rioter who had just stabbed a soldier with his own bayonet and pulled the trigger. The musket did not fire. Five wild-eyed citizens leaped on the Zouave, yanked the bayoneted musket from his hands, and ran him through.

A few feet away, Colonel Ellsworth and Corporal Brownell were fighting side by side. Ellsworth had just shot a rioter through the heart and Brownell dropped one with his bayonet When they saw the Zouave go down, they turned on his killers. The colonel blasted two of them with his revolver and swung the gun on another, but the hammer came down on a spent shell.

Buck stabbed one of them with his bayonet, cracked another on the jaw, then pivoted to stab the one Ellsworth was facing. However, the little colonel had slammed the man on the temple with his gun barrel, putting him down. Another rioter came up behind Brownell, wielding a knife. Ellsworth saw him and shouted, "Buck! Behind you!"

Buck pivoted, but not in time to dodge the deadly blade. It slashed across his face, burning like a red-hot iron. Reacting quickly, Buck seized the man's arm and brought it down on a raised knee. Bone snapped, the man howled, and the knife clattered to the street.

Blood streamed down Brownell's cheek as he continued to fight alongside his commanding officer. The Union troops stayed in close ranks as much as possible as they battled the mob and worked their way toward the railroad station.

Finally they reached the station, but the frenzied throng tried to block them from boarding the train. The Union officers braced their men for a final push and commanded those who had reloaded to fire point-blank into the mob. The fusillade cut a path, leaving bleeding bodies in its wake, and the soldiers boarded the train, carrying and aiding their wounded. The train pulled out with members of the mob shouting obscenities, throwing missiles, and firing through the windows with muskets they had wrested from the soldiers' hands.

As the train left Baltimore behind, the troops began tending to their wounded. Colonel Ellsworth tended to Brownell's slashed cheek, doing what he could to stop the bleeding.

At Fort Sumter, no one had been killed. The riot in Baltimore left a dozen citizens dead and scores wounded. Four soldiers had died and over a hundred were seriously wounded.

Baltimore's bloody riot was an accurate omen of what was coming. America had tasted civil war on its own streets. No person would be guaranteed shelter from its effects, whether in uniform or out of it.

CHAPTER FIVE

✦

Government authorities in Washington learned of the riot in Baltimore long before the train arrived with the soldiers. Baltimore's mayor had sent a wire, advising them that some of the soldiers had been killed in the clash with the pro-Southern civilians, and that a large number had been wounded. The wounded ones would need immediate medical attention when the train arrived in Washington.

The nation's capital city had only one small hospital, which was not equipped well enough to care for the number of soldiers who had been wounded. A vivacious and civic-minded young woman named Clara Barton—an employee at the U.S. Patent Office—quickly organized a makeshift hospital in the rotunda of the Capitol. Using congressional messenger boys, Clara called for doctors to come with medicine and equipment, and to bring as many nurses with them as possible. Realizing she would still be short on help, Clara sent word through the Capitol and across the city, asking for volunteers to help care for the wounded soldiers.

When the train arrived at the Washington depot at five o'clock in the afternoon, President Abraham Lincoln was there to meet it. He met with the three commanding officers, and was relieved that his friend Colonel Elmer Ellsworth was unscathed.

Wagons, carriages, and surreys were provided by concerned citizens to carry the wounded soldiers to the Capitol. They were amazed to find the makeshift hospital ready for them. Most of the troops went directly from the depot to an army camp just outside the city. The commanding officers and a few unharmed soldiers accompanied the wounded to the Capitol.

Among the volunteers who had answered Clara Barton's call were Jenny Jordan and Patricia Winters. Mary Lincoln had encouraged Patricia to go, saying she would tutor the boys herself. Jenny, who was at her desk when the call for help came, responded immediately, since she was already in the capitol building.

Soon soldiers with blood-soaked uniforms were lying in rows on the floor of the rotunda. There were twenty wounded men for each doctor, and almost as many for each nurse. Those most seriously wounded were tended to first, while Clara directed her volunteers to make the other soldiers as comfortable as possible while they waited. Others were still being brought in .

Colonels Jones and Ellsworth, along with Captain Frame, moved amongst their wounded men. The smell of salves and antiseptics was strong in the place. President Lincoln and some of his Cabinet members stood on the stairs that led to the Capitol's second floor and observed with grave interest.

Corporal Brownell came through the large doors at the front of the rotunda, carrying a wounded Zouave in his arms like a man would carry a child. The Zouave had taken a bayonet in the upper thigh, and his bright-colored, baggy trousers were soaked with blood.

Clara was helping a soldier lay a wounded comrade on the floor when she spotted Buck coming in. Hurrying to him, she said, "Right over here, Corporal."

As Clara led the way, she looked over her shoulder and said, "He seems to be losing a lot of blood. Was anything done for him during the train ride?"

"Yes'm," replied Buck. "We wrapped it as best as we could, but the gash is pretty deep. He'll need a doctor to stitch him up as quick as possible."

Clara nodded, showed Buck where to lay him, and glanced toward Jenny, who was just finishing up a temporary bandage on the broken, bleeding hand of a soldier nearby.

Clara called, "Jenny, as soon as you're finished there, I need you to come and cut away this soldier's pantleg."

"Be right there," Jenny answered.

Clara knelt beside Buck, looked down at the wounded man, and said, "I'll have a doctor here as quickly as possible, soldier. In the meantime, Miss Jordan will tend to you."

The Zouave, a private named Wally Springer, tried to smile. "Thank you ma'am. I appreciate your wonderful help."

"We all do," Buck said, giving Miss Barton an amiable smile. "They told us on the train that you headed this operation up, ma'am. You *are* Clara Barton?"

"Yes."

"You're not a nurse?"

"No, Corporal—"

"Brownell, ma'am. Buck Brownell."

"No, Corporal Brownell, I'm not a nurse. I've never been able to afford the cost for schooling. I work in the U.S. Patent Office, but I've volunteered my services here in the city when there've been disasters of one kind or another."

"That's very kind of you, ma'am."

Clara smiled. "Thank you. I see some more men being brought in. Miss Jordan will be here in a moment, and I'll see that a doctor is sent over as soon as one is available."

As Clara walked away, Buck said, "Wally, you'll be okay. It looks like the bleeding has eased off." Just then Buck looked up to see Jenny

Jordan drop to her knees on the other side of Wally Springer. She had a pair of scissors in her hand.

For a brief, magical moment, the eyes of Jenny and Buck locked and held. Corporal Brownell, roughneck Zouave and tough trainer of soldiers, was spellbound. His heart seemed to stop dead in his chest, yet his temples were pounding.

Jenny managed a sweet smile and said, "I'm Jenny Jordan."

Buck was so stricken that his brain seemed to go flat on him. For a moment he couldn't think of his name.

The wounded private saw the corporal's predicament and spoke up. "His name is Corporal Francis Brownell, ma'am. Mine's Wally Springer."

Jenny broke the spell by pulling her gaze from Buck and looking down at the wounded man. "Are you in pain, Wally?" she asked.

"A little bit, Miss Jenny, but it's not bad."

Leaning over him and tugging at the bloody pantleg, she aimed the scissors a few inches above the gash and said, "I'll try not to hurt you, but I have to cut this pantleg off so the doctor can get to the wound."

"That's all right, ma'am," said Springer, also taken by Jenny. "It'll be worth it just to have such a pretty lady taking care of me."

"Aren't you the flatterer?" she said lightly as she began to cut.

Buck watched Jenny work the scissors through the blood-soaked cloth and said, "I assume because you're not in a nurse's uniform that you're not a nurse, ma'am."

"You're right," she replied, concentrating on her work.

"You sure handle those scissors like you've done it before."

"Up until a short time ago I was a seamstress, Corporal Brownell," she replied without looking up.

"That answers it. So what do you do now?" He had noticed that she wore no wedding ring, so he wasn't afraid she would tell him she was now a housewife.

"I work for the government. I am a receptionist here in the Capitol for the Senate Military Committee."

"Sounds like an interesting job," Buck said.

Jenny finished cutting the pantleg and said, "It has its moments." Then looking up at Buck, she asked, "Would you help me, Corporal? He'll have less pain if the two of us slip this pantleg off together."

"Sure, just tell me how you want it done."

Suddenly Jenny caught sight of the gash on Buck's cheek. "Oh, Corporal!" she gasped. "You're wounded too...and it looks pretty bad. We'll get one of the doctors to check on it."

Buck's fingertips found the gash. "Oh, it's all right, ma'am. It's starting to scab over. It hasn't bled since this morning."

"But it looks swollen," she said, studying the wound. "I'll clean it in a moment, then we'll get a doctor to look at it. I think there might be some infection."

"Whatever you say," Buck grinned.

Jenny instructed Buck on how to help her slide the severed pantleg downward and over Springer's boot. Carefully, they worked together and had it done within a minute. Then she said to the private, "I'll get some alcohol and clean around your wound, Mr. Springer. Be back in just a minute."

While she was gone, Springer asked, "Corporal, you ever see a woman as pretty as her?"

"Not that I can remember."

"Kinda took your breath away, didn't she?"

"You might say that."

"*Might*, nothing. She had you so mesmerized, you couldn't even think of your own name."

Before Buck could comment, Jenny returned, carrying cloths

and a bottle of alcohol. On her heels came a doctor and his nurse. The doctor did a quick examination of Buck's wound and told him he would have to take stitches. He asked Jenny to clean the wound while he and the nurse took care of Springer. Jenny took Buck a few steps away to a straight-backed wooden chair and sat him down.

While she worked, trying her best not to hurt him, Jenny said, "It's awful what happened to you and the other soldiers in Baltimore. I understand some of our men were killed."

"Yes, ma'am."

"I'm afraid what happened there is just a small foreshadowing of what lies ahead. I wish there wasn't going to be a civil war."

"I do, too, Miss Jenny, but I don't think there's anything that can be done to stop it." He paused, then asked, "Do I detect a slight Southern accent in your speech?"

"Mm-hmm. I'm from Virginia."

"I see. Your parents still live there?"

"No. My mother is dead. Daddy and I live here in Washington. You may have heard of him—Lieutenant Colonel Jeffrey Jordan?"

"*Colonel Jeffrey Jordan!*" Buck exclaimed. "The Mexican War hero?"

"One in the same," she said proudly. "He's now military adviser to the Senate Committee on military affairs."

"Do you suppose I could meet him sometime? I've heard a lot about what he did in the war."

"I suppose that could be arranged. Now, hold still, Corporal. I've got to clean very close to the gash."

Buck winced as the alcohol touched its fire to the open wound.

"I'm sorry," Jenny said quietly, "but this has to be done."

"I know. Sorry I jumped."

Jenny soaked the cloth from the bottle, then leaned close to apply the alcohol. Buck's heart was doing strange things with Jenny so close to him. He found her invigorating. Never had a woman so stirred him.

On the other side of the rotunda, Patricia Winters found herself wrapping a broken forefinger on the right hand of Lieutenant John Hammond of the Sixth Massachusetts. One of the doctors had set the finger, explained to Patricia how to splint it and wrap it correctly, then moved on to another patient.

While Patricia worked at getting the finger wrapped just right, the lieutenant looked at her admiringly and said, "The doctor called you Patricia, Miss. May I ask your last name?"

"You may," she smiled. "It's Winters. You know...like the cold time of year."

Hammond smiled. "And where are you from, Miss Patricia Winters?"

"Springfield, Illinois."

"Springfield, Illinois? Are you acquainted with our president?"

Patricia smiled, took a second to brush a lock of dark-brown hair from her forehead, and replied, "You might say I am."

"Now, what does that mean?"

She giggled. "I work for Mr. Lincoln."

"Really?"

"Mm-hmm. *And* Mrs. Lincoln."

"Doing what? Don't tell me you're a maid in the White House."

"No. I'm governess to their two sons, Willie and Tad. Have been for nearly six years."

"Governess, eh?" he said pleasantly surprised.

"Mm-hmm."

"Are the boys really like the papers make them out to be? I mean, Willie quiet and reserved and Tad a regular pistol?"

"Exactly," Patricia laughed. "I love them both, of course, but that Tad is the charmer. I have to be careful. He can turn on that personality of his and talk me into all kinds of things."

"So you like your job."

"Very much so."

"Not planning on nuptials, then, I take it."

"Oh, I wouldn't say that," she said, tying a small knot to finish the wrapping. "When Mr. Right comes along, I'll marry him and give up my governess job."

"Any prospects for a groom at the moment?"

"No. There wasn't anyone I felt serious about in Springfield...and I've been so busy since moving to Washington that I haven't had time to meet any single young men here."

"Don't the Lincolns ever give you any time for yourself?"

"Oh, yes. I mean...they do if I ask for it." Patricia could tell Lieutenant Hammond was attracted to her.

"Well, then, what would you say if I asked you to spend a little free time with *me*?" asked Hammond.

Patricia cleared her throat nervously. "Well...well I'd say...*yes!*"

"Good! How soon can you get some time off?"

"I can have Sunday. I was going to ask the Lincolns for Sunday morning off, at least, so I can attend church. There's a Congregational church not far from the White House. I thought I'd try it."

"Would you mind some company?" he asked quickly.

"Not at all," she smiled.

"What about *after* church? I mean...maybe a picnic and a walk through the park?"

"All right. I'll make us a picnic lunch."

"How...ah...how do I get my buggy through the gates at the White House so I can pick you up?"

"That'll be easy. I'll be waiting at the gate on the east side at ten-thirty."

"Okay, Miss Patricia. I'll be there at ten-thirty sharp!"

When the doctor had finished stitching and bandaging Buck's face, he told Buck to come to his office in a week so he could examine the wound. If it was healing properly by that time, he would take the stitches out.

Jenny had gone to help Clara Barton with another patient while the doctor was working on Buck. Just as the doctor walked away, Jenny returned, smiling, and said, "Well, Corporal, it looks like you're all fixed up."

"Guess so," said Buck, who was still seated on the chair.

Jenny pulled up another chair and sat down. "We've got all the wounded men taken care of now. I have to get back to work upstairs shortly, but I thought I'd come back and see how you're doing."

"I'm fine, ma'am," said Buck.

"So...where are you from, Corporal? I know you're in the Eleventh New York Fire Zouaves, but if I understand correctly, that doesn't mean you have to be a native New Yorker."

"That's right. We have men in the Eleventh who are from Illinois and Pennsylvania, as well as New York. Myself, I'm from Saratoga Springs, New York."

"Your parents live there?"

"They're both dead, ma'am."

"Oh, I'm sorry."

"That's all right. How could you know? I have a sister who lives in California, and a brother who lives right here in Washington."

"Oh? Older or younger than you?"

"Both older. I'm twenty-six. Sis is thirty and has two children.

Robert is twenty-eight. Married, but no children yet."

"I'm interested in what caused you to join the Zouaves. I mean...they are just a bit different than your usual state militia."

"Well, let me explain that."

Just then Colonel Ellsworth drew up and said, "Well, Corporal, I see you've been patched up. Did this young lady do that for you?"

"No, sir," said Buck, rising to his feet. "She prepared the wound, but a doctor actually did the bandaging after he'd taken several stitches."

"So it'll be okay?"

"Doctor says I'll have a scar, but it'll be all right, yes," replied Buck. Then gesturing toward Jenny, he said, "Colonel Elmer Ellsworth, I would like you to meet Miss Jenny Jordan."

Ellsworth clicked his heels, bowed, and said, "Miss Jordan, it is a pleasure to make your acquaintance."

"Likewise, I'm sure," Jenny said warmly, smiling. "I've heard much about you, Colonel. Your exploits with the Zouave Drill Team are quite well known and very much discussed in our family. My father is Lieutenant Colonel Jeffrey Jordan. Perhaps you've heard of him?"

"Well, I certainly have. Talk about exploits! Your father is what I call a genuine hero."

"Why, thank you. I'll tell Daddy I met you, and relay your kind words about him."

Buck felt a tinge of jealousy over Jenny's warmth toward the colonel, and quickly reprimanded himself. He had no claim on her.

"Please do, ma'am," said Ellsworth. "And tell your father I would like to meet him some time."

While Jenny and the colonel discussed her father's valor on the battlefield, Buck wondered if she had a man in her life. He told himself that no woman as charming and beautiful as Jenny would find herself short of attention from men.

The conversation about Lieutenant Jordan trailed off, then

Ellsworth turned to Buck and said, "It's almost eight. We need to be getting out to the camp soon. I'll do a quick check on the rest of our Zouaves, then we'll go."

"Fine, sir," nodded Buck. "I'll wait right here." Ellsworth spoke a few departing words to Jenny and walked away.

Jenny rose to her feet and said, "Well, Corporal, I need to head for home. It's past my dinner time."

Buck had to satisfy his curiosity. "Miss Jenny," he said, "may I ask you a personal question?"

"Of course," she smiled.

"Is there a...a special man in your life? I mean...do you have a steady beau?"

"No, Corporal," she answered softly.

Surprised but pleased, Buck said, "Well, in that case, since you haven't eaten this evening, and neither have I...could I take you to dinner?"

"Well, I..."

Seeing her hesitation, Buck said, "Oh, you have to get home to prepare dinner for your father, don't you?"

"No. No, I don't. Daddy's eating dinner with friends."

"Then you can let me take you to dinner. There must be a good restaurant somewhere close by, isn't there?"

"Well, yes, but..."

"You said you wanted to know why I joined the Zouaves."

Jenny was feeling a magnetic pull toward the rugged Zouave, but was careful to mask it. "Oh, I do, but you heard the colonel. He wants you to go to the camp with him."

"I can talk him into letting me come to the camp after I take you to dinner."

A bit off balance at Buck's forwardness, Jenny laughed hollowly and said, "I doubt that, Corporal."

Patting her shoulder, he said, "You wait right here. I'll be back in a moment."

Jenny smiled to herself and watched as Buck hurried across the rotunda and approached Colonel Ellsworth. It took the colonel only seconds to glance across the wide room at Jenny, then nod his head. Buck whirled and hastened back to Jenny.

"Ready to go?"

Shaking her head in amazement, Jenny laughed, "Corporal, you're a real dazzler, you are!"

The restaurant was busy and full of chatter as Buck and Jenny sat at their candlelit table. "I'll walk you home after we've eaten, Miss Jenny," said Buck. "I hope your father will be home so I can meet him."

"He won't be. The friends he's visiting will keep him at their house past midnight. You'll have to meet him some other time. Now, Corporal, I want to hear why you joined the Zouaves."

Buck grinned in spite of the pain it caused. "Tell you what, Miss Jenny. I'd like it better if you would just call me by my name. You don't have to call me Corporal."

"All right, Francis," she said warmly.

"Not by that name, please. I don't know why my parents did such a thing to me. I guess they just didn't think about it."

Grinning broadly, Jenny said, "Sort of hurt your male ego?"

"Yes. Got me into lots of fights as a kid, too. When I was twelve, I started calling myself Buck."

"I see. Well, Buck does sound a lot more masculine than Francis, I'll admit. Okay, I'll call you Buck if you'll call me Jenny."

"It's a deal, ma'am," he said, reaching across the table to shake her hand.

"Not *ma'am*, Buck," she corrected him. "*Jenny*."

"Jenny."

She shook his hand, then said, "Now, tell me about joining the Zouaves."

Pleased that Jenny was interested, Buck told her of his boyhood fascination with the military and that he had joined the Regular Army immediately after graduating from high school. When the rough-and-ready Zouaves captured his interest, he asked for a transfer and got it. That was a year and a half ago. He enjoyed being a part of the famous drill team and liked working for the colorful Colonel Ellsworth.

As he walked Jenny home after dinner, Buck said cautiously, "Jenny..."

"Yes, Buck?"

"I'm...going to pay a visit to my brother Robert and his wife tomorrow evening. Would...would you like to go with me?"

"Oh, I'd like to, Buck, but I have so much to do at home tomorrow night. With my mother gone, I have to keep the house in good order and see to Daddy's needs. Tomorrow I have to get the washing and ironing done."

"I understand," he said, feeling disappointed. "Then how about Sunday?"

"Well, Daddy and I always go to church on Sunday. You'd certainly be welcome to come along. You could have Sunday dinner with us, then the two of us could take a stroll through Stanton Park in the afternoon. We go to Penn Avenue Methodist. Our pastor is a fire-eater. You'll hear some hell-fire and brimstone preaching."

"I'm used to that," chuckled Buck. "I was brought up in a Baptist church in Saratoga Springs. And even if I wasn't used to it, I'd gladly endure it for the pleasure of that stroll with you in the park."

CHAPTER SIX

✦

Corporal Buck Brownell stood on the porch of his brother's house in the light of the setting sun and knocked for the third time. He waited for the sound of footsteps from within, then sighed and turned from the door. He would look in the back yard. Maybe Robert and Kady were back there.

He had just stepped off the porch when he saw an elderly man looking at him from the front porch of the house next door. The silver-haired neighbor smiled and said, "You're one of them New York Zouaves, aint'cha?"

Buck knew his uniform was a dead giveaway. "Yes, sir. You wouldn't know where the Brownells are, would you?"

"Yep. I'll bet you're Robert's brother, Buck."

"Yes, sir," nodded Buck, walking toward him.

"They're lookin' for you, son. They been visitin' some of Kady's relations down in Richmond, and just got back this afternoon. I'd heard about all them soldiers what got kilt and banged up in Baltimore, an' I heard that some of 'em was New York Zouaves. So when Robert an' Kady come home a while ago, I tol' 'em 'bout it. They got all upset, 'fraid that you mighta been kilt or wounded, so they lit out like bats out of a burnin' belfry. I s'pose they headed for the Capitol buildin', 'cause that's where I tol' 'em the wounded was bein' took care of."

"How long ago did they leave?"

The old man scratched his hoary head. "Well, I reckon it was at least a hour ago. Mebbe more like a hour an' a half."

"All right, sir. I'll head toward the Capitol. Maybe I can—" Buck's attention was drawn to a buggy bounding down the street, throwing up a cloud of dust.

"Looks like that's them a-comin' now," said the neighbor.

Buck watched the buggy slow and turn into the yard, then moved toward it as Robert jerked the reins and brought it to a halt.

"Oh, Buck!" gasped Kady, leaping from the buggy and running toward him. "I'm so glad you're okay!" Kady was weeping as she threw her arms around her brother-in-law and held him tight.

Patting her back with both hands, Buck said, "Hey, Kady, don't cry. I'm all right."

Robert drew up and said, "We were really scared when we learned that your outfit was in that riot, Buck." He moved in to throw an arm around his brother's neck, but stopped short when he saw the bandage. "What happened to your face?"

Kady pulled back and eyed the bandage through her tears.

"Just a scratch," chuckled Buck. "Fella was coming at me from behind with a knife. My commander, Colonel Ellsworth, saw him and hollered at me. I turned around and took the tip of the knife in my cheek. Better than taking the whole blade in my back."

"It was Colonel Ellsworth who told us you were coming to our house," Kady said. "First we went to the Capitol. They told us you'd be at the army camp, so we hurried out there. A sentry told us you were the colonel's aide, and when we found him, we'd find you. I'm glad the colonel knew where you were headed."

Buck patted his stomach and said, "Well, I was hoping I'd be in time for supper. There's just no cooking as good as my sister-in-law's."

"Well, I'll see what I can whip up," Kady said, smiling.

During the meal, Robert and Kady asked about the New York Fire Zouaves and the famous Colonel Ellsworth. It had been a thrill for them to meet the national hero.

"Speaking of national heroes," Buck said, "guess who I'm going to get to meet tomorrow!"

"President Lincoln?" queried Kady.

"I saw him at the depot and at the Capitol, but I didn't get to meet him. I hope I'll get to do that, also...but tomorrow morning I'm going to attend the Penn Avenue Methodist church with none other than Lieutenant Colonel Jeffrey Jordan himself!"

"How'd this come about, little brother?" asked Robert.

"I met his daughter, Jenny, at the Capitol yesterday. She helped one of the doctors take care of this gash on my face."

"She a nurse?" asked Robert.

"No, she works in the Capitol building as a receptionist in the Senate Chamber...the Military Committee on Foreign Affairs, particularly. You know Clara Barton?"

"Everybody in Washington knows who she is," said Kady. "Always helping people in trouble."

"Well, she had put out a call for women to come and help the doctors with the wounded soldiers, and Jenny was one of the volunteers."

Robert grinned. "So my little brother turned on his charm with Jordan's daughter and wrangled himself a meeting with the famous Mexican War hero!"

Kady laughed. "Well, I know a little bit about how the Brownell men can turn on the charm!"

Robert reached across the table, took her hand, and said, "Yes, and you love it."

"You're right. And I bet Miss Jordan did too!"

Looking at Buck, Robert said, "Maybe if you get in good with Jenny and her famous father, we can meet him too."

Waggling his head, Buck said, "Well, I'll see what I can do."

The three of them laughed together, then the conversation turned to the civil war hanging like a black cloud over their heads. Each hoped it would not last long. Buck said that Union military experts were confident that one good bloody battle would crumple the Confederate army, and it would all be over.

Sunday morning brought a clear sky, a soft breeze, and the sweet smell of cherry blossoms along Maryland Avenue, where the Jordan home stood a half-block from Stanton Park.

Jenny was in her bedroom, applying extra powder to her face in an attempt to disguise the dark circles under her eyes. She had not slept well for two nights, ever since her father had told her of his spy ring activities. She feared he would be caught and executed.

A shadow fell across the open door behind her. Jenny looked at her father reflected in the mirror, and said, "I'll be ready in a moment, Daddy."

"Honey, I'm sorry this thing has upset you so, but you know it's the patriotic thing for me to do. You and I are Southerners. We must be loyal to the Confederacy."

"It's not the loyalty part that bothers me, Daddy," she said, dabbing the powder puff under her eyes, "it's the risk you're taking. I'm a Virginian, and proud of it. If I was a man, I'm sure I'd be in a Confederate uniform by now. It's just that...well, unless somehow they take a different attitude toward spies in this war, you'll face a firing squad if you're caught. Not only do I fear it first and foremost for you, but also for Rose and her girls, and for John Calhoun."

"But, honey, like I told you...I'd be in danger of getting killed if I were a soldier. Colonel Jackson agreed that what I'm doing is no more of a risk than I'd be taking in battle. John Calhoun loves the South as much as I do, and he's willing to take the risk. And as for Rose and her girls, I doubt seriously that any of these Northerners would execute women."

Jenny placed the powder puff in its box, turned, and said, "Daddy, I think they would. Men do strange things in war time. Women spies were executed on both sides in the Revolutionary War...and it happened in the Crimean War, too. Why should military leaders in this war be any different?"

"I just can't feature it, that's all. Anyway, I'm in the thick of it. If my espionage can help shorten the war and give the South the victory, it'll be worth whatever risk is involved."

A knock was heard at the front door.

"That'll be Buck," Jenny said excitedly, turning back to the mirror and smoothing the hair at her temples.

"I'll go to the door," Jordan volunteered.

"It's all right, Daddy," breathed Jenny, rushing past him. "Just be nice to him, won't you?"

Jeffrey Jordan followed slowly. He would allow his daughter to greet her guest before he arrived on the scene. He had not voiced it to Jenny, but he hoped she would not get too interested in this young Zouave. He was a Northerner. He felt the same way about Captain Jack Egan, who had been showing up on the doorstep too often lately. Egan was also a Northerner. Jordan wished Jenny would date only Southern men.

Jenny approached the door, took a second or two to smooth her hoop-skirted Sunday dress, then took a deep breath and opened the door. Corporal Brownell stood there in his well-pressed Zouave uniform, red tasseled fez in hand.

"Good morning, Jenny," Buck said, smiling broadly.

"And good morning to you, Buck," Jenny responded, showing him a warm smile. "Please come in."

As Buck moved past Jenny into the entry way, Lieutenant Jordan put in his appearance. His face was grim.

"Corporal Buck Brownell," said Jenny, stepping up beside him, "this is my father, Lieutenant Colonel Jeffrey Jordan"

"Colonel, sir, I am proud and pleased to meet you," smiled Buck, offering his hand.

"I'm glad to meet you," Jordan said, shaking Buck's hand with a touch of cool reserve. Jordan caught Jenny's apprising gaze on him and smiled in return. Putting a little more warmth in his voice, he said, "So you are in the same outfit as Colonel Elmer Ellsworth."

"Yes, sir. He's my commanding officer."

"I admire the young man."

"All of us who serve under him do too, sir. So does President Lincoln, as you probably know."

"Yes," said Jordan. Then he turned to Jenny. "Well, daughter, I guess we'd better head for church."

The Penn Avenue Methodist church was only a couple of blocks past Stanton Park. During the few minutes it took to walk it, Buck asked about Lieutenant Jordan's exploits in the Mexican War. Jordan was pleased with Buck's interest and warmed up to him even more.

That afternoon, Buck and Jenny took their planned stroll in Stanton Park, enjoying the warm sunshine and the allurement of the cherry blossoms that bedecked the trees that lined the paths. Buck wanted to hold Jenny's hand, but would not let himself be that bold. They both smiled and greeted other people they met along the way. Many were young couples holding hands. Some of the men were in uniform, but there were no other Zouaves.

When Jenny stopped to admire a bed of bright-colored flowers, Buck cleared his throat and said, "Jenny...I asked you Friday evening if you had a steady beau—"

"And I told you I don't. There are just three or four men that I see once in a while."

"Any one of them more than the others?"

Jenny was pleased that Buck was so interested. "I guess I probably spend more time with Jack Egan. He's an army captain, serving under Colonel William T. Sherman. Jack comes around more often than any of the others."

Buck felt a cold ball settle in his stomach. Being courted by a captain would give Jenny more social prestige than being courted by a lowly corporal. But Jenny seemed to like him. He would do all he could to make her like him even more. Somehow he would have to outshine this Captain Egan in her eyes.

On Tuesday, Jeffrey Jordan arrived home and entered the house to the smell of food cooking. Leaving his hat on a small table in the parlor, he moved into the kitchen. This had been one of Jenny's off-days from her job at the Capitol, and she had worked hard to prepare her father a special meal.

Jenny was at the stove, stirring gravy in a pan. Jordan approached her, kissed a cheek, and said, "Guess what news came to the president today."

"I haven't the slightest idea, Daddy," she said, concentrating on her task. "Why don't you just tell me?"

"You know we've been wondering about Colonel Robert E. Lee?"

"You mean if he'd go over to the Confederate army?"

"Yes. Well, he did."

"That's good!" she said with enthusiasm. "He'll become a leader with the Confederacy in no time."

"You're right," nodded Jordan. "He just signed up with the

Confederates this morning, and Jefferson Davis made him a general before noon. There's talk that he'll be made commander-in-chief within a day or two."

"They couldn't have picked a better man," smiled Jenny.

Jordan moved to the counter that held the wash basin and began washing his hands. "I sent word to Colonel Tom Jackson today and let him know that the spy ring is taking shape. John Calhoun and I are ready to collect classified information and pass it on to Rose, and she's already enlisted a couple of young women for her team."

Jenny poured hot gravy into a bowl and set it on the table. "Daddy, I just keep thinking of what will happen to you if you're caught. I just can't bear the thought of you...dying at the end of a rope or in front of a firing squad."

Jordan dried his hands on a towel, moved toward his daughter, and said, "Honey, we've been over this already. Let's don't belabor it. I'm willing to take my chances, as are John, Rose, and her girls. This is war, and war has its risks." He was about to take the towel back to its rack when he noticed there was only one place setting on the table. "Aren't you eating?" he asked.

"Yes, but not with you this evening," Jenny replied softly. "Buck is taking me out to dinner."

"Buck, again? You just spent most of Sunday with him. Jenny, listen...with this war about to blast open, I don't think it's wise to get attached to any young man, but especially a Northerner. Just go easy, okay? With Egan, too."

"Daddy, I really don't care that much about Jack. But Buck...well, he's different. I've never met anyone quite like him. He's—"

"Jenny, I am your father. I don't want you getting hurt. Right now is not the time to fall in love."

"Daddy, you can't lock me up in a cage just because there's a war on. I am human, you know."

Taking hold of her shoulders, Jordan looked into her eyes and said, "I'm your father, Jenny. I care what happens to my little girl. Just ease up with Buck...and keep a close watch on your heart, okay?"

"I'll be fine, Daddy," she said, hugging him. "Now, you sit down and eat your supper. I have to go get ready."

Buck Brownell picked Jenny up while her father was finishing his meal. The two men exchanged greetings only briefly, but Jordan was kind to the young Zouave for his daughter's sake.

Buck and Jenny enjoyed dinner at a fancy restaurant, then he took her to a concert. When he brought her home in the rented buggy at ten-thirty, they sat in front of the house and talked for some time.

Jenny was reluctant to go inside, but she knew she had to get up early for work the next morning. She looked at Buck in the light of the street lamp that burned nearby and said, "Buck, it's been a very nice evening. Thank you so much the wonderful dinner and the concert."

Hopping from the buggy, Buck hastily rounded its back side and took Jenny's hand to help her down. When she was on her feet, he kept her hand in his, and said, "Thank you for honoring me with your company, Jenny. I've never enjoyed an evening this much."

Buck let go of her hand and walked her to the porch, then guided her up the steps. Jenny put her hand on the doorknob, then turned and looked up into Buck's shadowed face. Jenny had never felt toward any man like she was feeling toward Buck. For a brief moment, they looked into each other's eyes. Buck's heart beat his rib cage unmercifully.

Buck hesitated, then touched his hat, smiled, and said, "Well, I know you need to get inside...and I need to get back to camp. So I'd better say goodnight. Could I take you to dinner Saturday night?"

"You certainly may," she replied warmly.

"Seven o'clock?"

"That'll be fine," she said, and turned the knob.

Buck waited till she closed the door, then made it back to the buggy in five bounds. As he drove away, his heart was still pounding.

Francis Eady "Buck" Brownell was sure he was falling in love with Jenny Jordan.

At the army camp the next morning, Buck was teaching the newest Zouaves how to become better marksmen. Colonel Ellsworth stood nearby, looking on. Buck was a crack shot and the envy of the rest of the regiment. When the training session was over and the Zouaves were scattering different directions, Brownell sat down on a tree stump and began cleaning his musket.

Ellsworth drew up and said, "Good session, Corporal. You have a real knack at teaching others what you know."

"Thank you, sir."

"Corporal, since you're my aide, I really care about anything that might happen to you."

Buck stopped what he was doing, looked up at Ellsworth, and said, "Yes, sir? Am I in some danger I don't know about?"

"Well, I don't think you would call it danger...but I think you're in a precarious situation that you ought to know about."

"Yes, sir?"

"You've been seeing Jenny Jordan quite a bit lately."

"That's right."

"It just so happens that I was talking to a couple of men from General Sherman's outfit a little earlier this morning. It seems there's a captain in their outfit who's sweet on Jenny and has dated her a number of times."

"Yes, sir. Jenny told me about him. His name's Jack Egan. Has he something to do with this precarious situation you mentioned?"

"These two men told me that Egan has been away for a couple of weeks. He just returned, and someone informed him that some Zouave has been seeing Jenny. Apparently he was irate when he heard it."

Buck shrugged his wide shoulders. "He doesn't own her."

"Well, I just thought I'd tell you that Egan has vowed to make mince meat of this Zouave when he finds out who he is. I thought I'd let you know that Egan is on your trail."

"Thank you, sir. I appreciate the warning, but I'll tell you right now...the only person who can keep me from seeing Jenny Jordan is Jenny Jordan."

"I thought you'd respond that way," grinned the colonel. "Just watch yourself."

"You can count on it," nodded Buck.

On Thursday, Corporal Brownell was sitting under a shade tree after a good workout with a small unit of the Zouaves, drinking from a canteen. A number of the men of the Eleventh New York were doing a marching drill on the grassy field nearby. Buck's attention was on the marching Zouaves when a shadow fell over him. He looked up to see a lantern-jawed captain eyeing him coldly.

"I'm Captain Jack Egan. You *Corporal* Brownell?"

Buck noted the emphasis on his rank, and stood up in respect for Eagan's captain's insignia. "I am," nodded Buck. "How'd you know who I am?"

"Asked a couple of those sweaty Zouaves over there. I understand you've been seeing Jenny Jordan," Egan said, clipping his words short.

"That's right," Buck replied.

"I want to talk to you about it."

"Talk."

Egan clinched his jaw. "I'm here to warn you to stay away from her."

"You have no claim on Jenny. She can see anybody she wants to!"

"Well, you're not to see her anymore!"

"Did Jenny say that?" demanded Buck.

"*I* said that!" boomed Egan, scowling. "I'm telling you to stay away from her!"

"I'll quit seeing Jenny when *she* tells me to stay away, and not before!"

"That attitude will only get you hurt, Brownell. I'm going to marry Jenny, do you understand?"

"Funny. Jenny hasn't mentioned such a thing at all. Maybe you'd better go check on that. And while you're checking, tell her I'm still planning on picking her up at seven Saturday night."

Egan stared hard at Brownell, then whirled and walked away. He had taken about a dozen steps when he turned and pointed a finger at the corporal. "You stay away from her, you hear?"

Buck did not reply. He simply stared back with wintry eyes.

CHAPTER SEVEN

✦

The sun was shining through a thin layer of clouds at mid-morning on Friday, April 26. The Federal army campground just outside of Washington to the northeast was patrolled by sentries at all times, and the only place allotted for an entrance was at the southeast corner, near a small creek. Soldiers were moving amongst their tents, washing clothes in the creek and clustering here and there in small groups. They had all taken part in marching drill and calisthenics earlier and were relaxing in different ways.

Guarding the entrance were privates Les Turner and Harold Byers. They were discussing the news that ex-U.S. army colonel Robert E. Lee had officially been appointed commander-in-chief of the Confederate military forces.

Byers spat angrily and said, "Dirty traitor! We oughtta put together a special unit and go kidnap him. He needs to be brought back so he can face a firin' squad!"

"I'm having a hard time about that, Harold," Turner said quietly.

"What do you mean, you're havin' a hard time about Lee's desertion?"

"Well think about it. Where you from?"

"You know I'm from Cumberland, Maryland."

"All right. Let's say that Maryland had seceded and joined the Confederacy. Which army would you belong to now?" When his partner did not reply after several moments, Turner said, "See what I mean? Isn't so easy to give an answer, is it?"

Byers gave him a grim look, then turned his attention to a rider who was trotting toward them aboard a bay gelding. The horse had a white blaze with four even white stockings to match, but neither of the guards noticed the beauty of the horse. Their eyes were glued to the woman on its back.

She drew up and flashed an engaging smile. "Good morning, gentlemen. My name is Jenny Jordan. You may have heard of my father, Lieutenant Colonel Jeffrey Jordan?"

The privates exchanged glances, then looked back up at Jenny. "Yes, ma'am," they said in perfect unison.

"I would like to see Corporal Buck Brownell. He's with the Eleventh New York Zouaves."

Byers grinned wolfishly, looked at Turner, and said, "I've never minded my name all these twenty-two years, Les, but right now, I wish my name was Buck Brownell!"

Turner chuckled, then looked up at Jenny and said, "I'm sorry, ma'am, but civilians aren't allowed in the camp unless they have a written order from a proper authority."

"Well," said Jenny, "how about one of you fine gentlemen finding Corporal Brownell for me while I wait here?"

"Sorry, ma'am," said Byers, "but we can't leave our post. And that's probably best, 'cause there'd be a bloody fight between Les and me as to which one got to stay here with you. However, maybe I can holler at somebody and—"

"Oh!" gasped Jenny, suddenly noticing an army wagon rattling up from her left. "Here's Corporal Brownell now!"

A smile spread across Buck's face as he pulled rein and hauled the wagon to a halt, the horses blowing. "Hello, Jenny!"

Jenny's mount bobbed its head at the wagon team and nickered, dancing about a bit. Steadying the animal, Jenny returned the smile and said, "Hello, yourself."

The two guards looked on with envy as Buck asked Jenny, "Aren't you working today?"

"No. Sometimes I switch off with my alternate. She owed me a day for a time I filled in for her, so I decided to take today off. I just rode over to see how you are. I see the doctor removed your stitches."

"Yes," nodded Buck, touching the reddened scar gingerly. "I just came from there." A flood of warmth washed through Buck. Jenny cared enough about him to ride to the camp and see about his wound.

"Does the doctor think the scar will be permanent?" Jenny asked.

"He says there'll be a tiny white ridge, and with my dark skin, it'll show some."

"Well, as far as I'm concerned," she said sweetly, "the scar won't hurt your looks at all."

Turner and Byers snickered. Buck's face tinted.

Jenny took a deep breath, let it out with the word, "Well..." and added, "I guess I'll be getting back home."

Buck hopped from the wagon, stepped up beside the bay, and looking up at Jenny, said, "I sure appreciate you coming out here to check on me."

Smiling down at him, she responded softly, "You mean a lot to me, Buck. I hope you know that."

The rugged Zouave's pulse throbbed. Struggling for breath, he said, "You mean a lot to me, too."

Tugging the rein to turn her mount, Jenny said, "I'll see you tomorrow night."

"You sure will," he replied.

Buck could hear the two guards laughing to themselves as he watched Jenny ride away. When she disappeared into a deep-shaded stand of trees, he wheeled to face his fun-loving tormentors.

Byers was elbowing Turner and still snickering as he said in a mocking falsetto, "You mean a lot to me, Buck. I hope you know that."

Turner grinned and said, "You mean a lot to me, too."

Buck showed them a mock-grimace and clipped, "You two are just green with envy."

Both guards burst into laughter, slapping each other on the back. Buck shook his head, climbed into the wagon seat, and snapped the reins. As the wagon rolled away, he heard Turner say, "As far as I'm concerned, the scar won't hurt your looks at all!"

Buck was grinning to himself and shaking his head again, but did not look back.

Saturday night came, and while Buck and Jenny sat eating in the Capital City Restaurant, they discussed the reports of skirmishes between Union and Confederate soldiers in various parts of northern Virginia. They talked of the military buildup on both sides and discussed their views on when and where a major battle would take place.

"The way I see it," Jenny was saying, "it'll probably happen somewhere along the banks of the Potomac."

"Could be," nodded Buck. "The river could very well be a point of contention...probably at one of the main bridges."

"That's what I'm hearing in the Capitol."

"On the other hand, the big battle just might be fought over the railroad. Maybe at one of the junctions. Talk at camp among the big brass is that to cripple the Confederate forces, the Union army will have to take control of the railroads."

Jenny sipped a cup of hot tea then set it in its saucer. "You said *the* big battle, Buck. Are you thinking the same thing I'm hearing from the

Senate Military Committee...that one big battle will settle the war?"

"Yes. That's the consensus around the camps. Among the officers, I mean."

"Well, that agrees with the opinions I'm picking up at work from the men on the Senate Military Committee. They feel that once there's a full-scale battle, the Confederates will find out they're up against a military force much better equipped and much better trained. They'll fold the first time they face the Union army."

"You're a Southerner, Jenny. Do you think the Committee is right?"

A pained expression claimed Jenny's features. Giving her shoulders a listless shrug, she replied, "I don't know. I've given it a lot of thought. The Union has some good military leaders, that's for sure—General Scott, Colonel McDowell, Colonel McClellan, and the like. But since Colonel Lee has become commander-in-chief of the Confederate forces and we—*they*—also have such men as General Beauregard and Colonel Jackson, the South may not be the pushover the Committee and the Union military leaders have imagined."

Noting the slip of Jenny's tongue, Buck leaned forward, laid his arms on the table, and said, "You're having a hard time with this, aren't you?"

"You mean being born a Southerner but living in the North and working for the Federal government?"

"Yes."

Her lower lip quivered slightly. "Yes, Buck. I am having a hard time with it. I...I feel a loyalty to Virginia. It's my home state. Since Virginia is part of the Confederacy, now, I can't help but feel torn."

"I understand. I'm sure I would have the same sentiments if New York had seceded."

"Thank you," she said, smiling weakly.

"Of course, I'm plenty glad you're on my side. I sure wouldn't want you to be my enemy."

Jenny wondered how Buck would feel toward her if he knew her father was the key man in a planned Confederate spy ring. She took a nervous sip at her tea and said softly, "I wouldn't want that, either."

Buck decided to get Jenny's mind off the North-South problem. Leaning back in his chair, he said, "Guess I ought to tell you about your friend, Captain Jack Egan."

Jenny raised her eyebrows. "Oh? Jack? What about him?"

"He paid me a little visit Thursday."

"Oh? You didn't say anything about it yesterday."

"I didn't think about it yesterday. I had my mind on the beautiful lady who rode all the way out to the camp to see about my face."

Jenny's features flushed. After a moment, she said, "Jack's been away from Washington for a short while. He came to see me Wednesday night. Someone informed him that I've been seeing a Zouave while he's been gone. He asked who it was, and I told him." Pausing briefly again, she squinted, cocked her head, and asked, "What was his little visit about?"

"He wanted to warn me to stay away from you."

Jenny's mouth dropped open. Her dark eyes went wide, and displeasure lay tightly across her face. "He *what*? What right has Jack Egan to warn you to stay away from me?"

"That's what I asked him. And I told him he had no claim on you, and that you could see anybody you wanted to."

"Good for you!" Jenny blurted. "Of all the nerve! So what did he say to that?"

"Well, I also told him that I'd quit seeing you when you told me to stay away. He said that attitude would get me hurt."

Jenny's back straightened. "He threatened you with bodily harm? Why, that impudent cad!"

"That's not all. He also told me he's going to marry you."

Jenny's jaw slacked and her eyes became even wider. Drawing a sharp breath, she blared, "If he was here, I'd slap his lying mouth! Marriage has never even been mentioned between us...and if he had brought it up, I would have told him I'm not interested in marrying the likes of him!"

Jenny's outburst drew the attention of people around them. When she saw it, she blushed brightly and slid down a little in her chair.

"I figured you'd be a little upset at the captain's announcement of your engagement," Buck said, smiling. "I'm glad you are. I assume it's all right, then, for me to ask you for another date?"

"Yes, it is."

"Okay. How about church tomorrow morning?"

"It's a date," she smiled.

Buck paid the waiter, and when they stood to leave, Jenny felt the eyes of the patrons around them fastened on her. She was glad when they were outside and in the buggy.

Buck and Jenny talked for a few moments in the buggy after it was parked in front of her house, then she said, "Well, Corporal Brownell, it's time for this girl to hit the hay."

Buck helped her from the buggy and walked her to the door. He looked into her eyes in the dim light of a nearby street lamp and said, "I'm looking forward to our time together tomorrow."

"So am I."

The night, dark and still around them, was silent except for the faint sound of countless crickets giving their nocturnal concert. Suddenly words were unnecessary. Buck slipped his arms around Jenny, drawing her close to him. She tilted her face upward and her two hands came flat against his chest. She felt his hands on her back, pulling her closer. This is the way she stood when he kissed her, long, sweet, and tender.

Releasing her, Buck whispered, "Goodnight, Jenny."

"Goodnight," she sighed, then turned and entered the house, softly closing the door.

Buck Brownell's heart was hammering his ribs as he stepped off the porch and headed down the walk toward the buggy. He was almost to the street when movement in the dark shadows slightly behind him caught his eye. He jerked his head around and slowed his pace.

A dark form glided into the soft ring of light cast by the street lamp. Buck stopped when he recognized Captain Jack Egan, though he was out of uniform.

"I saw what you did, Brownell!" Egan shouted in a strangled voice.

Buck felt the hair on the back of his neck bristle. "It's none of your business what I did. What are you skulking around here for?"

Egan moved within arm's reach. "I told you to stay away from Jenny!"

"You're not my commander, Captain," countered Buck.

"I gave you fair warning. You're going to wish you'd heeded me, Brownell!"

"Need I remind you that it's a serious offense for an officer to strike an enlisted man? It could get you in serious trouble."

"Don't you threaten me with army regulations, Brownell."

"There's another problem here, Captain—if you swing at me, I'll have to swing back. And if I strike an officer, I can be court-martialed."

"You won't have to worry about that, Brownell. I'm not in uniform, so you won't be swinging at an officer. I'll be the civilian. You be the soldier. We'll settle this man to man!" Even as he spoke, Egan's fist flashed toward Buck.

Buck dodged and countered with a hard right to Egan's jaw. The captain went down. Cursing, he scrambled to his feet and swung at Buck's head. Buck jerked his head to the side, and Egan's fist grazed his temple. Buck lashed back. Egan raised both forearms, blocking Buck's blows. Egan gave ground, then swung a haymaker that caught Buck flush on the jaw and sent him reeling. Thinking he could finish Buck off, Egan moved in quickly. Buck countered with a blow to the captain's stomach, doubling him over, then landed a solid uppercut to Egan's jaw that sent him to the ground once again.

Unaware that neighbors across the street had heard the ruckus and were standing on their porches, Brownell stood puffing over Egan and said, "I don't want to take...this any farther...than you force me to, Captain. When you're ready to stay down...I'll get in the buggy and...drive away."

Jack Egan was amazed at how hard the lighter man could punch, but he was determined to teach Buck a lesson. Rising to his feet and shaking his head to clear it, he growled, "You will stay away from Jenny, Brownell...and it'll be me who makes you."

Egan grunted and sprang at Buck, eyes wild and jaw set, his fists swinging wildly. Buck dodged one fist, took the second one on his shoulder, and lashed back, striking Egan on the nose. The punch stunned Egan, sending him backpedaling and blinking against the water that flooded his eyes.

Brownell was after him. Egan took a blow on the jaw, which propelled him backward against the light pole. His head hit the pole and rebounded. Buck cracked him again, and sent him sliding down the pole to a sitting position. Egan sat there groaning, his head rolling. Blood was bubbling from both nostrils.

Buck stood over him for a few seconds and decided the captain had had enough. He wheeled toward the buggy and the nervous horse, and looked back toward the Jordan house. The windows on the first floor were dark, and only one window on the second floor showed light through gauzy curtains.

Still oblivious to the gaping neighbors, Buck untied the reins from the hitching post and lifted the long leathers over the horse's head. Speaking softly to calm the animal, he started to climb aboard the buggy. Suddenly, without warning, Egan's full weight slammed him into the buggy.

Buck yelped with pain as the side of the vehicle punched his ribs. He took a wild blow that put him on the ground. The frightened horse nickered and trotted down the street some twenty yards, pulling the buggy, then came to a halt, snorting.

While Brownell was on the ground, Egan—still somewhat dizzy but determined—sent a savage kick to Buck's stomach. Somehow Buck managed to roll away from the next kick that was aimed toward his face. He sprang to his feet. This time, he would put Egan out cold before turning his back on him.

Buck braced himself as the heavier man, his nose spurting blood, came at him. Brownell bobbed and weaved as he avoided two, three, four swings, then caught Egan flush on the nose again. The blow drove Egan backward. Buck hustled after him, unleashing two blows to his jaw. Egan's head whipped hard both ways and his knees buckled. They were under the street lamp, and Buck could see Egan's eyes glaze.

Two more rapid punches and Egan fell flat, unconscious. Brownell stood over his vanquished foe, sucking hard for air, making sure the captain was out cold. When Egan made no move to get up, Buck stepped around him and walked down the street to the buggy.

Inside the dark parlor of the Jordan house, Jenny peered past the edge of the curtain she had barely pulled aside and watched Buck climb into the buggy and drive away. She stared at Captain Egan, who was beginning to stir, then dropped the curtain and headed up the stairs.

When Jenny reached the landing and started down the hall toward her room, she saw her father come through his door and wait for her in the vague light of a lantern that burned low on a small table in the hall. Standing there in his robe, his hands on his hips, Jordan spoke in a level tone as she drew near. "I saw the fight, Jenny. This kind of thing must not happen again. I want you to tell both of those men you want nothing more to do with them."

Jenny's face registered her disbelief. "You can't do this to me, Daddy...you can't make me send Buck away. He fought Jack because Jack thinks he has some kind of hold on me. I like Buck, Daddy. I like him a lot. I...I've never met anyone quite like him. He—"

"Jenny, with circumstances as they are—I mean with this war building, and all—you mustn't get romantically involved with *any* man...especially a soldier. Just about the time you fall in love with one, he'll get killed. You can't put yourself in that position. Do you understand what I'm saying? I'm trying to save you some heartache."

Jenny's countenance fell. "Yes, Daddy, but—"

Gripping her shoulders firmly, Jordan said, "Honey, listen to me. This war won't last for long. Please...no more thoughts of romance until this thing is settled and our lives can get back to normal."

Jeffrey Jordan chose not to voice it, but he did not want his daughter hooking up with *any* Northerner. They were Southerners, and the family would stay Southern if he had anything to do with it. He must especially not allow Jenny to become close to a Union soldier now that he was a Confederate spy. Buck Brownell may be different than any man his daughter had ever met, *but he was the enemy.* Jenny must not cohort with the enemy.

Anguish showed in Jenny's eyes. "But, Daddy, I can't just send Buck away. I can't—"

"I'll handle it, Jenny," Jordan cut sharply across her words, increasing the pressure on her shoulders. "I know what's best for you."

"But, Daddy—"

"You're still not of age, Jenny. Until you turn twenty-one, you're under my authority and under my roof. I don't want you involved with a soldier with this war building up, and I already told you why. Now, the next time Buck shows up here, I'll talk to him."

Jenny had no desire to rebel against her father's authority. Neither did she want his displeasure. She understood the risk of falling in love with Buck, only to see him killed. But strong feelings for the handsome young Zouave had already taken root within her. How could she stand the pain of suddenly not seeing him anymore? And what would it do to Buck? He would be hurt, too. Tears filmed Jenny's eyes and her lower lip began to quiver.

"Now, honey," said Jordan, "don't turn on the water works. Haven't I always done right by you?"

"Yes," she nodded, as the tears started to flow.

Releasing her shoulders and wrapping his arms around her, Jordan held her close and said, "Jenny, you're young. You've got plenty of time to fall in and out of love over and over again. Just remember that my seemingly hard hand, here, is for your own good."

When Jenny sniffled but did not reply, Jordan asked, "Do you and Buck have another date set?"

Jenny nodded against his chest. "Tomorrow morning. Church."

"All right, then. You stay up in your room, and I'll meet Buck at the door when he comes."

Jenny knew better than to argue with her father. She would not be allowed to talk to Buck herself. She could only cling to the hope that Buck felt the same toward her as she did toward him, and that when the war was over, he would once again show up on her doorstep.

"Daddy," she said with a quiver in her voice as she looked up at him, "will you tell Buck why you're doing this?"

"Yes, of course. Now, you get to bed. It's late."

Corporal Buck Brownell's heart was aflutter on Sunday morning as he left the buggy and made his way up the walk toward the porch. Had he raised his line of sight, he might have seen the curtain pulled slightly aside at Jenny's window on the second floor. Instead, he bounded up the steps and rapped the brass knocker.

Heavy footsteps from inside greeted his ears, followed by the rattle of metal hardware and the door swinging open. Smiling broadly at

Jenny's father, Buck said, "Good morning, Colonel Jordan. Jenny ready?"

A solemn look settled over Jordan's face. "No, she's not. She won't be going to church with you."

Surprise registered in Buck's dark eyes. "Oh? Is she—"

"Today, or any other Sunday," clipped the colonel. "In fact, she won't be seeing you any more at all."

The hard look on Jordan's face and the sharp, clipped words caught Buck off guard. For a moment, he was unable to speak. While he struggled for words, the thickening silence between colonel and corporal ran forward.

"You may leave now," Jordan said huskily.

"Don't I get a reason for this...this sudden end to my seeing your daughter, Colonel? If it's because of what happened here in front of your house last night, sir, it—"

"It's not that."

"Well, then...could I at least talk to Jenny, sir?"

"You may not," the colonel responded coldly. "But if it'll set your mind at ease, the termination of your relationship with my daughter is *my* doing, not Jenny's."

"May I ask, sir, what I've done that would cause you to stop me from seeing Jenny?"

Jordan decided to nip the situation in the bud and keep it from ever rising again. "It's not what you've *done*, Brownell, it's what you *are*."

"And what am I, sir?"

"As Jenny's father, I have set my sights much higher for her than a common soldier. She must move in high social circles and eventually marry a man of means. I mean to see to it that her life bends in that direction, and I am starting right now."

Buck felt as if he had been hit with a battering ram. "But, sir, what if this is not Jenny's desire?"

"That makes no difference. She is not of age, and she still lives under my roof. She will do as I say. She may not like it or even understand it right now, but one day she'll thank me for it." Backing into the house, he added, "Good day, Corporal. And good-bye."

The door closed in Buck's face. He turned and stood there a moment. He wondered why Jenny's father had waited until now to stop her from seeing any man not on the social level he wanted for his daughter. As he descended the porch steps, Buck told himself there was more to it than Colonel Jordan was revealing.

Not wanting to cause trouble for Jenny, he moved quietly toward the waiting buggy, feeling sick at heart. As he drove slowly away, tears flowed at a window on the second floor.

CHAPTER EIGHT

✯

After the attack on Fort Sumter on April 12 and the passage of the ordinance of secession by the Virginia legislature on April 17, both the North and the South marked time. Neither was prepared to assume the offensive.

Conscious that they could never hope to match the military strength of the Union, the Confederacy chose to exploit the advantages of defensive operations and the use of spies to counteract the offensive of the enemy. President Jefferson Davis and his advisers agreed that there was little to gain by invading the North. The Confederacy was merely asking to be let alone. If President Abraham Lincoln and the Union military leaders were not willing to back off and let the Confederacy go its way in peace, it was willing to fight. The Confederate offensive at Fort Sumter was meant to demonstrate that fact.

The Federal government's military task was fixed and unavoidable. The Union must move into the South and conquer it. This required a more elaborate military organization than was possible to create in a few weeks. It meant training soldiers, building up immense quantities of weapons and ammunition, developing and maintaining long lines of communication, imposing blockades on the South, and wresting major ports and rivers from Southern control.

Union military strategists wanted to launch a major offensive as soon as possible down the Mississippi River, but circumstances at hand made it inadvisable. The proximity of the first armies that were being organized dictated that Virginia must be the first theater of war.

As the days came and went, the enlistment of great numbers of soldiers, the training of troops, and the buildup of war matériel continued.

On Saturday afternoon, May 4, 1861, a large crowd of Washington, D.C., residents gathered in an open field twenty miles due west of the capital city on the west bank of Bull Run Creek, some five miles northwest of Manassas Junction.

The field belonged to Frank Lewis, a Union sympathizer who was enthralled by Colonel Elmer Ellsworth and his Eleventh New York Zouaves drill team, which he had seen perform once outside of Gettysburg. Lewis had invited the Zouaves to perform on his place, and the citizens of Washington were turning out in droves.

About a mile and a half west of the Lewis farm, John Henry, the thirty-one-year-old son of Mrs. Judith Henry, an invalid widow who owned the large house on Henry House Hill, stood in the yard with neighbor Mike Durbin. As they looked across the fields toward the Lewis place, Durbin patted his big black Newfoundland dog and said, "John, Frank told me he invited the Eleventh New York Zouaves to give a drill team show in his field this afternoon."

"I've heard about those Zouaves," John nodded. "I'd sure like to get a gander at 'em in action, but...wouldn't we be sort of traitors to go and watch 'em?"

"Not like Frank is for inviting 'em out here. He told me even ol' Honest Abe might show up."

John watched the movement of vehicles and riders. "'Course, ol' Frank is from the North—Pennsylvania. We ain't. Can't blame a fella for havin' an attachment for his home state."

"Yeah, I know." After a long pause, Durbin said, "I'm plannin' to join up with the Confederate army next week. What you gonna do?"

"Can't," replied John. "With Pa dead, I have to take care of the place for Ma. I guess you know Louise and I moved in with Ma a couple weeks ago so's my sister Mary Sue's husband could join up."

"Yeah. Carl's already done it?"

"He's in trainin' over by Richmond. Mary Sue's livin' in Ma's house, too. I ain't got no choice. I gotta stay."

The Newfoundland pawed at his master and whined for attention. Durbin leaned over and patted the dog's head and neck, and said, "Pal, I declare, do you think all I have to do in life is pet you?"

While the dog wagged his tail and whined in reply, John looked at him and said, "I thought the thing he likes best is ridin' in the hay wagon with you."

"It is. But if he ain't ridin', he wants pettin'. I can't go anywhere without him taggin' along."

"So, when you go into the army, who's gonna look after Jo-Beth and the place?"

"Jo-Beth's kid brother is comin' to stay with her and do the chores."

"I almost forgot Jo-Beth had a little brother. What's his name again?"

"Orville."

"Oh, yeah, Orville....So what do you think? Should we sneak over to the Lewis place and watch those Zouaves from the ditch bank?"

"Why not?" grinned Mike. Then looking down at his dog, he said, "Can't take Pal over there. He'd probably give us away."

"You can leave him in the barn. I'll go and tell the women where we're goin'. Be right back."

While John was in the house, Mike tricked Pal into the barn, then shut the door. The Newfoundland began to whine and scratch at the door. When John returned, he and Mike started across the sweeping green pasture toward the Lewis farm.

They were about a mile from Henry House Hill when John happened to look over his shoulder. He stopped, laughed, and said, "Lookee there, Mike."

Mike turned to see an ebony streak on the grassy field. Pal was running after him, his ears flying and his long black fur waving in the wind.

John shook his head. "How do you reckon he got out?"

"Well, knowing him, he either squeezed through a knothole or knocked your barn door off its hinges. I tend to lean toward the latter."

"So now what?"

"I'll have to forego the show. If I took Pal over there, he'd probably run right into the middle of the marching ranks."

Old Glory and the New York state flag flapped in the breeze at the head of the long, even lines of colorful Zouaves as all eleven hundred marched in front of the crowd some ten thousand strong. A military band played intermittently between announcements by Colonel Ellsworth.

In the audience was President Lincoln, his family, governess Patricia Winters, and Lincoln's secretary John Hay. Seated next to the president was the stout and stalwart Major Irvin McDowell. Lincoln was considering promoting the forty-two-year-old Mexican War veteran to brigadier general and making him field commander over the army of thirty thousand men gathered in camps around Washington.

In Lincoln's mind, the field commander would carry on his shoulders the onerous duty of invading Virginia to put down the Confederate rebellion. The president had been informed that just a few miles from where he sat—at Manassas Junction—General Pierre G.T. Beauregard was collecting troops.

Also in attendance were several units of fighting men, including the Sixth Massachusetts under command of Colonel Edward F. Jones, and the large Third Brigade of the Union army's First Division, under the command of Colonel William T. Sherman. Sitting astride his mount next to Sherman was Brigadier General Daniel Tyler, commander of First Division.

Lieutenant John Hammond of the Sixth Massachusetts—who had dated Patricia Winters four times since meeting her—found a spot next to her on a grassy slope where she was seated with the Lincoln boys. While the crowd thrilled at Ellsworth's drill team, Patricia thrilled at Hammond's touch when he took her hand in his.

Not far from the president and Mrs. Lincoln sat Lieutenant Jeffrey Jordan and Jenny. Also in the crowd were Senator Henry Wilson and Rose O'Neal Greenhow. Next to Rose were four pretty young ladies she had secretly engaged to do spy work.

Sitting on the grass next to her father, Jenny kept her eye on Corporal Buck Brownell, who was performing amid the Zouaves on the field. Suddenly Jack Egan eased down beside her. Jenny glanced at him, then said quietly, "Please find a seat somewhere else, Jack."

"Now, wait a minute. What'd I do wrong?"

"Well, for starters, you took it upon yourself to tell Buck he couldn't see me any more. You had no right to do such a thing."

Egan opened his mouth to speak, but Jenny cut him off. "And what's more, where'd you get the brass to tell Buck you were going to marry me!"

"Well, I—"

"Well, you're wrong, Captain Egan! Now leave me alone."

"But Jenny, I—"

Jeffrey Jordan eyed Egan with disdain. "Are you deaf, Captain?"

Ignoring Jordan, Egan hissed at Jenny, "Why'd you two-time me for that scum-bucket corporal? What do you see in him?"

Jordan leaped to his feet and stood over Egan as spectators in the area looked on. "On your way, Captain!"

"Okay, Colonel, I'll go. But I don't think I'm being treated right."

"Until this war is over and done with, Jenny isn't going to get involved with *any* man...especially a soldier. So the best thing for you to do, Captain, is find another girl."

Egan pulled his gaze from the stubborn eyes of Jordan and looked at Jenny. He found the same stubbornness there. Cursing under his breath, he stomped away.

The crowd cheered as Colonel Ellsworth led his brightly clad soldiers in snappy acrobatic maneuvers with musket and bayonet, all done in time to the music of the band. After a while, Ellsworth stood his brigade at attention and introduced Corporal Brownell, who would now demonstrate his skill at speedily loading and firing his musket at a stationary target, then a moving target.

Jenny bit her lower lip to keep from crying. Her heart seemed ready to burst with sorrow. She had fallen in love with the rugged Zouave corporal, and she would never forget him.

A few feet away, young Tad Lincoln looked on with awe as Buck continued his demonstration. Pressing close to his governess, who still held hands with Lieutenant Hammond, he told her he couldn't wait to grow up. He wanted to be a Zouave.

At the close of the performance, the crowd leaped to its feet and gave the Zouaves a five-minute ovation. Colonel Ellsworth then introduced Abraham Lincoln, and the crowd cheered and applauded some more as the president moved to the forefront. When it was finally quiet enough for him to be heard, Lincoln praised Colonel Ellsworth and his military achievements and Corporal Brownell for his expertise with firearms. Again the people cheered.

Lincoln stroked his beard and told the crowd that the Confederates better watch out. With rough-and-ready men like the Zouaves fighting for the Union, the Rebels didn't have a chance. Those words brought the loudest ovation. The people of Washington were certain the Confederates would be brought to their knees in the first major battle.

Colonel Ellsworth thanked the enthusiastic throng for coming, and dismissed them. Lincoln and those in his party rode away, with Colonel Ellsworth riding in the presidential carriage.

As the crowd was dispersing, Jeffrey Jordan leaned close to his daughter, and said, "Wait here, honey. I need to see Rose for a minute." Jenny nodded and let her gaze scan the milling crowd. She was trying to find a particular handsome face.

Rose O'Neal Greenhow was watching her four girls climb into her private carriage when she saw Jeffrey Jordan coming her way. She said to the young women, "I'll be with you in a moment," then moved out to greet her fellow spy, extending a hand.

"Hello, Colonel," she smiled, as Jordan took her hand.

Jordan felt the slip of paper press his palm as he greeted her in return. "Nice to see you, lovely lady. Did you enjoy the demonstration?"

"Very much so!"—then in a half-whisper, "Here are the names of the two new girls. We're ready to start carrying messages as soon as you're in a position to give them to us."

"It'll be a few more weeks, I think," Jordan whispered back. "It all depends on how fast Lincoln moves. By ready, I assume you mean you've made contact with Generals Lee and Beauregard, and they're expecting your girls to deliver the messages."

"Yes. Their military leaders have also been informed."

"Good. Then we're ready to roll."

"Definitely...and Henry doesn't suspect a thing."

"You're a doll, Rose," grinned Jordan. Casting an eye toward the carriage, he asked, "Will four girls be enough?"

"Not once we get under way. I'll have to recruit more when we're rolling, if the war lasts that long."

"Let's hope the experts are right, and it'll be a short one—only it's the Union that gets whipped in that big battle, and not our side."

"Amen," Rose whispered. "We'd better break it off. We'll meet again at the time and place we agreed on. Maybe by then, you'll know more than you do now."

Senator Wilson, who had been amid the dispersing crowd speaking to friends, drew up just as Jordan was turning to leave. "Hello, Colonel," Wilson said amiably. "Nice to see you."

Jordan shook his hand. "Nice to see you, Senator. What did you think of the demonstration?"

"Great! It was just great! I'm sure glad we've got those Zouaves on our side."

"Me too." Jordan smiled at Rose, told her he would see her soon, and headed for his surrey.

Threading his way through the crowd, Jordan spoke to several people who greeted him. As he drew near the surrey, Jenny was standing beside it, talking to Corporal Brownell. Jordan shot his undimmed hostility at the corporal as he drew up. "I thought I made it clear you are to stay away from my daughter!"

Jenny's face paled.

Buck said calmly, "I wasn't trying to get a date with her, Colonel Jordan. I was just greeting her and asking how she is doing."

"I don't want you coming around her at all, Corporal."

Buck and Jenny looked at each other. He could see the hurt in her eyes, and at that moment, he knew she was in love with him.

To Jordan, Buck said, "I apologize, Colonel. I didn't mean to rile you. But a man has to do what he has to do." Turning back to Jenny, he spoke softly, but loud enough for her father to hear. "I'm sorry, Jenny. I didn't mean to cause trouble. I only wanted to say hello...and...and that I love you."

The joy Jenny felt at Buck's words was marred by her father's outburst. "How dare you speak to my daughter in such a way when I just told you I want you out of her life!" To Jenny, he said, "Get in the surrey!"

While Jenny climbed into the surrey, Buck said, "It is not my intention to anger you, Colonel, but when a man loves a woman, he wants her to know it. I must tell you, sir, with all due respect...I am in love with Jenny, and I always will be."

A young Zouave soldier was showing his musket to a group of teenage boys nearby. One of the boys asked if he could hold the weapon just for a minute. The Zouave told him to be very careful, advising him that the gun was loaded. The youth assured him he would be, and took the weapon in his hands with delight. The Zouave's attention was drawn to Colonel Ellsworth, who was coming his direction, surrounded by another group of youths.

The boy with the musket decided to show his friends how well he could handle a gun. He would cock the hammer, then ease it back down. "Hey, guys," he said, earing the hammer back into firing position, "look at this!" Before he got the hammer locked, his thumb slipped and the hammer came down on the powder charge.

The shot ripped across the rump of Jeffrey Jordan's horse. Jenny was just settling on the seat when the frightened animal bolted. The abrupt movement of the surrey threw Jenny off the seat, to the back of the vehicle, and left her dangling partway over the right side. She screamed and held on for dear life as the surrey bounded over the open field, swaying dangerously. The terror-blinded horse was headed for the bank of Bull Run Creek.

While everyone else stood slack-jawed and wide-eyed, Buck dashed to a horse a few yards away, leaped into the saddle, and put the animal into an instant gallop. Colonel Ellsworth watched Brownell thunder away, and stomped to the Zouave who had let the teenager handle his musket. The Zouave looked sheepish as Ellsworth dressed him down for his foolish move. The boy with the musket was weeping and apologizing.

Buck's hat sailed from his head as he rode across the field in pursuit of the surrey. Somehow Jenny had been able to get herself back inside the bounding, careening vehicle and was gripping the seat to keep from being thrown out. The terrified horse raced blindly toward the grassy bank of Bull Run.

The creek was no more than a hundred yards away when Buck pulled alongside the surrey and shouted, "We'll only get one chance, Jenny! Do what I tell you! Get ready to jump." The frightened woman nodded, then let go of the seat and with difficulty, crawled to the side. Drawing as close as possible, Buck leaned from the saddle, held out his right arm, and yelled, "Jump, Jenny! Quick!" Jenny took a deep breath and leaped into the curve of Buck's strong arm.

Buck drew her to himself and held her tight as he skidded his horse to a halt. Jenny wrapped her trembling arms around his neck and said with shuddering words, "Thank you, darling! Thank you! You saved my life!"

Both watched the bounding surrey as the wild-eyed horse scudded toward the bank of Bull Run Creek, then made a sudden turn to the left. The surrey careened, overturned, came loose from the harness, and rolled into the creek. The horse thundered along the bank with the singletree dragging behind, then bounded over a hill and disappeared.

Buck's horse danced about a little while Buck held Jenny close and kissed her.

"Sorry," he said, "but I had to do that—despite what your father says."

"Don't be sorry. I let you, didn't I?"

Buck grinned. "Here. Let me slide you behind me. Wrap your arms around me and hang on. I'll take you back to your father."

Moments later, Buck and Jenny rode up to a cheering crowd. Buck smiled at them, slid from the saddle, then helped Jenny down. Jenny's father moved up and with reluctance, said, "Thank you,

Corporal. You no doubt saved Jenny from serious harm...maybe even saved her life."

"I'd do it again in a minute, sir."

Jordan took Jenny into one arm, leaned close to Buck and said, "I saw you kiss her, too. That I didn't like."

"I love her, sir. I told you...I'll always love her."

"I love you too, Buck," Jenny said boldly, avoiding her father's hard eyes.

Jordan turned quickly to Rose Greenhow and asked, "Can Jenny and I ride back to town with you?"

"Of course."

Jordan hastily ushered his daughter away from Buck toward Rose's vehicle. Jenny looked back with sadness and love in her eyes.

Buck stood with Colonel Ellsworth and watched the Greenhow party boarded the carriage. As it rolled across the field toward Washington, Jenny ventured a backward look over her shoulder at the man she loved. Tears glistened on her cheeks, reflecting the light of the lowering sun.

CHAPTER NINE

✦

Extensive training continued at the Union army camps around Washington, D.C. As more new recruits arrived, Colonel Elmer Ellsworth went to General Winfield Scott, chief of the Federal army, and offered to let Corporal Buck Brownell move about the camps and give extensive training in the use of firearms and bayonets. Brownell's reputation had earned him a great deal of respect amongst Union military leaders. General Scott appreciated Ellsworth's offer and took him up on it.

Early in the second week of May 1861, General Scott began visiting each camp to inspect the troops and speak to them. He happened upon the camp where Buck was doing his training. General Scott, along with his accompanying officers, approached the training site and observed with keen interest for over two hours. When the training session was done, General Scott stepped up to Brownell and extended his hand. "Young man," he said with exuberance, "I like the way you work. I'm General Winfield Scott."

Meeting Scott's grip, Buck smiled broadly. "I know who you are, sir. I've admired you from a distance for a long time. Your record in the Mexican War has more than impressed me."

Scott was aging and showed it. His health had been poor for the past few years, and he had put on a great deal of weight. He introduced his aides to Brownell, then excused himself to meet with the camp's officers before addressing the troops.

Twenty minutes later, a bugle called the troops together, where they stood at attention in perfect ranks while General Scott made his inspection. When that was done, the men were told to sit on the ground in a huge semicircle so the army chief could address them from the bed of a wagon.

Scott stood before them while the morning breeze toyed with Old Glory on a flag pole nearby. He took about ten minutes to give them a pep talk about the upcoming confrontation with the Confederate army, which no doubt would come before the end of summer.

When he had them eager to take on the enemy, Scott took a drink of water from a canteen handed him by an officer, then swept the faces of the troops with tired old eyes, and said, "Now, in order to build an efficient fighting force, there have to be rules, and there has to be discipline to enforce those rules. I'm from what they call the old school, men, and we're going to run this army the old-fashioned way."

There were some light-hearted chuckles, and the men exchanged mirthful glances.

Clearing his throat, the general proceeded. "Let me now give you some details concerning rules and discipline. Drunkenness, gambling, profanity, and absence without leave will be punished without exception. I emphasize the words, *without exception.* God is not a respecter of persons, and neither is General Winfield Scott. Neither are your commanding officers. Such conduct as I have just listed will result in punishment at the discretion of the commanding officers. The severity of the punishment will coincide with the degree of the infraction, running anywhere from extra duties to solitary confinement."

The mirth felt moments earlier among the troops began to subside.

Scott went on. "Blacklists of persistent offenders will be kept, and their names will appear on duty rosters for the purpose of digging latrines, burying dead mules and horses, and other such disagreeable tasks. Continued misconduct will result in actual physical punishment, employed to make examples of the offending soldiers...that others may fear.

"Physical punishment will be on the rack, or a lashing with a leather strap on a bare posterior while your fellow-soldiers watch. If that does not square the habitual offender around, the next step is court-martial. And believe me, gentlemen, you do not want to face a court-martial!

"Next, let's consider the most serious crime a Union soldier can commit—desertion. Deserters are the scum of the earth. They will be hunted down and shot by a firing squad. Let every ear hear this good. There will be no leniency. Deserters will die for their crime. Better to take a bullet from the enemy than face a firing squad made up of your comrades. During the Mexican War, I had thirty-four deserters shot, and after number thirty-four, there were no more desertions from the U.S. army in that war.

"This may seem like a harsh punishment, but it is the only sentence that equals the crime. Besides, I found out in the Mexican War that hard-line punishment resulted in overall fewer discipline problems, and without a doubt saved the lives of many soldiers in the remainder of that conflict. Thus, it will be done the same in this war."

The general's solemn words laid a sober atmosphere over the men in the camp.

"Now, let me deal with one other subject. All of you need to know Union army policy on this subject so if and when it happens, you will understand. I speak of spies. What I am about to tell you has been military policy for centuries around the world. President Lincoln has put his stamp of approval on it, and it holds firm.

"Any and all Confederate spies will be executed by firing squad within twenty-four hours of their capture. Spy executions will be overseen and conducted by the highest-ranking officer in command at the scene of the apprehension. That officer will not need to contact his superiors. The deadline holds. His duty is to see to it that the execution is carried out as ordered."

General Scott wished the men well, and turned the assembly over to the officer in charge. Announcement was made that immediately after the noon meal, Corporal Brownell would conduct a class on bayonet fighting. The men were dismissed and headed for the cook tents.

In early May, the South decided that Richmond, Virginia, would become the capital of the Confederacy. The capital had been in Montgomery, Alabama, but that was proving to be quite inconvenient since the war was shaping up to begin in Virginia.

While the Union was building up its army around Washington, the Confederates, under the capable leadership of General Robert E. Lee, were doing the same at two strategic places in Virginia. At the heart of Lee's defense was his twenty-thousand-man force positioned at Manassas Junction near Bull Run Creek, some twenty-five miles southwest of Washington. Virginia's two mainline railroads intersected there. This unit was under the command of Brigadier General Pierre G.T. Beauregard, hailed by Southerners as the Confederacy's first national hero for his leadership in the victory at Charleston Harbor.

Lee's other army was the twelve-thousand-man force stationed at Harper's Ferry under the command of General Joseph E. Johnston. Lee's thinking was that his two armies were strategically positioned so that no matter which spot the Yankees attacked, Beauregard and Johnston could use the railroad to join up quickly and defeat one section of the Union army before another could march to its aid.

At Harper's Ferry with General Johnston was Colonel Thomas J. Jackson, who—like General Lee—was Virginia born and bred. Handpicked by Johnston, Jackson was his man for training troops. The colonel, famous for his teaching years at Virginia Military Institute, believed that regardless of the patriotic spirit in a man or his will to fight, he was useless on the battlefield until he was well trained and knew how to carry out orders. Colonel Jackson's training program was rough and rigid, but his men loved him for it. Given enough time, Jackson assured General Johnston he would develop a crack fighting force.

On May 14, Major Irvin McDowell was made a brigadier general and, as President Lincoln had planned, assigned top field commander. On May 23, Virginia's popular vote ratified the ordinance of secession that had been passed by the legislature on April 17. Virginia was now officially enemy territory.

An immediate offensive was planned by General Scott in the Senate Military Committee chambers, with President Lincoln present. Scott explained that his objective would be to seize and hold a buffer zone between Richmond and Washington to protect the Union capital. Scott's "buffer zone" was a large area just south of Washington that included one town—Alexandria, Virginia.

Scott knew Alexandria was guarded by seven hundred Confederate troops. He told Lincoln and the Committee that he would send Colonel Orlando B. Willcox and his First Michigan Regiment to capture Alexandria. The Rebel garrison there was to be captured, run off, or shot down, whichever was necessary to lay hold on the town. Scott had great confidence in the Eleventh New York Fire Zouaves, under the leadership of Colonel Ellsworth. He would assign the Zouaves to help Willcox accomplish his mission.

The assault would be at dawn the next morning. Willcox's regiment would enter Alexandria by land and Ellsworth's Zouaves would approach from the Potomac River on three steamers with the sloop of war, *Pawnee*, as their escort.

President Lincoln and the senators liked Scott's plan and voiced their approval. Secretly, Lieutenant Colonel Jeffrey Jordan was upset.

The planned assault was too soon for any of Rose O'Neal Greenhow's girls to carry a message to the Confederate military authorities. Alexandria was open prey for the Union forces.

Just before the break of dawn on May 24, 1861, Colonel Willcox and his First Michigan Regiment crossed the Potomac over Long Bridge north of Alexandria, while Colonel Ellsworth and his Zouaves drifted downstream toward the Alexandria wharf on three river steamers, escorted by the *Pawnee*.

Colonel George Terrett, commander of the small garrison at Alexandria, learned that Willcox's troops were marching toward the town from the north. He attempted to assemble his soldiers in the center of town to brace for a battle, but was unsuccessful. The Rebels were billeted all over Alexandria in their own homes.

They had another problem. Terrett's force was low on ammunition. It had no more than two bullets per man.

Willcox's regiment entered town on King Street, the main north-south thoroughfare, some fifteen minutes before Ellsworth's Zouaves arrived. It was several blocks from the river to Alexandria's business district.

When the Zouaves neared the center of town, Corporal Brownell—in keeping with Colonel Ellsworth's instructions—was shoulder-to-shoulder with his commander. Buck's bayonet was fixed, and he carried his rifle at the ready.

When they heard shots in the direction of the railroad station, Ellsworth shouted to his men, "Spread out! We'll work our way toward the station. Keep your eyes open!" The sun was peeping over the eastern horizon by the time the Zouaves reached the depot of the Orange & Alexandria Railroad and found Willcox and his men with thirty-five Rebel prisoners. A dozen other Confederate soldiers lay dead, scattered about.

"What happened, Colonel?" Ellsworth asked.

"Seems they had a bit of a warning," replied Willcox. "Most of the seven hundred got aboard a train that was about to leave town and took off. Their commander went with them. I guess the rest of these boys were rousted out of their beds too late to catch the train."

Brownell chuckled and said, "Well, Colonel Willcox, you did all three things General Scott had written in our orders. Didn't he say to capture them, run them off, or shoot them down?"

"I guess he did, at that."

"So what now, Colonel?" queried Ellsworth, who stood a head shorter than Willcox.

"Let's secure the town. I'll have some of my men take these prisoners to the local jail. The rest will take positions in the residential areas. You take your Zouaves and secure the business district."

"Fine," nodded Ellsworth. "You and I can get together once we've made sure the citizens are under control. Let's have a cup of coffee at one of the cafés."

"That's a deal, Colonel. Coffee it is."

Turning to his men, Ellsworth divided them up, assigning a detail to stay and occupy the depot. Another detail would move onto the town's main thoroughfare and watch over the shops and stores. Two other details would guard the north and south entrances to the town. Leaving himself a unit of eight men, the colonel said to them, "All right, men, you and I will take over the telegraph office. Let's go."

Alexandria was swarming with Union soldiers as the towns people looked on from their windows and porches. They seemed numb with shock.

When Ellsworth and his small detachment reached the edge of the business district on King Street, the colonel's attention was drawn to a large flag flying atop the Marshal House Inn. He slowed, then halted. His unit stopped with him and studied the unfamiliar design.

"That's the new Confederate flag, isn't it, sir?" said one of the Zouaves.

"Looks like it. I heard a couple of weeks ago that they had adopted a new one." Running his gaze over the faces of his men, he said, "Alexandria is now occupied by Union forces. It is no longer a Confederate town. That flag has to come down. We'll put the Stars and Stripes up there later, but that Rebel flag is coming down now."

"I'll get it, sir," Buck volunteered.

"Sorry, my friend," Ellsworth grinned, "but yours truly is going to handle that little chore himself."

"Whatever you say, sir."

Looking around at the others, Ellsworth said, "Halstead, Schmidt, Grover, and Elkins. Go occupy the telegraph office. I'll take these four with me. We'll meet you over there shortly."

While the designated four hurried up the street toward the telegraph office, Ellsworth led his four men into the plush lobby of the Marshal House hotel. The eyes of the elderly man behind the desk bulged at the enemy soldiers crowding through the door. There was no one else in sight.

Ellsworth had dressed himself for the assault in a resplendent new uniform. Pinned on his chest was a gold medal attached to a bright red ribbon. The medal was inscribed with words in Latin: *Not For Ourselves Alone, but for Our Country.*

As Ellsworth approached the desk, the clerk stammered, "Wh-what do you want?"

"Only that you don't try to give us any trouble, Mr.—What's your name, sir?"

"Ollie Evans," gulped the old man.

"Well, Mr. Evans, we'll not harm you if you stay right here and remain quiet. All we want is to take down that abominable Confederate flag you're flying on the roof. Alexandria is now under Union authority. The Confederate flag must be removed from the roof."

Evans said no more. His wrinkled face was sheet-white.

Turning to his men, Ellsworth said, "Frye and Manley, you stay here and guard the door. If anyone comes in, hold them at gunpoint until Lynch, Brownell, and I return."

"Yes, sir."

Frye and Manley watched the three Zouaves mount the stairs and disappear. Then Manley moved to the door and looked out on the street. Two male citizens were in a heated argument with five Zouaves across the street and down a few doors.

"Stan, come here," said Manley. "Looks like a couple of hotheaded yokels are about to tie into some of our boys."

Frye hurried to the door and eyed the scene. "Hope they're not foolish enough to try to take on our guys."

While the two Zouaves concentrated on the street trouble, Ollie Evans ducked through a door behind the desk and hobbled as fast as he could through the office. Reaching a side door, he moved into the rear of the lobby and cast a glance at the two Union soldiers. They were intent on the action down the street and had not missed him.

Gritting his teeth against the arthritis pain in his legs, he quietly moved up the stairs. He was puffing hard when he reached the third floor and limped down the hall to the manager's private apartment. Tapping on the door, he called in a subdued voice, "Mr. Jackson! Mr. Jackson!"

Light footsteps sounded inside the apartment, the doorknob rattled, and the door opened slightly. "What is it, Ollie?" came a young feminine voice.

"Mrs. Jackson, I need to talk to your husband, quick!"

"He's watching the trouble down on the street," said the manager's wife, "and he's very upset. Can I give him the message?"

"Miss Lily, there's trouble right here in the hotel! I gotta tell him about it."

Still in a robe, Lily Jackson widened the door, turned and called,

BELOVED ENEMY

139

"James! It's Ollie. He says we've got trouble right here in the hotel."

Thirty-two-year-old James Jackson appeared, his face pale, and asked, "What kind of trouble, Ollie?"

When the three Zouaves reached the fourth floor landing, Colonel Ellsworth quickly found the dark, narrow staircase that led to the roof. Buck was on his heels as he hurried up the stairs, with Jim Lynch right behind him. It took the colonel a few seconds to find the bolt latch in the gloom and slide it free. Sunlight flooded the dark space when the door came open.

"You two wait here," said Ellsworth. "I'll be right back."

Buck and Jim pressed into the doorway together and watched as their leader left the small platform and began to climb the steep slope of the roof toward the flagpole. The colonel's leather-soled boots slipped a few times, but he soon reached the peak. When he stood up, gripping the flagpole, a rousing cheer came from King Street below. Several Zouaves stood over two crumpled forms and cheered their colonel's appearance atop the hotel. Colonel Ellsworth detached the Confederate flag and wadded it up, then turned and carefully made his way back to the platform.

When Ellsworth was back inside, Lynch said, "Go ahead, sir. I'll close and lock the door." Ellsworth thanked him and descended the stairs behind Brownell to the fourth floor landing.

Buck paused on the landing in front of the colonel, waiting for Lynch to catch up. He eyed the Confederate flag, grinned at the colonel, and said, "You going to hang onto that for a keepsake?"

"Might do that. Spoils of war, they call it."

Lynch drew up behind them, and they headed on down the stairs. There were windows at each landing, allowing the bright sunlight to flood the hallways. Just as Buck reached the landing on the third floor, he saw a man with a double-barreled shotgun standing in an open doorway a few feet away.

Buck tensed. Instinctively he lunged forward and swung his rifle, batting the shotgun with the bayonet. One barrel of the shotgun roared. Colonel Ellsworth, who was still on the staircase with Lynch behind him, took the blast square in the chest. The impact slammed him against the wall.

The man snapped back the hammer of the second barrel and aimed it at Buck, but too late. A slug from Buck's rifle entered the man's forehead, whipping his head back and throwing the double muzzle of the shotgun sideways. The gun roared, missing Brownell, but ripping a huge hole in the wall.

While the civilian assailant lay dead, flat on his back, Buck whirled to see Lynch grasp for Ellsworth. The little colonel was dead on his feet. His body slid partway down the wall, then pitched forward with a heavy, headlong weight. He hit the landing with a thud.

Buck's heart pounded his chest. He dropped to his knees beside Ellsworth's lifeless form. Lynch was instantly beside him. Neither man said anything. They only stared at their leader who still clutched the Confederate flag. It lay partially under him and was spattered with his blood. Ellsworth's gold medal had been driven into his chest by the shotgun blast.

The dreadful, silent moment was shattered by the scream of Lily Jackson, who stood on the stairs, beholding with horror the body of her slain husband. Directly behind her, Frye and Manley came bounding upward. The grief-stricken woman dropped to the floor beside her fallen mate. A chilling wail escaped her lips.

Only a brief glance at Ellsworth told Frye and Manley that their beloved champion was dead. The New York Fire Zouaves' grief and anger was violent. Some of them had to be deterred by their comrades from setting fire to the town.

The popular young colonel's death plunged the North into mourning. Bells tolled in church belfries and flags flew at half-staff. President Lincoln was grief-stricken. In honor of his fallen friend, he ordered the funeral ceremony to be held in the East Room at the White House. There would be a procession to the White House from the funeral home in Washington where the body was quickly embalmed. Upon viewing the body at the funeral home, Lincoln sobbed, "Oh, my boy! My boy! Was it necessary this sacrifice should be made?"

At nine o'clock on the morning of May 25, Corporal Brownell rode in the presidential coach with the president and Mrs. Lincoln as the funeral procession began at the undertaker's parlor. Buck was given this honor by Lincoln because he had slain Colonel Ellsworth's killer. Mary Lincoln carried a laurel wreath that she would place on the coffin when it arrived in the East Room at the White House.

Mourners turned out by the thousands. Double lines of grieving spectators filled the streets. Companies and regiments of soldiers from the Washington camps marched slowly to the beat of muffled drums beneath furled flags and banners.

The president's carriage led the procession, with the hearse next in line, pulled by four white horses. Ellsworth's pall was the country's flag. Six Zouave bearers walked beside the hearse, followed by a small band of Zouaves. Only a few could be spared, for the Eleventh New York was occupying Alexandria along with the First Michigan.

The small band of Zouaves was weaponless, walking with heads bowed in grief, eyes fixed on the hearse, and tears staining their cheeks. Behind them came a riderless horse, its back draped with the blood-stained Confederate flag Ellsworth had taken down from the flagpole of the Marshall House Inn. Following the riderless horse came the president's Cabinet, the Senate Military Committee, and the army's military leaders and their wives in carriages and buggies.

An honor guard was positioned at the White House, ready to carry the coffin to the East Room. Once it was in place, the lid was opened, and the body lay in state for several hours. At precisely three o'clock in the afternoon, a closed-coffin ceremony was conducted. The president sat near the coffin with his wife by his side. Head in hand, Lincoln shed silent tears. On his other side was Buck Brownell.

With the Senate Military Committee were Lieutenant Colonel Jeffrey Jordan and his daughter, Jenny. While listening to the minister, Jenny set her soft gaze on Buck. Several times, Buck let his line of sight drift to Jenny to find her looking at him. The occasion would not allow him to give her a smile, but he hoped she could read in his eyes his love for her.

Buck made a silent vow to himself. *When the war was over, he would find a way to make Jenny his bride.*

When the ceremony was completed, Lincoln turned to Buck and requested that he leave with him and Mrs. Lincoln. While everyone else waited, Buck filed out with the Lincolns. He managed to glance tenderly at Jenny. The glance did not escape Jeffrey Jordan's notice. Jenny saw her father's scowl and felt the pain of it in her heart. A tinge of despair washed over her. Why should two people in love never be able to have a life together?

Colonel Ellsworth's body was taken by train to City Hall in New York the next day, where thousands filed past the coffin to pay their last respects. Two days later, another train bore Ellsworth's body home to Mechanicville, New York, for burial by his family in a grave overlooking the lazy Hudson River.

CHAPTER TEN

✦

The tragic death of Colonel Elmer Ellsworth had varied results in the North. Sermons, newspaper editorials, songs, and poems lamented his loss and proclaimed his heroism.

But in the midst of the mourning over Ellsworth's death, another hero was proclaimed—Corporal Buck Brownell. His shooting of the little colonel's killer catapulted Brownell to fame.

On Wednesday, May 29, a special ceremony was held on the steps of the Capitol, and President Abraham Lincoln presented Brownell with a medal for his heroism. The sudden thrust into eminence was a bit embarrassing to Buck, but he handled it well. Given the opportunity to say a few words to the crowd, he averred that any of the Zouaves would have done the same thing he did. After a round of applause, President Lincoln introduced General Winfield Scott, who stepped to the podium and surprised Buck with a promotion to lieutenant. This honor left the young Zouave nonplused.

Buck had noticed that Jenny Jordan was in the crowd. At the end of the ceremony, she stood for a long moment, watching, but because of the press of well-wishers around Buck, she did not attempt to approach him. While Buck greeted those who swarmed him, he let his eyes roam the crowd for Jenny. By the time the crowd was gone, so was she.

The next morning, the Senate Military Committee was assembled in its meeting room with General Scott and Brigadier General Irvin McDowell. Jeffrey Jordan was also present, sitting next to Senator Henry Wilson. Though Jordan was official adviser to the Committee, he was outranked in the assembly by Generals Scott and McDowell. Scott, however, had requested his presence in case he should have something to add to the plan that was about to be presented.

Scott, beefy and tired-looking, stood at a large Virginia map on the wall with wooden pointer in hand. At a small table, aloof from the committeemen, sat General McDowell.

General Scott held the pointer in both hands across his ample midsection and brought the meeting to order. "Gentlemen," he said in his customary authoritative tone, "you all know that under my direction, the Union army is planning for a large-scale confrontation with the enemy in northern Virginia. As I have pointed out to you and to the president, northern Virginia is the natural place for this major battle. At the moment, I'd say we're looking at such a battle in about a month. It will probably take place just about where General Pierre Beauregard is gathering his troops...at Manassas Junction, some twenty-five miles west-southwest of here. But don't quote me on it, yet. These plans are still in the making."

Clearing his throat, the general proceeded. "At the moment—because of the upcoming northern Virginia battle—I am quite concerned about *southern* Virginia." Turning toward the map and using his pointer to draw attention to the southern tip of the Virginia Peninsula, Scott said, "Right here is our Fort Monroe, under the command of General Benjamin Butler. Monroe needs to be better fortified." Looking toward McDowell, he asked, "Would you agree to that, General?"

"Indeed I would, sir," nodded McDowell. "Fort Monroe, because of its position, is strategic to the Union."

"Do you concur, Colonel Jordan?"

"Absolutely, sir. It is not only a threat to the Confederates with the prospect of Union land thrusts toward Richmond, but it is also a constant obstacle to Confederate boat and ship traffic on the James and York Rivers. It most assuredly needs to be bolstered up with men and guns."

"Exactly," smiled Scott.

Jordan felt a twinge of excitement. Before this meeting was over, he would have information for Rose Greenhow to pass on to General Robert E. Lee.

General Scott continued. Running the tip of the pointer upward along the west shore of the peninsula, he said, "I also want to make a military move up the peninsula from Fort Monroe and establish Union fortifications. We must be in control of the entire waterway once the large battle in northern Virginia is over. We are confident that one good, hard punch will knock the Confederacy down for good, but just in case there's any fight left in them, we must be prepared. We dare not allow them to control the waters of the peninsula."

There was a glass of water on the table where General McDowell sat. Scott moved to it, took a short drink, and returned to the map. Using the pointer again, he said, "In the path of my proposed military move from Fort Monroe northward—as you can see—is the village of Big Bethel. Big Bethel is the nearest outpost of the Confederate forces in that part of the state, which are headquartered up here ten miles further north at Yorktown on the York River. In command of the Rebel forces there is Colonel John B. Magruder. He fought under me in the Mexican War. Tough as harness leather. He won three commendations for bravery."

Scott called for any questions that the men might have. There were none. The Committee was waiting to hear the time and details of the attack.

"I am going to assign Brigadier General Ebenezer Pierce of the Fourth Massachusetts Infantry to lead the attack," said Scott. "There will be three other regiments—the First Vermont, the Third New York, and the Fifth New York Zouaves." He gestured toward the Union field commander, who sat at the small table. "General McDowell and I have already discussed these units. He is in full agreement with me that these units are the most ready for combat that we have."

McDowell nodded. One of the senators raised his hand.

"General, since you're sending in Zouaves, why not send the Eleventh New York? Certainly they have to be among the very best. Is it because they haven't yet been assigned a new leader since Colonel Ellsworth was killed?"

Scott looked toward McDowell and asked, "Would you like to reply to that, General?"

"Of course," nodded McDowell, standing up. "We *are* sending the Fire Zouaves, Senator McGivens. There is a report being printed now for the Committee. Just yesterday, I merged the Eleventh New York Fire Zouaves with Colonel Abram Duryee's Fifth Zouaves. This move, of course, was with the approval of the president and General Scott. My reasoning is that there is just no one among the Fire Zouaves who can fill Colonel Ellsworth's boots. Since Colonel Duryee is matured and experienced in battle from the Mexican War, I felt it would be best that the Fire Zouaves be placed under his command."

"Good move!" called out one of the other senators. The rest of the Committee agreed.

With the Fire Zouaves brought to mind, Jordan thought of Lieutenant Buck Brownell. He hoped Jenny would soon get the man out of her thoughts.

Laying the pointer on a slender shelf beneath the map, General Scott ran his weary gaze over the interested faces and said, "Our scheduled time to launch the surprise attack on the garrison at Big Bethel is at dawn on Monday, June 10. With the Confederate outpost there in

Union hands, it will be removed as an obstacle."

A few other minor questions were presented and answered to the satisfaction of the Committee, and the meeting was closed. The men filed out of the Senate Chamber past Jenny Jordan's desk.

After everyone had gone, Jenny's father finally appeared and said, "I've been looking for John Calhoun. He's not in his office or any of the other offices within the Chamber. Do you happen to know where he is?"

"Yes, Daddy. He's downstairs posting some mail. He should be back shortly."

"Okay. I'll wait."

"If you're busy, I can give him a message for you."

"No, that's okay. I have to talk to John myself."

Jenny looked around to see if anyone was within earshot. Seeing no one, she said, "Daddy, did you learn something significant in the meeting?"

Bending over Jenny's desk, Jordan said in a low tone, "Did I ever! Four regiments of the Union army are going to pull a surprise attack on the Confederate garrison down at Big Bethel. I've got to get the message to General Lee. The safest way is for John to carry it to Rose Greenhow. She'll take it from there."

"I guess Rose's girls are champing at the bit to do their spy work," said Jenny. "They'll get their chance now."

Jenny's mind went to the man she loved. The question was out of her mouth almost before she had formed the words in her mind. "Daddy, do you know what regiments are going on this attack?"

"Yes. The Fourth Massachusetts, the First Vermont, the Third New York, and the Fifth New York Zouaves."

Jordan saw the relief come over Jenny's face and knew why she had asked. Sitting down in one of the two chairs in front of her desk, he leaned close, subduing his voice so it didn't carry down the hall, and said, "Jenny, you've got to get Buck Brownell out of your system."

"Daddy, I only asked—"

"You asked because you thought the Eleventh might be in on the mission, and you're concerned about Buck." Looking her straight in the eye, he said levelly, "Tell me I'm wrong."

Jenny's face flushed. "You...you're not wrong. Daddy, you can't legislate what goes on in my heart. I'm very fond of Buck. He's a good man and a gentleman, and he's—"

"He's the enemy, Jenny! You're a Rebel and he's a Yankee. You've got to forget him, do you understand?"

"But, Daddy, I can't just erase Buck from my mind! I can't snatch him from my heart like he never existed. Surely you can understand that."

"Look, honey, it was your Buck Brownell who shot and killed that innkeeper over in Alexandria. James Jackson was a Southerner, Jenny! Do you understand? James Jackson was merely trying to protect his nation's flag when he threw that shotgun on Ellsworth. He died for the Confederate flag, daughter, and he was your fellow-Virginian! This...this man you're so fond of put a bullet through his head and made a widow of his wife!"

"Buck didn't start this war, Daddy! He was with Colonel Ellsworth inside the hotel by orders. When he shot Mr. Jackson, it was because he fired first. What was Buck to do...just stand there and let the man kill him, too?"

John Calhoun drew up, cleared his throat, and said, "Excuse me. Am I getting into a family squabble here?"

"No squabble," Jordan replied, standing up and giving Calhoun a smile. "Jenny and I were just having a friendly discussion. I've been waiting to talk to you, John. Got some very important information for you."

"Good. Come on into the cubbyhole I call my office."

As Calhoun headed for the Chamber door, Jordan leaned close

to his daughter and said, "You're right, Jenny. Buck didn't start the war. But he's a Northerner, and don't forget it!" He took two steps toward the door, then came back and said, "And just so you know, the Eleventh New York Zouaves have been merged with the Fifth New York Zouaves because of Ellsworth's death. Your Lieutenant Brownell *is* going to be in on the sneak attack at Big Bethel."

Tears welled up in Jenny's dark eyes as her father followed after Calhoun. Her lower lip quivered as she stared after him and whispered, "I can't help it, Daddy. I *love* him. I do."

On the morning of June 4, Colonel John B. Magruder was in a meeting with his subordinate officers at the Confederate stronghold near Yorktown on the Virginia Peninsula. They were seated around a large table. Bright sunlight was shining through the open windows of the meeting room, and a warm breeze fluttered the sheer curtains. The discussion centered around how soon the skirmishes in Virginia would turn into major battles.

The door was standing open, allowing the morning breeze to cool the room. The discussion was interrupted by a light tap on the door frame. Seated at the head of the table, Magruder swung his gaze to the door to see a young corporal, who said, "Pardon me, Colonel. I'm sorry to disturb you, sir, but I believe you will agree that what I have to tell you is of utmost importance."

"That's fine, Corporal. What is it?"

"I have two young ladies out here, sir, who insist on seeing you. They say they have a message of vital importance. They were sent by a Mrs. Greenhow of Washington and have classified information about a Union attack on Big Bethel."

"Oh, yes!" Magruder exclaimed, rising to his feet. "A wire came from General Lee informing me that a couple of Confederate spies were on their way. I...ah...didn't realize they would be women."

The corporal grinned and winked. "They are definitely that, sir."

"Well, don't keep the young ladies waiting, Corporal. Show them in."

"Yes, sir."

The corporal stepped outside and ushered the two young women through the door. Instantly the officers were on their feet.

Rose Greenhow's spies were in their early twenties. They wore fancy hoop-skirted dresses with wide-brimmed hats and carried parasols. Moving to them, Magruder smiled and said, "Ladies, I am Colonel John Magruder."

"Hello, Colonel Magruder," one of them said. "I am Bettie Duval, and this is Susan Rand."

Magruder told them he was delighted to meet them, and introduced his officers with the sweep of his hand. He then asked the young ladies to be seated at the table.

When all were seated, Magruder said, "I received a wire yesterday from General Lee, informing me that two spies sent by Mrs. Greenhow would be coming with some vital information. He didn't say exactly when, nor did he tell me the spies would be lovely young ladies."

"Was there anything else in General Lee's message, Colonel?" asked Bettie.

"Yes," nodded Magruder. "I was puzzled by it, but I assume you can clear it up for me. It simply said, 'Look for the circled R.' "

The ladies exchanged glances, smiling at each other.

Bettie said, "Two things we had to know before we proceeded any further, Colonel, was that you fit the description we were given, and that you would be able to tell us about the circled R. General Lee sent the message in a secret code, did he not?"

"He did."

"So when we show you a message with a circled R on it, you will know it is authentic."

"I assume the R stands for Rose."

"Yes, that's right." Then turning to her companion, Bettie said, "All right, Susan." Susan scooted her chair back and rose to her feet. Immediately the group of officers stood up.

Susan smiled and said, "Please be seated, gentlemen."

As the men were easing into their chairs, Bettie helped Susan remove the lengthy hatpin and took the hat from her head. Susan then unpinned her long, upswept hair and let it begin to fall. From its folds, she took a well-concealed paper and handed it to Colonel Magruder. "Here you are, sir. Bettie and I hope this will save the lives of many Confederate soldiers."

Allowing her hair to remain in graceful curls on her shoulders, Susan sat down, and Bettie did the same, laying the hat on the table.

Magruder's face went grim as he read the message. When he was finished, he lifted his gaze to the men around the table, and said, "The Yankees are going to attack our garrison at Big Bethel next Monday, June 10, at dawn. They're coming with forty-four hundred troops."

"Forty-four hundred!" echoed a captain. "Sir, we've only got twenty-five hundred in the whole peninsula!"

"I know," said Magruder, "but because of this message, we've got six days to get ready...and the Yankees won't have any idea that we know they're coming. Even if we can't match their numbers, we'll have the edge with the element of surprise. We can't pull all of our troops from the peninsula down to Big Bethel, but with this much of a forewarning, we'll be ready for them."

"Who obtained this information for us, Colonel?" asked a lieutenant. "It had to be someone on the inside in Washington."

"It doesn't say, and I understand why. If these young ladies had been caught and the message found, the Yankees would know who to put before a firing squad in Washington."

Another lieutenant, Burl Newman, looked at Bettie and said, "You ladies are aware that if you had been caught, you would no doubt have faced a firing squad. It's just about a universal law anywhere in the world that spies are executed when they're caught."

"Yes, Lieutenant," nodded Bettie. "We know the risks involved. So does Rose, and so do the spies who obtained this information. We are all loyal Southerners and feel honored—just as you soldiers—to serve the Confederacy."

"God bless you and the spies in Washington," said Magruder.

"Ladies," spoke up Lieutenant Newman again, "how did you get past the Union soldiers...and how did you get down here?"

Bettie and Susan smiled at each other, then Bettie said, "We got past the Union soldiers by being a bit flirtatious and telling them we were going south to visit someone very special to us. That's you, Colonel Magruder."

Magruder blushed.

"You see, gentlemen," interjected Susan, "we figure men spies wouldn't have a chance getting past the Union lines. The Yankees would be too quick to suspect men. They'd search them...maybe even follow them if they found nothing on them. But Mrs. Greenhow came up with the idea of using female spies, and as you can see, it worked. She's already recruited two more girls to bring messages if the war lasts very long. And I'm sure if more are needed, she'll get them. Men are such pushovers for batting eyelashes and coquettish smiles."

There was a round of laughter. Magruder shook his head in wonderment. "I hope someday I can meet this Rose Greenhow. She must be some kind of woman."

"That she is, sir," Susan said.

"We hired a boat to bring us down here," said Bettie, answering Newman's second question. "Mrs. Greenhow paid for it."

"Bless her heart," breathed Magruder. "And you'll be going back the same way?"

"Yes, sir. The boat is waiting at the dock, and we must be heading back shortly."

"How about some good ol' army coffee and maybe a little something to eat before you go?" asked Magruder.

The ladies accepted the coffee, but politely turned down the offer of food. When they finished their coffee, they were escorted to the dock by Colonel Magruder. He thanked them and assured them their efforts would save Confederate lives. They climbed aboard the small boat and sailed northward.

Magruder went right to work. He left what troops he felt were necessary to slow any enemy advance on Yorktown and moved the rest of them to Big Bethel. He also sent for one of his best regiments, the First North Carolina Infantry under the command of his close friend, Colonel Daniel H. Hill, who had also fought with distinction in the Mexican War.

Hill and his men had to march to Big Bethel from inland Virginia. They reached the small town on June 7, and along with the men already there, spent the rest of that day and all the next erecting formidable earthworks and felling trees to build defenses on both sides of the Back River.

Colonel Magruder joined the troops at Big Bethel on the morning of June 9. He approved of the work that had been done to fortify the place, then studied the Back River for a few minutes. He suggested to Colonel Hill that if the Yankees from Fort Monroe chose not to come across the bridge, they might ford the river east of the bridge. To guard against this, Hill led the men to build more earthworks. The troops were stretched to the limit to finish the work, but the construction was finished by sundown on Sunday, June 9.

The thirty-three hundred Confederate troops at Big Bethel had their cannons in place by nightfall and were ready for the attack which reportedly would come at dawn. They laughed among themselves, saying the Yankees thought they were going to surprise the Rebels. Instead—thanks to efficient Confederate spy work—the Rebels would have a bigger surprise for the Yankees.

At 4:00 A.M. on June 10, 1861, the forty-four hundred Union troops drew near Big Bethel. There was a three-quarter moon, but it was continually obscured by low, drifting clouds.

Brigadier General Ebenezer Pierce of the Fourth Massachusetts Infantry was in command of the attack force. Taking advantage of what moonlight he had, General Pierce stood near the bridge that spanned the Back River, studied the situation, and called the other unit commanders to him for a consultation. When Colonel Edward Fitzpatrick of the First Vermont, Colonel H.G. Smalley of the Third New York, and Colonel Abram Duryee of the Fifth New York Zouaves huddled with him to view the massive Confederate bulwarks, they were stunned.

"We weren't told about any fortifications like these, General," said Fitzpatrick.

Pierce rubbed his chin. "This is odd. Why would this little town have such ramparts? It's almost as if they were expecting us."

"But how could that be?" put in Smalley. "There's no way the Rebels could have known we were coming."

"Maybe they built these right after the incident at Fort Sumter back in April," suggested Colonel Duryee. "You know...figuring war would come."

"That must be it," nodded Pierce. "All right, gentlemen. We'll go in as planned...over the bridge. It'll be faster than fording the river just for the sake of moving in a little less conspicuously."

"I agree," said Smalley. "They won't be looking for us, anyway. Time we open fire, they'll still be sleeping."

The commanders returned to their units and prepared to cross the bridge. Lieutenant Buck Brownell was in charge of a company of two hundred Zouaves. When the colonel approached him, Brownell said, "Colonel Duryee, I'm concerned about those fortifications. Big Bethel isn't supposed to look like a fort."

"We were just talking about that with General Pierce. We believe they built all that earthwork right after the assault on Fort Sumter. They probably wanted to be in better shape against a Union offensive, if it should come."

"Could be. It makes sense, anyway."

The Union troops fell into rank and made their crossing of the bridge. Each regiment knew to fan out and to wait until General Pierce's signal at dawn to swarm the town.

Under Colonel Duryee's directions, Lieutenant Brownell led his company across a marshy area about a hundred yards from the eastern bulwarks. From there, they were to do as the other companies and rush the earthworks at General Pierce's prearranged signal.

In the dark moments just before the break of dawn, Buck could make out the rest of the Zouaves off to the north. He was thankful to be among many of the men he had trained for combat.

One of Brownell's corporals brushed up beside him and said, "Lieutenant, unless my eyes are deceiving me, I just saw the outline of a Howitzer being rolled atop that rampart right over th—"

Before the corporal could finish his sentence, the roar of cannons shook the entire area, and cannonballs whistled through the gloom. The flash of rifle muzzles from the ramparts joined with the roar and orange flare of cannon fire and there was instant bedlam. Cannonballs exploded and drove the Union troops behind anything they could find for cover.

"They knew we were coming!" one of Brownell's men shouted at him as they dived into a shallow ditch together. It was mushy and wet.

"No doubt about it," Buck agreed, then looked to see if the rest of his company was finding cover. They had been trained well and knew how to improvise. They were flopping into marshy ditches all over the open area.

While the Confederate howitzers thundered and muskets barked, the Yankees gallantly returned fire. The Union forces were finding it difficult to retaliate effectively because of the Rebel artillery.

The enemy was well-prepared for them and had them where they had not planned to be...on the defensive. After some twenty minutes of ear-splitting gunfire, the Yankees were hard-pressed to make a dent in the Confederate bastions.

Buck Brownell carried a bayoneted rifle as well as wearing the customary sidearm of an officer. While he loaded and fired the rifle, he noted in the dawn's early light that Colonel Duryee and the company of Zouaves he was with were pinned down directly beneath three relentless Confederate howitzers. The big guns were in a grove of trees on a rise a few yards to the north of one of the giant man-made earthworks. Duryee and his men were helplessly trapped and would all die if the howitzers were not soon put out of commission.

Buck looked up and down the line of the ditch where he lay in the muck and spotted three of his best men. Shouting above the thunder of battle, Buck called to Sergeant Eric Barnes and Corporals Willie Smith and Theo Watkins. Within seconds, they were huddled beside him.

Buck pointed out the desperate position of Colonel Duryee and his men and explained that they needed to take out the three howitzers. The chosen Zouaves were eager to help their lieutenant accomplish the mission. Rifles loaded and bayonets fixed, they listened as Brownell laid out his plan.

Buck told his men around him to lay a barrage of rifle fire toward the three howitzers so as to keep the crews' attention away from their rear flank. Each of the howitzers' crews had three men—one to pack powder in the magazine, one to ramrod the cannonball, and the other to fire the fuse. Barnes, Smith, and Watkins knew their task was a dangerous one, but they had absolute confidence in their leader. They would follow Lieutenant Buck Brownell anywhere.

Amid the deafening roar of cannonade and the rattle of musketry, Buck led his three men across the marshy field in a wide circle, working his way to the tree-studded rise where the howitzers stood.

Prone on the grassy, open slope, Colonel Duryee and another

Zouave were working on a young private whose left hand had nearly been blown off. The private had passed out from the pain. "Tie it off as best you can," Duryee said. "Get Worthington over there to help you."

Another Zouave crawled close and was ready to speak when a shell screamed in close by. Heads down, the Zouaves waited until the shrapnel hissed away and the dirt rained down around them, then looked up.

"What is it, soldier?" Duryee asked.

Rolling onto his side, the Zouave pointed toward the mound where the howitzers stood and said, "Look, sir—it's Brownell and three of his men. They're going after those Rebel cannons!"

"Good for them!" shouted Duryee. "Pass the word along. Tell the men to fire as much as possible toward the howitzers. Even if they don't hit anything, it'll help distract them."

While the battle raged, Colonel Duryee and the Zouaves unleashed their guns on the howitzer crews. They watched with keen interest as Buck and his men rushed the first gun crew from behind and killed them. Even having one cannon silenced was a great relief.

The second crew was knocked out a few minutes later. The third crew was grabbing for their rifles when they realized the Zouaves were coming for them. But it was too late. All three were cut down before they could fire a shot.

There was a rousing cheer from the Zouaves on the slope when the last howitzer was silenced. Buck and his men packed the muzzles of the cannons with sod. When they were firmly packed, they loaded the magazines with powder, lit the fuses, and hit the ground. All three howitzers were destroyed beyond repair.

The battle continued for over three hours. The Confederates had the advantage, and soon the Yankees had to pull out and retreat to Fort Monroe. They had no choice but to leave their dead behind. When the Confederates saw them leaving with their wounded, they ceased fire and did not pursue them.

At Fort Monroe, General Pierce had the wounded soldiers treated as much as possible, then sent them up the peninsula on boats to Washington, where they could get better care under the watchful eye of Clara Barton. He sent Colonel Duryee and Lieutenant Brownell's company of Zouaves along to protect the boats. Duryee would also make a report to Generals Scott and McDowell.

When they arrived at the main Washington camp, Clara sent out word to the women who had helped her after the Baltimore riot, asking them to meet her at the camp as soon as possible. A few went with her immediately, and the work of patching up some sixty-five wounded men began.

Colonel Duryee left Brownell and his company at the makeshift hospital to do what they could to help, and headed for General Winfield Scott's tent to make his report. General McDowell was called to hear the report also, and the three Union officers met in Scott's tent.

Duryee gave the details of the Confederate ambush, and reported that eighteen Union soldiers had been killed and sixty-five seriously wounded. He shared his conviction with Scott and McDowell that the Confederates had received details of the planned attack several days in advance. Someone in high places—or maybe more than one person—was a Confederate spy. The two generals agreed. There could be no other explanation. Scott would discuss it with the president as soon as he could get an appointment.

Duryee told the generals there was something else they needed to know. He then told them of Lieutenant Buck Brownell's daring and courage in taking out the three howitzers. He also named the three Zouaves who assisted Brownell, suggesting that all four should receive commendations. When the generals agreed, Duryee said that one of his captains had been killed in the battle and that he needed to fill his spot. He suggested that the new captain be Buck Brownell.

CHAPTER ELEVEN

★

Word spread quickly through Washington of the battle at Big Bethel, of the Union's defeat, and that the wounded men had been brought to the main military camp just outside the city. Jenny Jordan had been between work and home when Clara Barton sent messengers to round up volunteers. She was not aware of what was going on until she arrived home and was told by a neighbor. Jenny hurriedly saddled her horse and rode for the camp. She had to find out if Buck was all right.

Along the way, Jenny encountered one of Miss Barton's messengers, who informed her of the need for volunteers to help with the wounded soldiers. As she rode on, Jenny told herself she would be glad to help Clara, once she knew about Buck.

The sun was lowering as Jenny rode up to the camp's entrance. Two guards stepped up to greet her, blocking her way. One of them said, "Good evening, ma'am. What can we do for you?"

Knowing she would be allowed in only if she was there to answer Clara's call, Jenny smiled and said, "I'm here to help Miss Barton."

The guards relaxed and took Jenny's horse for her. She hastened to where the wounded soldiers were being tended to and approached

Clara Barton, who was giving orders to two women who had arrived a short time earlier. Clara smiled at Jenny and finished her instructions to the two women. When they moved away, she turned to Jenny and said, "Hello, Jenny. I appreciate your coming."

"Glad to do what I can to help."

Clara quickly put Jenny to work making sure the wounded men had water. Carrying a jug and some tin cups, she weaved her way amid the cots. Fear filled her heart when she didn't find Buck. She hoped he was not among those eighteen men reported killed. Returning to the water barrel to refill the jug, Jenny spotted a small group of wounded Zouaves clustered together. Pouring cups of water as she went, she finally reached the Zouaves. Two of them were being treated by nurses, but the rest were already bandaged.

Standing over the cots, Jenny smiled and said, "I have some cool water, here. Anybody interested?"

One of them, a youth of eighteen, grinned and said, "Only if you put the cup to my lips, Miss. I...uh...I have a broken arm."

Jenny knew flirtation when she saw it. "You can't use your other arm?"

"Oh, no, ma'am," grinned the youth. "It became paralyzed the moment I laid eyes on you."

"Thank you, soldier, but I'm afraid you'll just have to make that good arm work. I have too many other soldiers to tend to."

The youth's friends kidded him as Jenny passed out cups to each of them. As she was finishing, she steeled herself for the worst and asked, "Do you men know Lieutenant Buck Brownell?" There were six affirmative answers. "Is he all right? I...I mean did he make it through the battle?"

"Oh, yes, ma'am," spoke up the one with the broken arm. "Lieutenant Brownell came with us from Fort Monroe."

Feeling sweet relief and breathing a prayer of thanks, Jenny asked, "Do you know where he is?"

"Yes, ma'am," spoke up another. "He's in General Scott's tent. But when he comes out of there, he won't be *Lieutenant* Brownell anymore."

"What do you mean?"

"Well, ma'am, he was here with us when General Scott's adjutant came and told him he was wanted at General Scott's tent. After Lieutenant Brownell hurried away, the adjutant told us Lieutenant Brownell was being promoted to captain. That's what's going on right now in General Scott's tent."

Jenny smiled and said, "That's wonderful."

"Do you know the lieutenant...the captain well, ma'am?" asked another Zouave.

"Yes, quite well," Jenny smiled. "Well...I must get going. There are many more soldiers who need water."

As Jenny turned to leave, the soldier with the broken arm said, "Ma'am?"

Jenny set her dark eyes on him. "Yes?"

"Are you Lieut—I mean Captain Brownell's girl?"

Jenny felt an icy wave wash over her heart. Buck loved her. She knew that. But she couldn't let herself be Buck's girl. Choking on the lump that had lodged in her throat, she replied, "Sort of."

The Zouave grinned and said, "If I had a girl as beautiful as you, I'd have the courage to charge three blazing howitzers, too!"

Jenny knew what howitzers were. She could only imagine what kind of courageous deed Buck must have done. Eager to find General Scott's tent, she excused herself and headed again for the water barrel. A carriage load of women pulled up as Jenny filled her jug and replenished her supply of cups. She kept an eye on the new women until she saw them approach Clara Barton for instructions.

Hastening to the spot where Clara was giving orders, Jenny pressed in and said, "Clara, could you have one of these young ladies relieve me? I have to meet someone at General Scott's tent."

Clara agreed, and Jenny showed her replacement where she had left off. Jenny then hurried to the guards at the gate and asked the location of General Scott's tent. Moments later, she approached it and was met by a young corporal. "May I be of help to you, ma'am?"

"Well, I don't know. I'm looking for Lieutenant Buck Brownell."

"I'm General Scott's adjutant, ma'am," said the corporal. "Lieutenant Brownell is with the general and some other officers at the moment. Are you with the Barton crew?"

"Yes. I...I've been working among the wounded. Some of the Zouaves told me I could find Lieutenant Brownell over here."

"Well, ma'am, you can either sit on that wooden chair over there and wait until the lieutenant comes out, or you can return to your job with the wounded men. I'll come fetch you when he's available."

Before Jenny could reply, the tent flap came open and Buck Brownell emerged, followed by a Zouave colonel Jenny did not recognize. The instant Buck saw Jenny, a smiled spread over his face. Turning to the man who flanked him, Buck said, "I want you to meet somebody."

The adjutant entered the tent while Buck was introducing Jenny to Colonel Abram Duryee. The colonel told Jenny he was glad to meet her, then courteously excused himself and walked away.

In the light of the setting sun, Jenny set her eyes on the captain's bars that graced Buck's shoulders and said, "Congratulations, Captain."

"Somebody told you."

"Yes, some of your wounded Zouave admirers over there. I think it's wonderful, and I'm sure you deserve it."

"You must have answered Miss Barton's call for help."

"Well, not exactly. Daddy told me a few days ago that your Fire Zouaves were going to take part in an upcoming battle. I didn't learn what had happened until I arrived home from work this afternoon. I was...concerned about you. I had to come and see if I could find out how you were." Moving close and laying a hand on his arm, Jenny said, "I'm so glad you're all right."

The newly made captain looked at the ground, then back at Jenny. "Thank you. I'm glad you care what happens to me."

"I...I have to go now. It'll be dark soon. I didn't leave a note for Daddy and he'll be worried about me."

"I'll walk you to your horse," said Buck, gripping her hand.

When they reached the camp entrance, Buck led Jenny to her horse. It was tied to a bush, along with several others. He raised the reins over the animal's head and dropped them in front of the saddle. He opened his hand, palm up, to help her aboard. When she took the hand, he squeezed it and pulled her close. "Jenny, I love you."

"And I love you, Buck," she said, her eyes misting.

Buck looked around to see if anyone was watching. When he saw that the coast was clear, he lowered his head and kissed her. Tears were visible on Jenny's cheeks when they parted. Fighting to keep her composure, she turned toward the horse.

Buck reached for her. "Jenny..."

Without turning around, she said, "Please, Buck. I must get home."

He carefully hoisted her into the saddle. When she settled in, she looked down at him through a wall of tears and said, "Thank you."

"When this war is over—"

"We can never have each other, Buck," she said, drawing a shuddering breath.

Buck reached up and grasped her hand. "Jenny, you can't let your father control you all your life."

"You don't understand."

"Jenny, your father will probably marry again someday. Then he won't even want you around the house. You have your own life to live. We love each other, Jenny, and we could be happy together. This war won't last forever. Please tell me that when it's over, we can be together."

Jenny's throat was constricted and she was crying so hard, her chest was heaving. Choking out the words, she said, "I'll always love you, Buck." Then she slipped her hand from his grasp and goaded the horse into a trot.

When she knew she was out of sight of the camp, Jenny pulled the horse off the road into a stand of willows and wept her heart out. Tears flowing, Jenny caught her breath convulsively, giving vent to the emotions tearing at her soul. She felt like a liar and a hypocrite before Buck, knowing her father was pretending loyalty to the Union while engaged in espionage for the Confederacy.

Jenny loved Buck desperately, yet what could she do? She was a daughter of the South and owed it her loyalty. She owed her father her loyalty too, and she knew how he felt about her keeping company with Buck.

Bent over in the saddle, Jenny sobbed and prayed, "Dear God in heaven...what am I to do? Please help me! I could ask You to take away the love I have for Buck, but I want to love him. I want to be his wife and to bear his children. But I also love my Daddy...and I love the South. Oh, God, I don't know what to do. I don't know what to do." Her words trailed off into groans of despair.

In the days that followed, a heavy-hearted Buck Brownell plunged into his work of training the new recruits as they arrived daily. Jenny was hardly out of his thoughts. Often he prayed that one day, in spite of Jeffrey Jordan, Jenny would be his.

As the Confederates continued to gather troops at Manassas Junction, the North fumed and fretted over the presence of Rebel troops at the very doorstep of the nation's capital. President Lincoln felt the pressure of it, and after the embarrassment at Big Bethel, he determined to take action. In a private meeting with Generals Winfield Scott and Irvin McDowell, the president directed them to proceed immediately with their proposal to launch a gigantic assault on General Pierre G.T. Beauregard's force at Manassas Junction.

Scott and McDowell went to work. Since the scheme was already in the embryonic stage, it didn't take them long to come up with a well-contrived plan. On Friday, June 14, the plan was presented to the president, his Cabinet, and the Senate Military Committee. Jeffrey Jordan sat in the meeting and smiled inwardly. He would send every word of the plan directly to General Beauregard through Rose O'Neal Greenhow's girls.

In the plan, the Federal army would divide into three columns to increase its pace and mobility, and advance west-southwestward on roughly parallel routes. It would seize the Confederate outposts at Fairfax Court House sixteen miles from Washington and at Centreville, five miles beyond. Two of the columns would then push ahead and make a diversionary attack on the center of the Confederate line at Bull Run Creek.

The third column would skirt the Rebels' right flank and strike southward, cutting off the railroad to Richmond and threatening the Confederate rear. The Rebels would then be forced to abandon Manassas Junction and retreat some fifteen miles to the next defensible line, at the banks of the Rappahannock River. The Northerners, and especially the citizens of Washington, could then breath easier, and the morale of the Confederacy would be severely damaged. Even beyond that, Generals Scott and McDowell were confident that the Rebel forces would be so completely overwhelmed that the whole war would come to an end and a Union victory proclaimed.

The president, the Cabinet, and the Committee agreed on the plan, giving Jeffrey Jordan, as the Committee's military adviser, opportunity to voice his opinion. When Jordan said he could not improve on the plan, it was finalized and the generals were given authority to proceed.

General McDowell, as field commander, was responsible to set the date for the campaign to begin. He told the gathering he already had a date in mind—Monday, July 8. He figured it would take five days to march the men to the point of attack, meaning the actual battle would occur on Saturday, July 13.

Chairman Henry Wilson ran his gaze over the faces of the group, and said, "I agree with Generals Scott and McDowell. This offensive will spell the end of the Confederacy. This ridiculous civil conflict will no doubt be history by July fourteenth."

Jeffrey Jordan laughed to himself. How shocked Senator Wilson would be if he knew that the woman he was courting was a Rebel spy and that General Beauregard would receive all the information on the Union plan through her hands. As with the other men in attendance, Jordan had been taking notes. He had it all down in his notebook. The papers he would pass through John Calhoun to Rose Greenhow would explain the plan in every detail, including a list—as given by McDowell—of every Union regiment that would be involved in the attack. Like at Big Bethel, the Confederates would have a big surprise for the Yankees on the morning of July 13.

It was just past midday on Thursday, June 20, when Bettie Duval and Lola Morrow drew up at a wagon blockade in the road as they were headed west out of Washington. A U.S. flag flapped in the breeze from a pole affixed to one of the wagons. The horse pulling their buggy snorted and blew, bobbing its head when two men in blue—one a private, the other a corporal—stepped up and smiled.

"Good afternoon, ladies," said the corporal. "May I ask where you're headed?"

"Nowhere in particular, Corporal," replied Bettie, who held the reins. "We're just out for a little ride...getting away from the city to breathe a little fresh country air."

As Bettie spoke, she and Lola flashed flirtatious smiles. Both wore hats that shaded their faces.

"You live in Washington, then, I take it," said the private.

"Yes," nodded Bettie.

"Maybe you should ride north out of town. You're heading into Confederate territory going this way."

"Could be dangerous, ladies," added the private.

Lola rolled her big blue eyes at them and said, "We appreciate your concern for us, gentlemen, but we're really not afraid the Rebels will harm us. There isn't any real country north of Washington for several miles. We like it out this way."

"But, ma'am," countered the private, "with things heating up between us and the Confederates, you don't know what might happen if you run into a Rebel patrol."

"We're not afraid, Private. The Southern gentlemen are known for being just that."

"But, ma'am—"

"Is there a law that says we can't drive into Southern country, Private?"

"Well, no ma'am, but—"

"Then we'll proceed," Lola smiled.

Both soldiers tipped their hats and watched as the buggy moved past the blockade.

A little over an hour later, the buggy rolled to a halt at a Confederate road block. Bettie and Lola could see the small depot at Manassas Junction from where they sat. To the south and east were thousands of Rebel soldiers milling about among hundreds of small white tents. In a field to the north were scores of soldiers in training.

Three Rebel privates moved up beside the buggy. The one who

seemed to be the oldest, greeted them warmly and said, "The road is closed from here on, ladies. I don't know where you're headed, but you'll have to find another route."

"Actually we were headed straight for this camp," smiled Bettie. "We have a message for General Beauregard."

"Well, now, pretty little filly, what kind of message could sweet young things like you have for the general?"

Bettie fixed him with a steady gaze and asked, "Private, did you hear about the battle over at Big Bethel?"

"Sure did, ma'am!" he grinned. "We sent those blue-bellies a-skeedaddlin' for cover. They got the surprise of their lives!"

"And why was that?"

"Well, our guys got word ahead of time that the blue-bellies was comin'!"

"And just how did Colonel Magruder get that word?"

"Why, it was a couple of female spi..."

"Spies?"

"Yeah. That...that's what you are, ain't it!"

"Yes," Bettie replied, lifting her graceful chin. "Now, may we please proceed so we can deliver our message to General Beauregard?"

"I could save you the trouble, ma'am," spoke up a second private, "if you'll let me take it to the general for you."

"Doesn't work that way," said Bettie, shaking her head. "We have orders to deliver it to the general personally. Otherwise, we are to return to Washington immediately."

The trio exchanged glances, then the older one said, "Mind if I jump on the side of the buggy, ma'am? I'll guide you to general Beauregard's tent and let him know you're here."

"Fine," smiled Bettie, snapping the reins.

The private hopped onto the buggy's lower step and rode to the camp, pointing the way to General Beauregard's spacious tent. When the buggy stopped, Bettie and Lola were aware of many soldiers looking their direction. The private left the buggy, halted at the flap, and called, "General, sir, it's Private Donnie Lee Cowper. I have two young ladies out here who wish to see you."

"I'll be right with you."

Cowper glanced back toward the buggy, then the tent flap parted and a tall, slender man with coal-black hair and mustache appeared in a double-breasted uniform with parallel lines of gold-plated buttons running from the shoulders downward to the bottom of his knee-length coat. He wore no hat.

"That's him," Bettie whispered to Lola. "I've seen pictures of him. He's forty-three and dyes his hair so the gray in his temples won't show."

Beauregard's Creole ancestry gave him strikingly handsome features with marble-black eyes and dark, smooth skin. He dismissed Cowper and moved toward the buggy with squared shoulders and back ramrod straight. A smile parted his lips as he halted beside the vehicle. For lack of a hat to tip, he bowed his head politely and said, "Good afternoon, ladies. General Beauregard at your service. And to what do I owe the pleasure of your visit?"

"If I said 'Circled R,' General would it mean anything to you?" Bettie asked.

"Yes," he replied quickly. "It would mean you ladies have a message for me from Mrs. Rose O'Neal Greenhow."

"You are so right," Bettie smiled. "May we step down?"

"By all means," nodded the general, stepping up and offering Bettie his hand.

When Beauregard had helped both women from the buggy, he invited them to sit at a table in the shade of a large oak tree, saying that the tent was a bit stuffy at that time of the day.

As they moved to the table under the watchful eyes of an innumerable company of gray-clad soldiers, the general asked, "Am I permitted to know your names?"

Halting beside the table, Bettie said, "Of course, sir. I am Bettie Duval, and this is Lola Morrow."

"I am happy and honored to make your acquaintance," smiled Beauregard. "Please sit down."

"Before we do, General," Bettie said, "we may just as well give you the message."

Lola wore her long, silken-black hair in an upsweep. Bettie removed Lola's hat and helped her drop the thick, shiny waves. Producing a folded set of papers, Lola handed them to the general, then she and Bettie sat down. Beauregard eased down onto a straight-backed chair, unfolded the papers, and laid them out on the table. The women remained quiet while he read them through silently.

When he finished, he shook his head and said, "Ladies, the Confederacy is forever indebted to you and Mrs. Greenhow...and, of course, to whomever garnered this vital information in Washington. Are you the two who carried the classified information to Colonel Magruder at Yorktown?"

"I am one of them sir," offered Bettie. "Another young lady was my partner in that venture."

"I see," he nodded. Then running his gaze between them, he asked, "Are you aware of the penalty if you're ever caught?"

"Yes, sir," spoke up Lola, "but since they won't let us put on a uniform and go into battle, we find great satisfaction in doing this job. We are honored to risk our lives for the Cause."

"Well, I'm very proud to serve the Confederacy with soldiers such as you. Together, we're going to give the Federals more than they can handle. Thank you."

"Our pleasure," smiled Bettie. "Now, sir, we must head back."

As the general walked them to the buggy, he lamented, "It really grieves me about this coming attack. You see, General Irvin McDowell was a classmate of mine at West Point, and I fought under General Winfield Scott in the Mexican War. This is a hard thing...to have them now as opponents."

"I'm sure it is, sir," Bettie said. "Didn't I also read that Major Anderson, whom you were ordered to fire upon at Fort Sumter, was one of your instructors at West Point, and that you had also been close friends?"

Beauregard bit down hard on his lower lip. "Yes, ma'am. Major Anderson and I are still very close friends. It just so happens that the way things are at the moment, we cannot pursue our friendship. I am hoping that when this awful ordeal is over, we can enjoy each other's company once again."

Leaving a sad-eyed Creole behind, Bettie Duval and Lola Morrow drove away.

CHAPTER TWELVE

✦

By Sunday morning, July 7, General Irvin McDowell was aware that his projected date for launching the offensive against the Confederates was unrealistic. It would take eight more days to be properly prepared. He would march his men toward Manassas Junction on July 16. The attack would be launched on Sunday, July 21.

McDowell explained the situation and announced the new dates in a brief meeting at the Capitol with the president, the Cabinet, and the Senate Military Committee early on Monday morning. Jenny was at her desk when the meeting broke up, and was chatting with three of the senators when her father appeared. Jeffrey Jordan waited till the senators were gone and the hall was clear, then sat down in front of Jenny's desk and said quietly, "I've been meaning to talk to you about something very important, but I wasn't in any rush because I thought there was plenty of time. This meeting I was just in has changed that. We need to talk before this evening."

Jenny studied her father's concerned features. "All right, Daddy. Talk."

"No, honey. Not here. How about during your lunch hour?"

"Of course."

"I'll be back a little before noon. We can grab a bite at a nearby restaurant, then go for a walk around the capitol grounds."

"Okay, Daddy."

Jordan returned later, as promised. They were seated quickly and were done eating by twelve-thirty. Then they headed out into the hot afternoon sun and began their walk.

"Jenny, I told you about the upcoming assault on the Confederate army at Manassas Junction."

"Yes. Next Saturday." Jenny felt a pang in her heart. Buck would be in on that offensive.

"Well, that's changed. It's going to be a week from Sunday. The twenty-first."

"What has that got to do with me, Daddy?"

Jordan paused while they met another couple on the walk. When the couple was past and out of earshot, he said, "Rose Greenhow has been after me for several days to see if I'd talk to you about becoming one of her girls."

"You mean me be a spy?"

"Yes."

"Oh, Daddy, I couldn't do it."

"Yes, you could. I was at Rose's house yesterday afternoon, and she's having trouble getting volunteers. She can't let those who are working with her be seen too often at the Union blockades or the Yankees will get suspicious. She needs more girls. She thought at first she wouldn't have any trouble getting young women with Southern loyalties to join her, but when the Washington newspapers printed the president's policy on Confederate spies a couple of weeks ago, it put a crimp in things."

"Yes, I read it," Jenny said tightly. "And I don't mind telling you as I did when you first started this spy business...it worries me, Daddy. Immediate execution. No quarter."

"We've already been over this, Jenny. You wouldn't worry about me if I were on the battlefield?"

Jenny was quiet for a moment. A pair of Orioles was chirping in a tree just ahead, but she didn't hear them. Jenny's mind was intent on the discussion at hand. "Of course, I would worry about you if you were on the battlefield. But since you won't be in combat, I have to worry about you getting caught as a spy."

Jordan reached down, took his daughter's hand, raised it to his lips, and kissed it. "I'm glad that you care enough to worry about me, honey."

"Care enough? You're my Daddy! I love you with all my heart!"

He kissed the hand again and said, "And I love you with all my heart, too."

They continued along the shady path, Jenny pondering what her father had asked her to do. Finally, he broke into her thoughts. "Honey, are you asking yourself how I could love you as I do and ask you to put yourself in the dangerous position of a spy?"

"Not really," she responded softly. "I realize I'm already in a risky spot. I know what you're doing as a spy, and I'm aware of John Calhoun's involvement...and I know what Rose and her girls are doing. I am already a conspirator because I haven't turned all of you in. If any of you get caught, it won't take the authorities long before they come after me. I could perjure myself in court and say I knew nothing about it—that you were able to carry on your espionage activities right under my nose without my ever suspecting anything—but you and I both know I would never be able to do it. If they didn't execute me, they'd surely lock me up in prison. No, Daddy, I'm not questioning your love for me because you want me to become one of Rose's girls. When I said I couldn't do it, I didn't mean because I fear getting caught. I'm just as much a Southerner as you are. But...but..."

Jenny's throat went tight and tears filmed her eyes.

Jordan stopped and looked at her. Gripping her shoulders, he said, "Jenny, you've got to forget Buck Brownell. How many times do I have to say it? He's the enemy."

"But Daddy—"

Gripping her harder, Jordan caught her eyes square with his own, held them there, and said emphatically, "Listen to me, honey! Your loyalty to the South must come first. When our Southern men and boys go into battle, they leave sweethearts, wives, children, and families for the sake of the Confederacy. On that battlefield, nothing else matters. The South comes first. The same principle applies to those of us who work as spies."

Jenny continued to weep, but she did not attempt to break the stare between them.

"This is war, Jenny. Our personal feelings must be put aside. Do you understand what I am saying?"

Jenny blinked against the hot tears and sniffed. "Yes."

"All right, then," Jordan said, releasing his hold on her shoulders. "I went to Rose's house this morning after we talked at your desk. I had to let her know of the change in plans for the assault on our forces at Manassas Junction. While I was there, Rose asked me about you. I explained that I would be talking to you about becoming one of her girls during your lunch break. And..."

"Yes, Daddy?"

"Well, I told her I know what my daughter is made of. I told her you would say yes."

"Oh."

"Was I right?"

Jenny swallowed hard. She knew she had no options.

Jordan could read his daughter's eyes and knew she was resigning herself to it. "Good!" he breathed. "I knew I could count on my little girl. Rose asked if you could be at her house right after supper tonight.

I told her I'd bring you over myself. I can pick you up and bring you home later."

Later that afternoon, Jenny was busy at her desk, trying to bury herself in her work, when she suddenly became aware of a form standing over her. Looking up, she saw a young Zouave private, holding a small brown envelope and smiling at her.

"Yes?" she said, returning the smile.

"Miss Jenny Jordan?"

"Yes."

Extending the envelope, the Zouave said, "Captain Buck Brownell sent me to deliver this to you, ma'am."

Jenny took the envelope, noting that it was sealed, and thanked him. He saluted her and quickly walked away. Jenny's hands trembled slightly as she used a letter opener to break the seal. Looking around, she saw people milling up and down the hallway. She reached into a drawer, drew out a small wooden sign that read: "Back in Ten Minutes," and placed it on the desk top. Then she moved into the Senate Chamber and entered the file room. Finding it unoccupied, she pulled out the folded slip of paper and read it.

Darling Jenny:

I love you more each day, and more than words could ever express. The only way my love for you can ever change is to grow stronger.

Please don't forget me.

Though I am still not high on the social scale demanded by your father, it should impress him some that I am now a captain. If you will wait for me until the war is over, I will approach your father and try to convince him that I am worthy of becoming his son-in-law.

Always,
Buck

Jenny leaned against a file cabinet and had a good cry. When she was able to dry her tears, she touched up her makeup and returned to her desk, clutching the letter close to her heart.

At five o'clock, Jenny emerged heavy-hearted from the Capitol and started down the long, wide stairs toward the street. Other employees were leaving, and several people were moving about on the Capitol steps. Suddenly Jenny recognized Captain Jack Egan threading his way toward her. When Egan reached her, Jenny did not stop.

Moving in beside her as she continued down the steps, Egan said, "Hey, Jenny, it's me, Jack. Hold up a minute!"

Jenny's pace remained the same. Egan caught up to her and leaped in front of her, blocking her way. "I want to talk to you."

Jenny faced him head-on. Her stare was like the insistence of a knife point. "Please get out of my way."

Holding his ground, Egan said, "Come on now. What about us?"

"There is no us. Please move."

"Look, Jenny, don't let your father's attitude get in your way of happiness. You and I can still see each other—"

Jenny's eyes flashed fire. "I'm not interested in seeing you any more, Jack. I lost all respect for you when you took it upon yourself to tell Buck he couldn't see me, and that you and I were planning marriage. Now...out of my way!"

"It's Brownell, isn't it? No matter how your old man feels about you getting involved with soldiers, you're still seeing that egotistical, backwoods corporal, aren't you?"

Jenny's shoulders shook and her nostrils flared. "Buck is not backwoods, and he's not egotistical. And what's more, he's not a corporal!"

"Yeah, I heard that he wrangled himself a lieutenant's bar for shooting that helpless civilian."

Jenny slapped Egan's face. The impact resounded across the Capitol steps like a gunshot. People stopped and looked. Surprised and stung, Egan hunched his shoulders as if he might strike her in return, but restrained himself.

"Buck didn't shoot a helpless civilian! And he's not a lieutenant anymore, either—he's a captain!"

Just then a huge, muscular man bumped Egan's shoulder and growled, "This soldier givin' you trouble, ma'am?" Egan saw two more just like him standing by. His eyes bulged.

"Yes," replied Jenny, "but he was just leaving. Weren't you, Jack?"

Egan licked his lips. "Yes. Yes...I was just leaving."

"Before you go," Jenny said tartly, "I want to make it clear that I don't want to see you again. Find some other woman, Jack. My heart belongs to Buck."

Egan took a deep breath, looked at the three men, and walked away without another word.

"Thank you," Jenny said, smiling at the big man with the bear-like voice.

"My pleasure, ma'am," he grinned, showing two broken teeth. And, uh...ma'am?"

"Yes?"

"If you and this Buck fella should ever break it off...look me up. My name's Garth Heegan. I work at the Fair Oaks Farm just west of town."

Jenny managed to keep a straight face as she said, "All right, Mr. Heegan. I'll keep you in mind."

That evening, Jenny rapped Rose Greenhow's brass knocker and waited for her to open the door. Rose greeted her with a warm smile, and Jenny turned and waved at her father, who sat in his buggy at the curb. Jeffrey Jordan waved back and drove off.

Rose put an arm around Jenny and ushered her into the parlor.

Sitting on a fancy overstuffed love seat next to a small table that held a glowing lantern was Bettie Duval.

"You remember Bettie, don't you, Jenny?"

"Of course," smiled Jenny. "We rode back from the Zouave demonstration together in your carriage, Rose. How are you, Bettie?"

"Just fine. Nice to see you again."

"Nice to see you, too."

"How about some tea, Jenny?" asked Rose.

"Maybe a little later, thank you. Right now, I'm too full. Daddy and I just had dinner."

Rose seated Jenny next to Bettie, then sat on a couch facing them a few feet away. Wasting no time, Rose reminded Jenny that her father had been there earlier in the day with information about the Union attack at Manassas Junction. When Jenny nodded, Rose said, "Your father told me you had agreed to become one of my messenger girls."

Jenny gave her a weak, "Yes."

"Well, honey, I've got a job for you immediately. You worked today, so you're off tomorrow, right?"

"Yes."

"I want you to go with Bettie and carry the message of the change in date to General Beauregard. Sometime in the future, I might send a girl on a mission alone, but not yet. We're finding it works quite well getting two girls past the Union lines. So, you and Bettie will go to Manassas Junction tomorrow."

Bettie felt Jenny tense up, and Rose saw it in her face.

Rose raised her painted eyebrows. "Is something wrong, honey?"

Jenny's hand went to her mouth. There was consternation in her eyes. "I...I didn't realize you would send me out so soon, Rose. I guess I thought there would be some training or schooling or something."

"You'll get your training by going with Bettie," smiled Rose.

"Bettie has already delivered two messages for me. She and Susan Rand carried the message to Colonel Magruder at Yorktown." She chuckled. "We all know what happened there."

Jenny's features paled. She thought of Buck...and of the Union men who were killed and wounded in that fiasco.

When Jenny did not comment, Rose said, "Bettie and Lola took the message to General Beauregard about the upcoming Union assault on our army over there. Now that McDowell has changed the date, we want General Beauregard to know it as soon as possible. That's why it has to go tomorrow."

"I understand," said Jenny.

Rose chuckled and said, "Big Bethel was one thing, but this is going to be one to really set the Union back on its heels. I'm sure by now Lincoln and his boys are wondering how they were outfoxed at Big Bethel. On this Manassas thing, we'll give them a whole lot more to wonder about. Because of our espionage, we'll make those blue-bellies eat dirt on this one!"

Bettie looked at Jenny and said excitedly, "This is great, isn't it? What a thrill to know it couldn't be done without us. This'll be written down in history. Someday we can tell our children and grandchildren about it!"

Rose was concerned over Jenny's lack of enthusiasm. Trying to put a spark under her, she said, "Jenny, if General Beauregard can counter this Union assault with enough strength, this may be the first and last big battle. Wouldn't it be great for you to look back on it and say that you helped bring this war to an abrupt end? And even if this isn't the last battle, it will still help bring the war to an end much quicker than otherwise. The Union has more men and weapons than the Confederacy, but by our espionage, we can offset that advantage. You are willing to help, aren't you?"

The web of apprehension that was closing in on Jenny's mind became quite evident on her face.

Rose studied her for a few seconds, then said, "Honey, are you afraid? Do you have some reservations about joining us that your daddy doesn't know about?"

There was a tremor in Jenny's voice. "No, Rose. My father is aware of anything and everything about me. As for being afraid...I'm not afraid as you might think. I have no fear for myself. It's just that..."

Rose left the couch and knelt in front of Jenny. "What is it, honey? What's bothering you?"

"You were there at the Zouave demonstration. So was Bettie."

Before Jenny could proceed, Rose stood, clapped her hands together, and exclaimed, "Ah—it's that handsome young Zouave who rescued you from the runaway buggy! Yes...I remember now. I even heard you tell him you loved him right in front of your daddy."

"Yes, I did. And I meant it."

Rose bent over and looked Jenny in the eye. "What does your father think of your being in love with a Union soldier?"

"He...he doesn't like it at all. But that doesn't change a thing. I love my daddy, but even he can't control my heart. I'm in love with Buck, and I can't help it. I don't want to help it."

Rose turned and took two steps, then wheeled about. "I assume you didn't know Buck before the war started."

"No, I met him the day I was helping Clara Barton when they brought in all those wounded men from the Baltimore riot. Buck had been stabbed in the face, and I helped patch him up. I didn't realize it at the time, but looking back, I know that's when I fell in love with him. I'm sure it was the same time Buck fell in love with me, too."

Rose sighed and said, "Jenny, honey, I don't mean to sound like a know-it-all, but you should have kept a guard on your heart. Falling in love in wartime is always risky...but falling in love with a Union soldier, you've really done it."

Jenny looked at Rose and said, "If the war goes beyond this

Manassas Junction battle, and I can carry messages that don't affect battles Buck will be in, I'll be glad to help you, Rose. Can't you get one of your other girls to go with Bettie tomorrow? Buck's going to be in the thick of this one. I...I just can't do it."

Rose was quiet for a moment, then she said, "The reason I wanted you for this job, Jenny, is that I don't want the faces of any of my girls becoming too familiar. I've chosen Bettie for this one because she has the most experience and is the best one to break you in. If the war goes on, it'll be quite a while before I send her again. I need a new face to go with her, and I need one that will captivate those Union soldiers at the road block. You're just so perfect for the job."

Jenny rose from the love seat, drew close to Rose and said, "Rose, I appreciate that, but please put yourself in my place. Buck was in that battle at Big Bethel. Thank the Lord in heaven, he wasn't killed...but he could have been. Do you realize if he had been killed, and if instead of Susan it had been me who went with Bettie to carry that message to Colonel Magruder...I would have been responsible for Buck's death! Please don't ask me to go with Bettie on this job tomorrow."

Rose and Bettie exchanged glances. Speaking to Bettie, Rose said, "Susan will go with you, I'm sure."

"Of course," Bettie smiled.

Jenny rushed to Rose, threw her arms around her, and said, "Oh, thank you!"

Rose hugged her tight, then held her at arm's length. Smiling, she said, "Your father didn't know that I had you in mind for this Manassas Junction job. We'll just tell him that you've agreed to work for me, and that if the war goes further, you'll go on whatever missions I ask you to. You and I will work those out by mutual agreement."

"Thank you, Rose," Jenny breathed a heavy sigh. "Thank you for understanding."

Bettie left the love seat, stepped up close, and said, "Jenny, what if the war goes on and you do work with us on espionage missions...then somehow things work out so you and Buck get together? How would he feel if you told him you've been a Confederate spy? You know...working underhandedly as his enemy?"

The thought was a new one to Jenny. Blinking, she paused, then said slowly, "I...I don't know. I couldn't marry him without confessing it. There shouldn't be any secrets between a husband and wife. I...I guess if by some miracle it came down to that, it would be a true test of his love."

"Well, honey," said Bettie, "I'm pulling for you. Sounds like you and Buck have got the real thing between you. I hope with all my heart it works out...and that Buck's love will be put to the test."

"Me too, honey," spoke up Rose.

Jenny managed a smile. "Just imagine," she sighed, clasping her hands under her chin, "a life together with my beloved enemy!"

CHAPTER THIRTEEN

✦

On Tuesday July 9, Bettie Duval and Susan Rand delivered to General Pierre G.T. Beauregard the message containing the new date for the Union assault at Manassas Junction. Beauregard expressed his deep appreciation; they were going to have a big part in the Confederate victory because he had been forewarned of the attack.

In Washington, however, where neither military nor civilians were aware of the espionage going on under their very noses, there was a growing confidence that the pending battle at Manassas Junction would be a total rout for the North. When word hit Washington of the Union victory in the battle at Rich Mountain, Virginia, on July 11, Northerners found even more reason for their confidence to build.

On Tuesday, July 16, General Irvin McDowell led his troops out of the Washington camps toward Manassas Junction. Word spread through the city and into surrounding towns, and soon the populace knew the assault against the Confederates was going to take place on the following Sunday. A great number of people, including politicians and their families, made plans to take picnic lunches and watch the rout from the high hills on the north side of Bull Run Creek, near the railroad junction.

One unit of men-in-blue marched directly through Washington and down Pennsylvania Avenue past the White House on their way to the battle site. Citizens along the streets cheered when they saw the Yankee soldiers carrying a Confederate flag that had been captured in the battle at Rich Mountain. The city was buzzing with excitement.

At the Robert Brownell house, Kady told her husband at the supper table that she was going to pack a splendid picnic lunch for Sunday.

"That'll be nice," Robert said. "From what I hear, we'd better get an early start. Sounds like half of Washington is going out there."

"I can't wait to see the show. I guess that's how just about every-body around here feels. They all want to get a look at the Rebels on the run."

"That *will* be a good show!" laughed Robert.

Kady set down her fried chicken and said, "Do you think we'll be able to see Buck during the battle?"

"You mean Captain Buck Brownell, the famous war hero? The one who took us to dinner last week?"

"That's the one."

"I sure hope so. I'm taking my binoculars. He shouldn't be hard to pick out amid the colorful Zouaves."

"Let's take our flag, too. We can wave it over our heads to cele-brate the victory."

"Sounds good to me, Mrs. Brownell," grinned Robert.

On Saturday, at the Jordan home, Lieutenant Jeffrey Jordan had been in his library reading since shortly after breakfast. It suddenly dawned on him that it had been nearly three hours since he had heard Jenny moving about the house.

Laying his book down, he left the library and went through the house. When he had covered the first floor without finding her, he mounted the stairs and headed for her room. The door was closed. Tapping lightly, he said, "Jenny? You in there?"

A few seconds lapsed before he heard a weak voice say, "Yes. Did you want something, Daddy?"

"Just missed you flitting about the house as usual. You all right?"

Again, there was a silent moment before the answer came. "Yes. I'm fine."

"You don't sound fine, honey. May I come in?"

"Of course."

Jordan opened the door and found his daughter sitting on the bed with an open Bible in her hands. Her eyes were puffy, and he knew she had been crying.

Moving closer, he asked, "What is it, sweetheart?"

"I'm just doing some praying and laying hold on some of God's promises. He says if we love Him, all things will work together for our good. And He says the effectual fervent prayer of a righteous man availeth much. So I was just asking Him to give me the faith to believe Him for some very important things I have on my heart right now."

"Things like the safety of a certain Yankee captain?"

Jenny swallowed with difficulty. "Yes," she replied, blinking.

Jordan rubbed the back of his neck and said, "Honey, I'm telling you for your own good—you must forget him. Even when the shooting stops and an armistice is signed, there are going to be hard feelings between the North and the South for generations to come. I want my little girl to marry a Southerner. It'll save her a lot of problems."

Closing her Bible, Jenny laid it on the bed and stood up. Deep lines creased her brow as she said, "But, Daddy, I'm in love with Buck. I can never love another man."

Jordan folded his daughter into his arms, held her close, and said,

"That's the way it seems, right now, but it'll change one day. You'll see."

Jenny clung to her father, hugging him tight, but thought, *You're wrong, Daddy. It will never change.* After clinging to him for a long moment, she eased free of his arms and said, "I guess you know there's going to be a big gathering on the hills overlooking Manassas Junction tomorrow."

"Yes."

"I'm planning to go with Rose and her other girls. Rose wants to see first-hand the results of her spy work. I want to see it, too."

"I'd like to see it, myself, but I have to be at the Capitol with the president, the Cabinet, and the Senate Military Committee. Lincoln wants us all to wait there together for the news of the Union's victory." He paused, then chuckled, "I'm really looking forward to seeing their faces when it turns out the other way."

At the White House, Mary Todd Lincoln was seated on a cream brocaded Queen Anne chair, watching her maid, Myrtle Wetherby, stretch a new Battenburg lace cloth over the dining room table. When they heard the parlor door open and close, and young Tad's chatter, Mary said, "Sounds like Patricia and the boys are back from their walk."

Myrtle laughed, "What was your first clue?"

Seconds later, the boys charged into the dining room with their pretty governess following.

"Mom!" exclaimed Tad, eyes dancing with excitement. "Guess what we found out!"

"I haven't the slightest idea," smiled Mary.

"A million people are goin' out to watch the war tomorrow mornin'! Not only grown-ups, but kids, too. Can we go, Mom? Willie an' me want to see the battle!"

"Willie and *I*," corrected Patricia, tapping Tad's shoulder.

Lifting his eyes to the governess, the boy grinned mischievously, looked back at his mother, and said, "See? Miss Patricia wants to see it, too! You want to go, too, don't you, Mom? Can we go? Please?"

Mary set her loving gaze on the lad and said, "I'm not feeling very well, honey. I think I'm coming down with something. I doubt if I will feel well enough by tomorrow to venture out."

"How about Papa? Can he take us?"

"He can't, Tad. He told me he'll have to be at the Capitol while the battle is going on tomorrow. There's no way he can take you. Besides, it might be dangerous with all that gunfire going on."

"It won't be dangerous, Mom. Else all those other kids' parents wouldn't be takin' 'em. One man we talked to said everybody'll be up on top of a high hill so no bullets or cannonballs can get to 'em."

Mary looked at Patricia.

The governess said, "That's the way I understand it, too, ma'am."

"Well, it really doesn't make any difference," Mary said. "There's no one to take them. If I'm feeling better tomorrow, we'll see about it then."

"Is there anything I can do to help you feel better, Mom?" asked Tad. "I'll do anything." Turning to his brother, he said, "Won't we, Willie?"

"Sure," nodded Willie.

Mary smiled weakly. "No, boys, there isn't anything you can do. We'll just have to see how I feel in the morning."

The boys, disappointed that the venture was doubtful, were led from the room by Patricia.

Early that same day at Manassas Junction, General Beauregard welcomed brigades led by Brigadier Generals Joseph E. Johnston and Thomas J. Jackson. The brigades arrived by rail from where they had been stationed in the Shenandoah Valley near Winchester. As soon as the Shenandoah troops jumped from the train, it pulled out to head for the Piedmont Station to pick up the Georgia Brigade commanded by Colonel Francis Bartow.

Many other brigades arrived before sundown, including the rugged South Carolina Third Brigade, led by hard-nosed Brigadier General Barnard Bee. By the time darkness had fallen, the forewarned General Beauregard had amassed an army of 32,500 men, ready and eager to fight.

On the other side of Bull Run Creek, General Irvin McDowell called his final council of war just after 8:00 P.M. at Union head-quarters near the small village of Centerville. Present in McDowell's tent were seventeen officers representing five divisions, which ranged from two to four brigades apiece, plus a cavalry brigade under the command of Major I.N. Palmer. In total, the Union force was 35,000 strong.

McDowell spread an elaborate map on the floor of his tent. By lantern light, he made the battle assignments to his commanders. Outside the tent, beneath an ebony sky bedecked with countless twinkling stars, the Union soldiers sat around campfires watching the flames cast flickering shadows into the fields and woods that surrounded them. Those who felt like talking did so in hushed tones, allowing the reflective ones to hear the cattle lowing in the nearby meadows and the sound of the night breeze rustling through the trees. From somewhere in the camp, a lone harmonica played a mournful tune.

Hundreds of the Yankee soldiers were writing letters by firelight to their loved ones at home, expressing hopes for survival, yet acknowledging the possibility that tomorrow they could die.

After the assignments were made and battle-related questions were answered inside General McDowell's tent, Colonel Erasmus D. Keyes said, "General McDowell, there is something that concerns me, sir...and I feel no doubt concerns the others here. May I address the subject?"

"Of course," nodded McDowell.

"My concern, General, is the defeat our forces met at Big Bethel, and the evidence that Confederate spies had fed classified information to Colonel Magruder. Can you tell us what has been done to ferret out the spies?"

McDowell cleared his throat. "The president, General Scott, and I discussed this at length. Mr. Lincoln then broached the subject while we were in a joint meeting of the Cabinet and the Senate Military Committee. The Committee was assigned by Mr. Lincoln to conduct an investigation. This investigation is still in progress, but at the last report a few days ago, they had been unable to turn up a clue as to who the spy or spies might be. The general consensus is that it has to be someone in the Cabinet, on the Committee, or possibly a clerk or secretary who works in the offices of these two groups."

For a moment there was dead silence. Then Brigadier General Daniel Tyler looked around at his fellow-commanders and said with feeling, "It's bad enough to think it could be a clerk or a secretary...but to think it could actually be someone in the Cabinet or on the Committee!"

"General McDowell, I hope Beauregard wasn't fed information like Magruder was," interjected Colonel William T. Sherman.

"What we're hoping," said McDowell, "is that since everyone within the Senate Chamber offices knows the investigation is underway, the guilty party or parties have pulled their heads in. That he, she, or they have been scared off."

"Even if Beauregard *has* been given information on our assault," put in Colonel Ambrose E. Burnside, "it won't make that much difference this time. Their army is scattered all the way up the Shenandoah Valley. We probably outnumber them two-to-one."

General McDowell asked if there were any more pertinent questions. There were none, and he dismissed them.

By ten o'clock the brigade commanders had collected their men and passed General McDowell's instructions on to them. There was nothing to do now but try to sleep.

Most of the Union soldiers found sleep impossible. Many sat and stared into the fires. Others lay quietly surveying the starlit sky. Some spent their time praying, while still others wrote down their thoughts, reflecting on the situation at hand. One young private wrote, "This is one of the most beautiful nights imagination can conceive. The sky is perfectly clear, the moon is bright, and the air is still as if it were not in a few hours to be disturbed by the roar of cannon and the shouts and cries of fighting and dying men."

Colonel Abram Duryee's Fifth New York Zouaves had been placed in First Division under Brigadier General Tyler, and assigned as part of First Brigade under Colonel Keyes.

At the section of the camp where the Zouaves were positioned, Captain Buck Brownell lay on his back near a fire and gazed into the heavens. Jenny Jordan was on his mind. The cattle had settled down for the night, and whoever had been playing the harmonica had stopped. There was only the low murmur of a few men in the area who preferred to talk. Above their subdued voices could be heard the music of innumerable crickets.

Buck looked by faith beyond the stars and whispered, "Lord, when the battle is fought tomorrow, no matter how it goes for either side...a lot of us are going to be killed. Only You know if there'll be a bullet out there with my name on it, or a hunk of shrapnel, or even a bayonet. I settled things with You back there in that Baptist church as a boy, and I'm not afraid to die. You know my heart. And since You do, You also know that I want to live. I've talked to You about Jenny and me many a time. You're probably tired of hearing me ask for some kind of miracle that would change her father's mind, but here I am again. If You see fit to let me live through this war, please make it possible for Jenny and me to be married. And Lord, if in Your wisdom You choose to take me out of this world in tomorrow's battle, or another one...I ask that You take care of Jenny and give her a happy life."

Buck's prayer was interrupted by a hoarse whisper, "Captain Brownell?"

Looking up, Buck recognized the face of Corporal Derek Flanders, one of the men in his company. Sitting up, he whispered back, "Yes, Flanders?"

"We've got a young Zouave over here in another company who's so all-fired scared, he's shaking all over. Colonel Duryee asked me to come and get you. He seems to feel you can help this kid."

"I'll try," replied Buck, rising to his feet.

While the captain and the corporal made their way among the campfires and men, Buck asked, "What's this boy's name, Flanders? Do I know him?"

"He's a fairly new recruit, sir—name's Danny Forbes. He told Colonel Duryee you taught his unit hand-to-hand fighting, but that the two of you hadn't actually met personally. He admires you a lot."

Colonel Duryee was standing over the frightened young private as Brownell and Flanders drew up. There was a fire close by. In order not to embarrass Forbes, the other Zouaves had withdrawn from the immediate area.

Danny Forbes was sitting on the ground, knees pulled up to his chin, and trembling like a leaf in the autumn wind. He was so frightened, his teeth were chattering. Brownell met Duryee's gaze and nodded. The colonel moved away, taking Corporal Flanders with him.

Buck laid a steady hand on the frightened soldier's shoulder, knelt beside him, and said, "Danny. Captain Brownell."

Danny's head came up, his face a mask of terror in the moonlight and glow of the nearby fire. "Y-yes, s-sir."

"Colonel Duryee told you he had sent for me, right?"

"Uh-huh."

"Got the jitters, eh?"

"M-more than th-that, sir. I'm just...just plain scared out of my wits! I...I'm ashamed of myself. I'm a...a coward. I was sittin' over there by the fire w-with some of the other fellas, and they were talkin' about f-facin' those Rebel guns in the mornin'...and I plumb fell to pieces. I mean, C-Cap'n, I started cryin' like a baby. I...I can't face those fellas ever again!"

"Hey, my friend," said Buck, squeezing the shoulder tightly, "you're only human. Your fellow-soldiers know that. If the truth were known, they're just as scared as you are."

Forbes blinked and drew a shuddering breath. "Then how come th-*they* haven't fallen apart?"

"We're all made different, kid," said Buck, hunkering down to look him in the eye. "You want to know something? I'm just as scared as you are."

Young Danny eyed him incredulously. "*You?*"

"Mm-hmm. And I can guarantee you, there isn't a man here who isn't scared. And over there at the Junction, every one of those Rebels is scared, too."

The truth was sinking in. Danny shook his head and said, "It's funny, Cap'n. When I signed up to be a Zouave, I was so eager to be a soldier and get into the fight. I never dreamed I'd have a moment like this."

"It's the same way with all of us, kid. How old are you?"

"Eighteen."

"Well, there are a lot of men your age and older going into battle for the first time in the morning. And there are some out here—on both sides—who fought in the Mexican War who've got the jitters, too. It's just a normal part of war, Danny."

Young Forbes sniffed, palmed tears from his face, and said, "So I'm not a coward?"

"No. You could've taken off through the woods and over the hills, couldn't you?"

"Yes."

"Did you?"

"No."

"Why not?"

"Well, because...even though I'm scared, I...I'm going to be here...to fight...in the morning."

"That proves you're not a coward. Being scared doesn't make you a coward. It's what you do when you're scared that shows what you're made of. You're made of the real thing, Danny. You've got what it takes to be a soldier. You're going to pick up that gun of yours and charge the enemy at dawn *because* you're a soldier."

Danny Forbes sniffed again and thumbed tears from the corners of his eyes. A smile worked its way over his face. He stood up, took a deep breath, and looked Buck—who rose with him—in the eye. "Thank you, Cap'n. I'm going to be all right."

Colonel Duryee had been waiting in the shadows. Both men heard the swish of his baggy trousers as he approached.

"Corporal Forbes will do just fine, Colonel," Buck told him. "He'll be ready to do his part in the battle tomorrow."

"That's right, Colonel Duryee," spoke up Danny. "Captain Brownell helped me get a grip on myself. I'm ready to face those Rebels and help whip 'em!"

"Atta boy!" gusted Duryee, placing a hand on Danny's shoulder. "I was sure you had it in you...and I knew Captain Brownell could bring it to the surface."

Duryee thanked the captain for his help, and Buck headed back toward his company, struggling with the butterflies in his own stomach, and thinking of Jenny Jordan.

General Irvin McDowell roused his army very early on Sunday morning, July 21, 1861, and had them marching toward a designated site east of Manassas Junction by 2:30 A.M. The adrenaline was flowing, and excitement was running through the men like an electric current as they prepared for battle.

Federal artillery batteries placed at strategic points along Bull Run Creek the day before opened fire at exactly 5:00 A.M., lobbing whistling shells toward Confederate lines.

The Rebels were ready. Return fire came immediately, and the Battle of Bull Run was under way.

CHAPTER FOURTEEN

The field of battle pivoted around the intersection of Warrenton Turnpike—which led straight to Washington—and Sudley Road. Bull Run was a meandering stream flowing south along the east side of the field. Warrenton Turnpike crossed Bull Run over Stone Bridge. There were also two fords where major roads crossed the creek: one was Blackburn Ford, which was on the main road from the north to Manassas Junction, and the other was Island Ford, crossed by a well-traveled road that led southwest to Sudley at New Market. Sudley Road was a direct thoroughfare southeast to Manassas Junction. In anticipation of a mass attack prior to the first message he received from Rose Greenhow's girls, General Pierre G.T. Beauregard had begun digging entrenchments along Bull Run from Warrenton Turnpike where it crossed Stone Bridge all the way to Union Mills, some six or seven miles to the southwest.

A small creek, known as Young's Branch, wound around the base of a high hill on which stood two farm houses. One was owned by an elderly invalid widow, Judith Henry, and stood atop the hill. The other, at a lower elevation, was owned by a free Negro named James Robinson. Warrenton Turnpike ran along the north base of the hill, which was called Henry House Hill by people of the area. Dozens of other farm houses dotted the area, but the Henry house and the Robinson house—because of their locations—were destined to play vital parts in the battle.

As the dull light of dawn gave way to the pink and yellow streamers of the rising sun, deep-throated cannons—Union and Confederate alike—roared like a thunderstorm. Trees and brush on both banks of Bull Run Creek were aflame. The musketry sounded like an endless string of firecrackers. The constant bellowing of the big guns, punctuated with the sharp sound of rifled cannons and the crack of Minié rifles, left no question that Death was riding his pale horse along the banks of Bull Run and over the brightening fields.

When there was a brief, intermittent pause in the roar, the screams and cries of wounded and dying men could be heard resounding over the rolling hills.

President Lincoln had been in the Senate Chamber conference room at the Capitol, along with his Cabinet and the Senate Military Committee since an hour before dawn. He was seated at the head of the table listening to the group of men chatting happily as sunlight struck the room's several east windows. Confidence of a quick and easy victory at Manassas Junction was running high.

Servants wheeled breakfast in on trays. During the meal, the almost festive atmosphere began to grate on the president. He held his peace until the meal was over and the dishes had been taken away. Most of the men were sipping coffee, laughing and joking about the certain defeat of the "hillbilly army." Lincoln rose to his feet and cleared his throat. It took only seconds for him to gain the attention of every man. The sudden quiet was welcome relief to Lieutenant Colonel Jeffrey Jordan.

"Gentlemen," said the tall, gaunt-looking man at the head of the table, "I don't mean to speak to you in a scolding manner, nor would I for a moment throw cold water on your enthusiasm. But I feel the tone being set here is a bit out of line. Possibly I should remind you that even if the battle that is now underway goes as we all anticipate, a high price is going to be paid for victory. This is not some sporting event taking place out there. The Confederates do have artillery, rifles, bayonets...and the will to fight. Many Union soldiers will die today and will not be around tomorrow to share with us in the victory celebration. Others will be crippled or maimed or blinded for life. It seems to me we should be thinking of them."

For a long moment the room was quiet as a tomb.

Taking a deep breath, Lincoln spoke again. "Gentlemen, within an hour or so, our first messenger from the battle scene will be coming in here to give his report. I propose that we have a time of silent meditation concerning our fighting men, and a time of prayer. We need to hold before God our brave soldiers who are even now suffering and dying at Bull Run."

Senator Henry Wilson, chairman of the Military Committee, rose to his feet and said solemnly, "Mr. President, I believe we are all in agreement with what you have just said. We understand your feelings and deeply appreciate them." Running his gaze over the faces all around the table, he added, "As we have this time of prayer, I will also ask that as Cabinet and Committee, we hold our president before God. His load is heavy, and this is the best way we can help him."

Lincoln gave Wilson a tight smile and said, "Thank you, Senator."

As the men in the group bowed their heads, Jordan silently prayed for the Confederate troops and President Jefferson Davis.

As usual, breakfast was quite early at the White House. The Lincoln boys and their governess were eating in the small dining room in the family's private quarters. Mary Lincoln was feeling worse than the day before and had not put in an appearance. Myrtle was skipping breakfast in order to attend to the First Lady.

Speaking around a mouthful of scrambled eggs, young Tad looked across the table at the governess and said, "Miss Patricia, even if Mom isn't up to takin' us out to see the battle, you could take us."

Patricia Winters was sipping coffee from a steaming cup. She swallowed it carefully and said, "Tad, how many times have I told you not to talk with your mouth full?"

The bright-eyed boy grinned and closed his mouth to finish chewing his eggs.

"Well?" said Patricia, raising one eyebrow.

Pointing to his mouth, Tad mumbled, "Mm-mm-mm-m."

Patricia laughed. "Sorry! I didn't mean to make you do it again."

In a tone of disgust, Willie said, "He'll do it again anyhow."

Tad swallowed and said, "I don't know."

Patricia raised both eyebrows this time. "You don't know what?"

"How many times you've told me not to talk with my mouth full. I don't count 'em."

Patricia looked at Willie, who said, "He's really dumb."

"I ain't neither!" spat the younger brother. "I'm smarter'n you!"

"Hah!" laughed Willie. "That'll be the day!"

"I can prove it."

"You can prove you're smarter than me?"

"Yep."

"Okay. Go ahead."

"Bet I can make you say *black*."

"No you can't."

"Oh, yes I can."

"No, you can't."

"What color is the American flag?" challenged Tad.

Willie got a smug look on his face. "Red, white, and blue."

Tad laughed. "See there? I told you I could make you say *blue!*"

"You didn't either! You said you'd make me say *black!*"

Tad threw his head back and cackled. "You just said it! See, I told you I'm smarter than you."

While Willie disgustedly returned to his breakfast, Patricia giggled and asked, "Tad, where'd you get that one?"

"From Uncle Elmer. He pulled it on me one day when we were alone...before...before he was killed."

Patricia saw the sadness that filled the eyes of both boys at the mention of Colonel Elmer Ellsworth. "You both miss Uncle Elmer, don't you?"

The boys nodded, then Tad said, "If Uncle Elmer was still alive, he'd be fightin' out there at Manssas—Manssas...out there at Bull Run Crick. He'd show them Rebels, wouldn't he, Miss Patricia?"

The governess nodded. "He sure would."

"Would you take us, Miss Patricia?" begged Tad. "Ple-e-ease?"

"Ple-e-ease, Miss Patricia?" chimed in Willie.

Patricia Winters wanted to oblige the boys. She also was concerned about Lieutenant John Hammond and wanted to be on hand where he was fighting. Thinking on it a moment, she said, "Tell you what. I'll go talk to your mother and see if she'll give me permission."

While the Lincoln brothers raised a cheer, the governess left the dining room and made her way to Mrs. Lincoln's bedroom. Myrtle was just coming out the door as Patricia approached.

"I need to talk to Mrs. Lincoln for a moment, Myrtle," said Patricia.

The maid thrust a forefinger to her lips. "Sh-h-h! She's asleep. You mustn't disturb her."

Patricia nodded and returned to the dining room. Willie and Tad were waiting with eager eyes. Disappointment showed quickly when the governess said, "I'm sorry, boys, but your mother is asleep and mustn't be disturbed. I couldn't talk to her."

Their voices blended together as the boys begged Patricia to take them anyhow.

"I can't take you that far without her permission. I'm sorry, boys, but we just can't go."

Young Tad—who knew he held Patricia's heartstrings in his hand—left his chair and hugged her, saying, "I sure do love you, Miss Patricia."

Looking down at him and ruffling his hair, she smiled and said, "I love you too, Tad. But my loving you can't get me permission from your mother to take you to Manassas Junction."

Still holding onto her, but pulling back far enough to look up into her face, Tad said, "It really would be all right if you took us. Neither of our parents showed any objection to the idea when we talked about it the other day."

"That's right," put in Willie. "Neither one. It'd be all right, Miss Patricia."

The governess wrestled with whether she should make such a move on her own. She did so want to please the boys—and to be there with John when victory was won. Tad continued to beg. After a few more moments, Patricia squeezed the delightful boy who held onto her and said, "Oh, all right! I'll take you."

"Yahoo!" bellowed Tad and hugged her hard. Standing on his tiptoes, he planted a thankful kiss on her cheek. Willie kissed her on the other cheek and thanked her, too.

A White House carriage and driver were always at the disposal of the young governess. The White House kitchen prepared a quick lunch, and soon Patricia and the Lincoln boys were on their way.

As early as daybreak, hundreds of Washingtonians were arriving on the hills overlooking the Bull Run battlefield from the north. They thrilled to the sound of artillery, muskets, and exploding shells. They could hear the shouts and cries of men in battle and were mesmerized at the sight of Union and Confederate troops in fierce, bloody conflict. All over the valley, puffy blue-white clouds of smoke drifted on the morning breeze. When the sun peeked over the eastern horizon and spread its yellow light over the battlefield, the scene became even more graphic. There were repeated flashes along the creek, on the rolling hills, and amongst the trees as the rays of the sun hit bayonets and brass cannon barrels.

The attitude of the excited civilians was that Sunday, July 21, 1861 would be a banner day for the North. The Southerners were going to be conquered handily, and their exhilarating outing would be topped off with happy celebrations. The vanquished Confederates who were fortunate enough to live through the battle would be sent home like whipped dogs with their tails between their legs. And the Civil War would be over!

Amongst the gathering crowd were many government leaders. One of the most popular was Senator Charles Sumner of Massachusetts. Sumner, a fiery man of deep conviction, had shown more anger at the audacious Confederate attack on Fort Sumter than any other man in Congress. He stood on the hilltop in the midst of his peers and loudly proclaimed his confidence that Richmond, the Rebel capital, would be in the hands of the Union "sometime early this week."

Sumner's boundless confidence affected his colleagues. Congressman Albert Riddle of Ohio announced his plans to "meet our brave men on the field in order to rejoice with them." Senator Alfred Ely of New York said he would be down there "hopping over Rebel corpses to congratulate the New York brigades for their part in the victory."

Several Washington ministers and their families were there with their gigs, buggies, surreys, and carriages collected in a group. The louder-spoken of the clergymen were in agreement that "the Lord would deliver the Philistines" into the hands of the Union "Joshua," General Irvin McDowell.

Jenny Jordan was there, seated in a surrey with Rose O'Neal Greenhow and three other young women: Bettie Duval, Lola Morrow, and Susan Rand. Jenny was studying the battle, trying to catch a glimpse of the man she loved, but the distance was too great. Even if she could make out the Zouaves, it would be next to impossible to know which one was Buck. From time to time her lips moved silently as she prayed for his safety.

Just after nine o'clock, Jenny's attention was drawn to the White House carriage as it topped the hill off to the east. She waved at Patricia, and saw the governess speak to the driver and point in her direction. The carriage soon pulled up alongside, and Jenny and Rose greeted Patricia and the boys. The White House driver told Patricia he was going to join some friends he had noticed in the crowd.

Patricia and the Lincoln boys were introduced to Bettie, Lola, and Susan, then turned their attention to the battle below. Soon Tad tugged at the governess's sleeve and said, "Miss Patricia, could me an' Willie get out of the carriage and watch the battle from that big rock over there?"

"Willie and *I*," corrected Patricia.

Grinning mischievously, Tad responded, "I really think you would be happier here with these ladies."

Patricia laughed. The little scamp had bested her at it again. "Okay. *You* and Willie can go sit on that rock, but don't stray off somewhere else. Stay right there, you hear?"

"Yes, ma'am," nodded Tad.

"Yes, ma'am," echoed the other brother.

Robert and Kady Brownell were not far from the White House carriage, standing with friends. Robert was busy with his binoculars, searching the landscape for some sign of the bright-colored uniforms of the Zouaves. A captivating scene spread before Robert as he took it all in through his binoculars. Looking south and sweeping the valley east and west, he saw densely wooded country, dotted at intervals with green fields, plowed sections, and farm houses under large shade trees, flanked by barns and various other outbuildings.

The wooded country, fields, and farms in the valley were bounded by a line of blue and purple ridges, terminating abruptly in escarpments toward the east front and swelling gradually toward the west into the lower spines of an offshoot from the Blue Ridge Mountains. On the east, the view was circumscribed by a forest that clothed the side of the ridge where the crowd had gathered and covered its shoulder far down onto the open fields.

A gap in the nearest chain of the distant hills directly south was known as Manassas Pass, by which the railway from the west was carried into the valley floor. Still nearer to the south was the junction of that line with the line from Alexandria and with the railway leading due south to Richmond. Robert marveled at the golden ribbons of rail glistening in the sunlight.

All across the breathtaking valley, undulating lines of forest marked the course of Bull Run Creek and its tributaries. Robert thought what he beheld through the glasses presented the most pleasant display of pastoral woodland scenery that the God of heaven had ever made. But the thunderous sounds that came on the breeze and the exhibition of battle no more than a mile away were in terrible variance to the tranquil landscape.

The woods far and near echoed with the roar of cannon, and tiny clouds of blue-white smoke marked the spots from whence came the sharp sounds of rolling musketry. Larger puffs of smoke floated high above the treetops, shading the rippling waters of Bull Run, and the boom of howitzers marked the lines of artillery. Clouds of dust shifted and moved through the forests, mingling with the smoky mists, and thicker dust-clouds marked the presence of shuffling feet and pounding hooves.

Robert removed the glasses, looked back at his wife, and saw that she was shading her eyes with her bonnet. "I think I just saw some Zouaves!" she shouted. "Maybe one of them is Buck!"

"Where?" Robert asked.

Pointing, Kady said, "Down there along the creek bank where it bends at that cluster of trees. There! See them?"

Robert brought the binoculars up and peered in the direction Kady was pointing. For a brief instant, he caught a glimpse of the bright-colored uniforms of a handful of Zouaves wading across Bull Run, then they disappeared behind the thick foliage. "It's Zouaves all right, but that's all I can tell. No way to know if Buck is among them. They're out of sight again."

It seemed that more cannons had arrived at the battle scene, for the deep-throated roars came more often. The spectators on the hillside became more excited. One portly woman who carried an opera glass stood near the Brownells and their friends. When the unusually heavy discharge of cannons rolled across the fields and over the hills, she grabbed the arm of the skinny little man next to her.

"Oh, Ralph!" she shouted. "This is splendid. Oh, my! Isn't that first-rate?"

"Yes, dear," said Ralph, who was not so impressed.

Peering through her opera glasses, she gasped, "Oh, isn't this a sight to see, Ralph? We'll be in Richmond by this time tomorrow!"

"Yes, dear," nodded the little man.

Loud cheers suddenly burst from the spectators as a Union officer came riding at breakneck speed up the grassy slope, waving his campaign hat. Dodging large rocks that lay scattered on the hillside, and threading his way amid the few trees and bushes, he drew near the crest and shouted, "We're whipping them good! It'll be over before long!" With the cheers of the crowd in his ears, he thundered back down the hill and soon disappeared in the woods.

"Bully for our side!" shouted Senator Sumner as the congressmen began shaking hands all around. "Bravo! Didn't I tell you so?"

Sitting quietly with Rose Greenhow and the other girls, Jenny listened to the cheering crowd, clenched her hands into fists, and prayed in a whisper, "Dear Lord, let this awful thing be over quickly. And please...please protect Buck."

On the battlefield, Captain Buck Brownell hunkered with his two-hundred-man company along the north bank of Bull Run Creek about three hundred yards northwest of Stone Bridge. Next to Buck was Colonel Keyes, his commander.

The sun was nearly halfway in the morning sky, shining a dull yellow through columns of smoke, as Keyes pointed across the creek at a two-story farm house and said, "Captain, take as many men as you think necessary and capture that house. We're going to need it for a hospital before this thing is over. We're beating the Rebels back now, but it's way too early to say we have them under control. Once you've secured the house, leave some men there to protect it and come back here. I'll leave further orders with one of your lieutenants."

"Yes, sir," nodded Brownell.

Quickly choosing a dozen men, Buck led them along the bank. They bent low, trying to keep from being seen by enemy artillery dug in on the other bank. Soon they came upon several dead Union soldiers and two dead horses where Confederate cannon balls had taken their toll earlier. The Zouaves tried not to look at their dead comrades, but found it difficult to tear their gaze away from the bulging eyes and gaping mouths of men who died so suddenly.

Leading them on, Buck thought of Jenny, wondering where she was and what she was doing. It was just about church time. That's probably where she was...sitting in her favorite pew, lifting her voice with the rest of the congregation in a rousing hymn.

Bullets suddenly began to chop into the brush all around them. Instinctively, the Zouaves flopped on their bellies, looking around to see where the barrage was coming from.

"Straight ahead of us, Captain!" shouted a Zouave sergeant just before a bullet struck him between the eyes.

Buck saw a half-dozen men-in-gray squatting behind a heavy bush on the creek bank twenty yards ahead. "Let 'em have it!" he shouted as he raised his revolver and began to blaze away.

Zouave rifles barked, cutting brush and finding flesh and blood targets. When the volley was over, the Zouaves left the dead sergeant behind and followed their captain as he ran to the spot, gun ready. All six of the Rebels lay dead.

"C'mon," breathed Brownell. "We've got a house to capture."

General Beauregard had set up his headquarters in a large tent near Mitchell Ford on Bull Run Creek, which was located on a seldom-traveled road between Centreville and Manassas Junction about a mile west of Blackburn Ford. Beauregard had expected the main enemy blow to fall at a spot about a mile-and-a-half north of Mitchell Ford where the main road that ran between Centreville and Manassas Junction—which crossed Bull Run at Blackburn Ford— intersected with the less-traveled road. He was perplexed and alarmed when he heard no firing from the area of the intersection where he had concentrated several brigades and three artillery batteries. He heard only a little firing to the east, where five of his brigades were supposed to be crossing Bull Run to make a circular sweep and attack the Federal camps around Centreville.

Instead, fierce sounds of battle grew steadily in the west, his lightly defended left flank. The Yankees had surprised him by attacking where he had least expected. This confused him, and for some time he made no countermove. Finally, he sent the brigades of Thomas J. Jackson, Bernard E. Bee, and Francis S. Bartow to reinforce his threatened left.

As the sun rose higher, the July heat and humidity began to take its toll. Canteens were running low on both sides, and men were leaving the battle lines to fill canteens at Bull Run and other smaller streams.

As the battle raged, General Joseph E. Johnston, second in command under Beauregard, became concerned as he saw the left flank beaten back in spite of the three brigades sent to bolster it. Riding to the headquarters tent, Johnston confronted Beauregard and asked why more help had not been sent to that vital part of the battle. Angrily, Johnston blared, "General, don't you realize the Yankees are having a heyday on our left flank? Their officers are riding around waving their hats and shouting that the Rebels are about to give up!"

Beauregard mopped sweat as he paced back and forth in front of the tent. "I...I just got confused for awhile, General. The Yankees did the unexpected. If they'd centered the attack where I thought they would, we'd have them on the run by now."

"We can still have them on the run," said Johnston. "All we have to do is shift more of our forces to the left. We've already surprised McDowell with the number of men we've got here."

"I know. I've already sent word for Ewell, Jones, Longstreet, and Holmes to come back on the south side of Bull Run. We'll have to forget hitting the Union camps at Centreville for now."

"I know it's important to hit those camps because of the reserves McDowell's got stashed there. Maybe we ought to pull Early and Bonham's brigades from the right and send them to the left. Let Holmes go with them, and send Jones, Longstreet, and Ewell on to Centreville."

"Sounds like a good idea," nodded Beauregard, who seemed to be settling down. "I'll just do it."

"Fine," grinned Johnston, who was two years younger than his commander. "I'm going out to the left flank right now."

It was a frustrating day for the brigades that Beauregard kept moving back and forth across Bull Run. The men never quite got their socks dry.

With substantial reinforcements sent to his threatened left flank, and his confidence rising, Beauregard mounted up and rode after Johnston to watch the battle.

CHAPTER FIFTEEN

✦

At the extreme northwest end of what had become the Bull Run battlefield was the small farm community of Sudley Springs, approximately two-and-a-half miles northwest of the Warrenton Turnpike at Stone Bridge where the fighting had become quite heavy by nine-thirty that morning. This was the left flank that concerned Generals Beauregard and Johnston, causing them to send several brigades to bolster.

Noting the Confederate buildup around Stone Bridge, General Irvin McDowell brought in reserves from the camps at Centreville, giving the Confederates more to handle. Meanwhile, McDowell decided to strengthen his right flank farther to the west in case the Rebels tried to send troops in a sweep around by Sudley Springs and move in on them from behind. McDowell was already finding out that Robert E. Lee and P.G.T. Beauregard had brought in thousands of troops to meet the Union assault. McDowell and his commanders were amazed and wondered how the Confederacy had learned of the very time and place they had so carefully planned the attack.

While the battle progressed, General McDowell sent for Colonel Ambrose Burnside and told him to dispatch a company of two hundred men westward toward Sudley Springs to counter any Confederate move in that direction. Burnside, in turn, sent his B Company, under the command of Captain Elrod Dunwaite, with instructions to call for help if he saw more Rebels coming than he thought he and his men could handle.

On a wooded hill above Sudley Springs was Sudley Church. The pastor, Reverend Clyde Walters, was at the door of the church at nine-forty, ready to greet his people if any chose to attend the services in spite of the fighting less than three miles away. His wife and two teenage children stood just inside.

While the sounds of battle met his ears, Walters was pleased to see a few buggies and carriages, along with some riders on horseback, turn onto the path that led up to the church. By ten o'clock, forty-nine adults and teenagers and eighteen children were gathered in the building as the song service began. The pastor counted only four families who were not present. Before it was time for him to preach, two more families had arrived.

Walters was not surprised to see every man of his congregation— young and old—carrying rifles and handguns. The people feared the worst from the Yankee soldiers, and the men were prepared to defend their families if the need should arise. Though Walters had objections to firearms inside the church house, he did not voice them. He was just glad to have his people there on such a frightful day.

General Beauregard caught up with General Johnston at Island Ford, where Johnston was in conversation with Brigadier General Thomas J. Jackson, commander of First Brigade, Army of the Shenandoah. Two of Jackson's officers stood beside him. As he dismounted, Beauregard recognized them as Captains Duane Gibson and James Black. Jackson had his hat off and was mopping sweat from his receding hairline and forehead. All four men greeted the field commander as he drew up.

"So how is it looking here, General?" Beauregard asked Jackson.

"We've got a hot scrap going on upstream at Bull's Ford, sir. And we're strung out on the bank all the way to Stone Bridge, where, as you know, it's hot and heavy. They sent in some reserves a while ago, so I brought up a few more companies to counter them. It's toe-to-toe, but we're doing more damage at the moment than they are."

Johnston interjected, "General Jackson was just explaining to me what he's about to do with a couple of companies."

"According to one of my scouts, sir," said Jackson, "there's some light Union activity going on over there toward Sudley Springs. I was just telling General Johnston that I'm sending Captain Gibson's company of 200 and Captain Black's company of 250 over there to head them off."

"Sounds good," nodded the field commander. "If you have instructions for the captains, please proceed. You and General Johnston and I will have a meeting of the minds once they're on their way."

It was ten-thirty when Captain Elrod Dunwaite and his company were hastening along the bed of an unfinished railway, heading south toward Sudley Springs. Suddenly a sergeant named Clifford Mayer pointed down the ridge where the tracks were meant to be laid and said, "Captain! Rebels!"

Dunwaite gave a quick command for his men to jump behind the ridge. His lieutenant, Boris Wyman, peered at the cluster of Confederate troops who were skirting a section of woods and heading directly toward them. Dunwaite was beside him.

"Looks like we're outnumbered, sir," said Wyman. "Shall we retreat back to that patch of woods we passed through a few minutes ago? We'll stand a better chance of holding them off."

Dunwaite shook his head. "No. We'll not retreat before any backwoods hillbilly squirrel hunters. We're more than a match for them right here. Since they haven't broken rank, it's apparent they didn't see us before we jumped off the ridge. Pass the word along. We'll hold our fire till we can count the freckles on their ugly faces. When they're close enough, I'll give the signal to open fire by firing the first shot. Go!"

Captains Gibson and Black led their companies shoulder-to-shoulder in ranks of sixteen. The morning sun was bearing down with the promise of more heat to come as the day wore on. Warm water sloshed in half-empty canteens on their belts and sweat streaked their faces. Gibson and Black were marching in the forefront, side by side.

"Your idea ought to fake them out, Captain," Black said. "Sure enough, they'll think we didn't see them."

"I'm counting on it," Gibson drawled. "If that Yankee leader up there can count, he knows he's outnumbered. But these cocky Yankees think we're a bunch of dumb country yokels who'll fold up the first time we meet in battle. If McDowell's had a chance to teach that Yankee leader up there any tactics, the man will wait till we're within spitting distance before they open fire. Well, we won't give them the opportunity. We'll split our companies just outside of musket range and swing a wide circle. If they try to turn around and high-tail it the other way, they'll have to cross Bull Run. That'll slow them good, and they'll be sitting ducks."

"I'll ease back and pass the word," Black said. "I'll tell them you will give the command to spread out."

Wyman and Mayer flanked their captain as the fiery rays of the sun lanced down from the cloudless Virginia sky.

"Exactly what point are you going to allow them to reach before we open fire, sir?" Wyman asked.

Dunwaite ignored the question for the moment. He was intent

on the approach of the enemy. Dust rose around the marching columns. The metal of their weapons flashed bright against the relentless sunlight. Then with his voice hard, precise, and biting in the dead-hot humid air, he said, "When the first lines reach that clump of berry bushes, we'll unleash on them. All it'll take is a taste of hot Yankee lead to put them on the run—that is, the ones who are still alive. And while they're running, the—"

The captain's words were cut off when he saw the tight ranks suddenly break, and the Confederate soldiers began to spread out outside of musket range, ejecting wild Rebel yells.

"Captain!" gasped Mayer. "What are they doing?"

Dunwaite studied the movements of the enemy for a few seconds. "They're fitting a phalanx together to tie us up in a noose. We're spread too thin against that many men. We've got to retreat before they get us locked in. We'll have to get across the creek quick!"

Captain Dunwaite gave the command for his men to head across the weed-infested terrain that stood between them and Bull Run. By the time they were within fifty yards of the meandering stream, the Confederates were on the railway ridge, firing their muskets.

Men in blue began to drop, while others whirled around to make a stand. A few kept running toward the creek. Whooping like Indians, the Rebels charged. Within a few seconds, it was an all-out battle. Muskets cracked and bullets cut the hot morning air.

Lieutenant Wyman soon found himself flattened on the bank of Bull Run in the shade of an old oak tree. Bullets were thwacking into the tree and the bush that sided it. Within a few seconds, Wyman was flanked by a half-dozen other men who had sought the same refuge.

Bill Quinn rolled next to Wyman and said above the battle's roar, "Lieutenant, I don't know about you, but I'm heading across the creek while the going's good!"

"So am I!" said Darrell Bateman.

On the other side of Bateman were identical twin brothers,

Privates Eddie and Freddie Spangler. Straw-haired and blue-eyed, they said almost in unison, "Me, too!"

Corporal Arland White gasped, "Lieutenant, I just saw Captain Dunwaite get it! Bullet through the head. Let's get outta here!"

"Let's go!" shouted Wyman, and plunged into the two-foot depth of water. Quickly the others followed, including the sixth man, Thaddeus Pauley.

Bull Run was forty feet wide at that spot. It took the seven men about a minute to cross it fighting the current. As they ran up a gentle slope with the sounds of battle behind them, they soon came to a double-rail fence, supported by X-framed poles. Carrying only his handgun, Lieutenant Wyman vaulted the fence with ease. The others, each carrying a bayoneted musket, found it more difficult to get over. Hanging onto their weapons, they slowly worked their way over the double rails. Wyman shouted at them to hurry.

Freddie Spangler watched his twin make it to the other side, but found the task cumbersome with the musket in his hand. Seeing that he was the last to get over, Freddie swung his musket over the fence and stood it against the top inside rail. The shiny bayonet glistened in the mid-morning sun.

Freddie hopped onto the first rail, gripping one of the X-framed poles to steady himself. He shifted his right foot to the second rail, but when he let go of the pole to drop to the other side, he slipped.

The rest of them were talking to Wyman about which way to go when they heard Freddie's high-pitched scream. Their heads whipped around in time to see the yellow-haired youth plunge downward. Eddie, eyes bulging, wailed his twin's name as Freddie impaled himself on the bayonet.

The men in blue stood paralyzed as Freddie kicked and screamed. First to find his legs was Eddie, but by the time he reached the fence, Freddie had stopped flailing. There were no more screams.

Captain Wyman laid a hand on Eddie's shoulder and said,

"C'mon, kid. There's nothing you can do for him now. We've got to get out of here."

Eddie broke into uncontrollable sobs. "No, Lieutenant! No! I can't leave him here!"

"We're going, kid," sighed Wyman. "You can stay if you want." With that, he hastened up the slope telling the others to follow.

Eddie Spangler looked back across Bull Run Creek at the smoke of the battle. Swallowing hard, he glanced down at his twin's lifeless form. Then he turned quickly and followed the others, not allowing himself to look back.

As the Confederates began to overpower the Yankees at the creek bank, many of the men in blue tried to get away across the stream. Bullets cut them down mid-stream, and the normally clear water was crimson with blood.

Smoke hung like a pall over the area, but when a sudden breeze rushed over the landscape, it cleared a wide spot. At that instant, Captain Duane Gibson's attention was drawn to the crest of the slope beyond Bull Run where he saw Lieutenant Wyman and his five men running along the ridge.

Gibson sent a man to tell Captain Black that he was taking a dozen men to run down some escaping Yankees. When he had picked his squad, they hastened downstream some fifty yards, then splashed across, ran to the double-railed fence, clambered over it, and charged up the slope.

As Lieutenant Wyman led his men along the ridge, Sergeant Quinn looked back over his shoulder just in time to see thirteen Rebels wading across Bull Run, headed in their direction.

"Lieutenant!" shouted Quinn. "They're coming after us!"

Puffing as he ran, Wyman looked back and saw Gibson and his

squad in pursuit. Quickly, he led his men off the ridge and down a steep slope into a mulberry thicket. They threaded their way through the mulberry bushes, the stiff branches clawing at their uniforms.

The thicket was about a hundred feet from one side to the other. When they emerged, they found a small tributary of Bull Run snaking its way through the grassy, daisy-strewn dell that lay before them. The small valley was about a hundred yards wide. Beyond its natural border on the other side was a gentle slope that lifted to a height of thirty feet and was topped by a road. Above the road, on a rounded hilltop amid a stand of tall trees, stood a stone church building. Parked in front and along one side were several buggies and carriages. Three or four saddled horses were tied to hitching posts.

Wyman shot a glance to the ridge behind them. So far there was no sign of the pursuing Rebels. Swinging his gaze back to Sudley Church, he said, "We're going to be all right, boys. We'll just attend us a little Sunday service. When those stinking Rebels get here, we'll tell 'em to go back where they came from or we'll kill us a bunch of Southern worshippers. Let's go."

Wading through the small stream and scurrying over the dell, the six Yankees huffed and puffed their way up the slope and across the road. The church door was open, as were all the windows, and they could hear the preacher delivering his sermon. They decided to stay hidden until they caught their breath. Wyman looked behind him and swore when he saw the dozen Rebels running along the ridge where they had been five minutes before.

Wyman cocked his revolver and said, "Okay, I'll go in first. Have your weapons ready. If any of the men in there are man enough to stand up to us, kill them."

Wyman charged for the open door and bolted inside with the others on his heels. "Everybody stay right where you are!" he bellowed, waving his revolver.

Women screamed, frightening babies, who began to cry.

Children, eyes bulging, moved close to their parents. The people sat stunned. The soldiers stood poised with their bayoneted muskets cocked and ready to fire. Throwing his gun on the preacher, who stood behind the pulpit, Bible in hand, Wyman roared, "Put the Bible down, holy man, and take a seat down here with your congregation!"

The threat of violence hung like a thick cloud over the room. Everyone waited and watched in breathless trepidation. Mothers with babies were attempting to quiet them. Terrified small children were beginning to cry.

Reverend Walters looked at Wyman and said in a level tone, "You have no cause to come in here like this, Lieutenant. There's no one in this house of God who represents a threat to you. I ask you politely to take your men and leave."

"I'm not asking you, holy man, I'm *telling* you—come out from behind that pulpit and take a pew. *Now!*"

Walters knew the enemy soldiers had not yet spotted the muskets that lay at the feet of the men in his congregation. He hoped they wouldn't. And even more, he hoped no one would attempt to shoot it out with them. As he laid his Bible on the pulpit and started off the platform, he said to Wyman, "What do you want from us?"

"I want you to sit still and shutup. We've got a little problem here to handle, and—"

At that instant, a man sitting by a window leaped to his feet with a cocked revolver aimed at Wyman and shouted, "Drop your gun, Yankee, or you're a dead man!"

There were more screams as Bill Quinn swung his musket on the man and fired. The man took the slug in his chest, but reflex squeezed his trigger. The shot struck Wyman in the forehead, snapping his head back as he bounced off the end of a pew and crumpled in the aisle. While the shocking echoes filled the room, the preacher yelled for everyone to get down. His command was not needed; they were dropping between the pews almost as one person.

But not all of them. Defiant men, indignant at the soldiers for barging into the house of God, brought their muskets and revolvers to bear on the intruders. There was an outburst of yells and shots, mingled with screams and childish wails, as guns roared and bullets struck flesh, chewed into wood, and shattered windows. For the next half-minute the church building was a scene of desperate fighting, the ferocious, joyless task of killing.

When the shooting stopped, five of the six Yankees lay dead on the floor. The sixth, Eddie Spangler, hung partially on a pew. His cap dangled from one ear, exposing a mop of yellow hair. Four slugs had taken his life.

There was a wild maelstrom of weeping and wailing. Two newly made widows knelt beside the lifeless forms of their husbands. One of the dead was the man who had thrown his gun on the Yankee lieutenant. One other man was wounded, but not seriously.

The dazed congregation looked up through the smoke cloud that hung in the room to see Captain Duane Gibson and his men filing through the door. The preacher left the wounded man with two of the women and met Gibson in the aisle.

"I'm Pastor Walters, Captain," the preacher said solemnly. "These Yankees burst in here a few minutes ago, barking orders, and waving their guns at us. One"—Walters choked on the word—"one of my men produced a revolver and commanded the leader to drop his gun. One of the other Yankees opened fire, and...and you see the results. I was hoping it wouldn't come to this."

Gibson raised his hat, sleeved sweat, and ran his gaze over the six corpses in blue. "Well, that's a half-dozen we won't have to fight again. How many of your people were hit?"

"Only three, thank the Lord. Two of my men are dead, and another wounded. It was only the hand of God that kept the women and children from being hit."

"I'll say 'Amen' to that, Reverend. This could have been a real disaster."

Walter's wife and children moved up beside him. Closing all three in an embrace, he said, "I pray the whole Yankee army will be vanquished today, Captain."

"Well, keep praying, Reverend," said Gibson as he turned to leave. "We've given the Federals plenty of resistance so far, but there's a long day ahead."

CHAPTER SIXTEEN

✶

I n the thick of the battle at Stone Bridge was Confederate Colonel
Nathan G. Evans, who was looked upon by Generals Lee and
Beauregard as a "Rebel among Rebels." Evans, an insubordinate,
hard-nosed, egotistical South Carolinian, swore like a sailor and always
carried whiskey in a flask on his belt. Hot-headed, with a hair-trigger
temper, he loved to fight.

Though Lee and Beauregard were not fond of the colonel's way,
they admired him for his fighting spirit. The men who followed him
had the same crusty mannerisms and the identical love for fighting.
The "Evansites" were a breed of their own. It was for this reason that
Lee made Colonel Evans commander of his own brigade, and rather
than give it a number like the others, dubbed it "Evans's Demi-
Brigade."

Also in the fire and smoke at Stone Bridge was the First
Louisiana Special Battalion under the command of Major Roberdeau
Wheat. Wheat and Evans were very much alike in their appetite for
fighting. The Special Battalion was better known as "Wheat's Tigers,"
notable for wearing bright-red shirts, and more notable for their bel-
ligerence and the same rugged fighting spirit as Evans's Demi-Brigade.

Wheat had recruited his unit from the wharves along the New Orleans waterfront.

About a mile-and-a-quarter west of Stone Bridge was a farm owned by the Matthews family. Like so many of the farms in the area, the house, barn, and outbuildings sat atop a hill, overlooking the rest of the property. Thus, the hill on Union army maps was called Matthews' Hill.

As the morning wore on and the fighting grew more intense, Union field commander General Irvin McDowell sent Brigadier General David Hunter's Second Division out of Centreville in a wide sweep north and westward. Second Division was made up of two brigades. First Brigade was commanded by Colonel Andrew Porter, and Second Brigade by Colonel Ambrose E. Burnside.

The twenty-eight hundred men of Second Division were to cut south at the unfinished railway about a half-mile east of Sudley Springs and swing around Matthews' Hill. This would bring them up on the Confederates' rear flank without being seen. From there they could surprise them with artillery bombardment, then launch a devastating infantry attack.

General Beauregard, however, had posted Captain E.P. Alexander—the engineer officer in charge of his signals unit—on a nearby lofty hill just before dawn. Colonel Evans had a signal corpsman stationed at the fringe of the Stone Bridge battle site to keep an eye on Captain Alexander for word of more Union reinforcements being brought in.

The blazing sun looked down at the carnage on the banks of Bull Run and the dust and smoke at Stone Bridge. Bodies were scattered about on the blood-soaked ground, while others bobbed lifelessly in the crimson waters of the creek. The wounded lay bleeding in the heat with no one to tend to them. Sometimes the men in the thick of the fight could hear their cries, which usually faded into moans, then into silence.

Evans's lookout man crawled to him near Stone Bridge and shouted above the din, "Colonel! Captain Alexander just sent a signal. He estimates there are about twenty-five hundred Union troops coming from the north just this side of Sudley Springs. Captain Alexander thinks they're going to circle Matthews' Hill and come in behind us!"

Evans had been told only minutes before that General Beauregard was now using a farmhouse about five hundred yards southeast of Stone Bridge as his headquarters. "All right," nodded Evans, pointing that direction. "I want you to make your way to that farmhouse out there by the road. See it?"

"Yes, sir."

"General Beauregard is in that house. Relate Captain Alexander's message to him. Tell him I don't have time to wait for his approval, but that I sent you so he'd know what I'm doing. Tell him I'm going to take my brigade and Major Wheat's, and head for Matthew's Hill to meet those Yankees. Got it?"

"Yes, sir," replied the corpsman, and hastened away.

Evans knew that even with the eleven hundred men in his brigade and the five hundred in Major Wheat's battalion, they would be greatly outnumbered by the oncoming Union force...but he dare not take any more troops from the present battle site. Within twenty minutes, he and Major Wheat were leading their men toward Matthews' hill. Wheat was bringing along four howitzers, and Evans had six.

The heat was becoming unbearable as Evans and Wheat led their men across the green fields. Evans was glad to have Wheat beside him. Rob Wheat was a veteran of the Mexican War; he had also been a much-publicized filibuster in Central America, and a bloody mercenary warrior for Guiseppe Garibaldi during the war for Italian unification. Standing six feet four inches in height and weighing three hundred pounds, Wheat was an imposing figure in the thick of a fight.

Crossing shallow Young's Branch with their men and equipment, Evans and Wheat soon deployed their infantrymen and howitzers from the top to about halfway down the side of Matthews' Hill under cover of dense woods. They had a clear view of the open fields and lower half of the hill that Hunter and his eager troops would have to cross.

While they were digging in and anchoring the howitzers, Colonel Evans had two of his men check to see if anyone was in the farmhouse or any of the outbuildings. He wanted to give the Matthews family an opportunity to vacate the premises before the Federals arrived. He was not surprised to learn that the family was already gone.

The Confederates had barely positioned themselves for the battle when the columns of Union troops appeared, coming across the fields like a swarm of ants. General David Hunter was leading them on horseback, and Colonels Porter and Burnside rode their mounts not far behind, each in front of his brigade.

In the shade of the dense woods on Matthews' Hill, Evans and Wheat waited. Their men were all in place, ready to unleash their fire power. While Wheat sipped water from a canteen, Evans took a snort of whiskey from his flask.

Smacking his lips, the colonel extended the flask toward Wheat and said, "Good stuff, Major. Want some?"

"Not right now. I want to go into this fight with a clear head."

Evans chuckled as he corked the flask and hooked it back on his belt. "That's exactly what it does for me, Major. Clears my head."

The oncoming swarm was now about two hundred yards from the base of the hill. Instructions had been given to the men with the howitzers to open fire at Colonel Evans's command. Evans was sure

Captain Alexander was right. The blue-bellies were planning to circle the hill and attack the Confederates at Stone Bridge from behind. Once the howitzers opened fire, the Union commander would know he had lost the element of surprise. If he ordered his troops to take the hill, the Confederate muskets would cut loose.

Evans lifted his hat and wiped the perspiration from his forehead. "When that front line gets another fifty yards closer," he said to Wheat, "we'll blast them."

Wheat nodded and pulled his revolver. "I'm ready."

Evans drew his sidearm and moved to the edge of the trees. He let about fifteen seconds pass as he eyed the enemy's front line of soldiers, then moved into the sunlight where the howitzer operators could see him. Lifting his hat high over his head, he brought it down swiftly, shouting, "*Fi-i-r-r-e!*"

The howitzers boomed in a planned staccato. Shells whistled downward and Yankees—with a helpless look of horror—began to scatter as the shells struck and exploded. All six were aimed well, and plowed into the ranks, blowing bodies every direction. There were shouts and curses as the Yankees followed their leader's command and began to swarm up the side of the hill.

Rebel muskets opened fire while the howitzers were being reloaded. Waving his revolver and trying to keep his frightened horse in check, General David Hunter shouted at the top of his voice, encouraging his men as they hurried up the slope. As they climbed, they fired their muskets at the puffs of smoke that appeared against the dark shade of the trees.

The first Rebel howitzer was reloaded quickly and fired again, just ahead of the others. A shell exploded a few feet from Hunter's horse, blowing him out of the saddle. The horse screamed and fell over dead.

Instantly, Colonel Burnside was kneeling beside Hunter, who was seriously wounded in the neck and left cheek. Burnside quickly called for two soldiers to carry the wounded general from the field of fire. As they picked him up, Hunter grasped Burnside's sleeve and said, "You're in charge. I'm leaving the battle in your hands."

While the Matthews' Hill and Stone Bridge battles raged, Union General Daniel Tyler's First Division was fighting brigades three, four, and six of the Confederate army along Warrenton Turnpike about two miles northeast of Stone Bridge. Fighting in Tyler's First Brigade under Colonel Erasmus D. Keyes were the Fifth New York Zouaves, led by Colonel Abram Duryee. Under Duryee, Captain Buck Brownell commanded a company of three hundred. General Tyler's Third Brigade was led by Colonel William Tecumseh Sherman.

It was almost eleven o'clock when Buck found himself in a gully some three hundred feet from the Turnpike, where the Confederates were dug in and fighting fiercely. The Yankees had found other gullies and low spots in the open field and were firing in return.

The gully Buck was in was about forty feet in length. Fighting right next to him was one of Colonel Keyes's captains, Kenneth Merritt. Beyond Merritt were several of his men, and on Brownell's left was a string of Zouaves. The rest of Brownell's men were in gullies and ditches all around him. Though Buck was not aware of it, some thirty yards to his right, in another long gully, was Captain Jack Egan, who had been in Sherman's brigade since the war began.

While muskets barked and bullets buzzed angrily in the air, Egan noted where Brownell was positioned. A boiling hatred seethed through Egan toward Brownell. He had dreamed of putting a bullet through the heart of the man who had stolen Jenny Jordan from him.

Buck was bent low, reloading his musket when he heard a bullet strike flesh next to him and saw Captain Merritt slump down. Buck turned him over and saw that the slug had shattered the clavicle on his right side and had ripped open an artery. Merritt was conscious, in a great deal of pain, and blood was pumping from the severed artery. Buck whipped a bandanna from his pocket, wadded it up, and pressed it to the bleeding wound.

Lieutenant Bradley Runyon of Sherman's Third Brigade eyed his captain, then looked at Brownell and asked, "What do you think, sir?"

"I think we need to get him out of here or else he'll bleed to death."

Buck had noted a farmhouse a short distance off the Turnpike, about three hundred yards from where they were positioned. "There's a farmhouse up the road a ways. If we could get him to that house, we could leave a man with him to keep the pressure on the artery. When this battle's over, we can get him to a doctor."

"Sounds good to me," nodded Runyon. "For sure we can't keep that compress on him here. Not if those Rebels decide to rush us."

Eyeing the distance to the farmhouse, Buck said, "We'll have to crawl about two hundred yards. One of us will have to drag him while the other holds the compress." Looking down at Merritt, he asked, "Think you can stand it, Captain? It's bound to be painful with that collarbone broken."

"I can take it," replied the wounded officer through his teeth.

"Okay," said Buck. "You just hold on. We'll get you to safety."

"I'll drag, if you'll hold, sir," Runyon said.

"Fine. You can stay with him once we get him to the house."

"Not me, sir. I need to be out here with my men. You can stay with him."

"Can't," said Buck. "I need to be here with my men, too. You have a man along the line you want to take along?"

Looking along the line to his right, Runyon called a young private, Lanny O'Dell, to him and explained the situation.

"Okay," Brownell said. "Let's go."

Passing the word both ways about what they were doing, Brownell, Runyon, and O'Dell began their difficult task.

Enemy bullets whirred over their heads and plowed sod around them as they made their way over the grassy field toward the farmhouse. Jack Egan observed them from his position not far away.

Sweltering in the humid heat, the three men soon had the wounded officer within a hundred yards of the farmhouse and past the line of fire.

As they paused to catch their breath, Buck said, "I'll pick him up and carry him if one of you will hold the compress."

"I'll do it, sir," volunteered O'Dell, handing his musket to Runyon.

The lieutenant had just pulled his revolver from its holster for safety's sake, contemplating their journey across the hundred yards of open field. Slipping the gun back into leather, he cocked the musket and said, "Let's move."

Buck handed the blood-soaked cloth to O'Dell, knelt down, and picked up Merritt. "Hard part is over, Captain. We'll have you in a safe place in a few minutes."

Once O'Dell had a firm hold on the artery, they hastened across the field to the two-story house. They were drawing near when they saw movement at an open window on the ground floor.

"Somebody's in there, all right," commented Runyon. "Shortest distance is to the back of the house around that shed."

They rounded the corner of the old unpainted shed and headed toward the back porch. The door was standing open. Suddenly a tall, slender elderly man stepped through the door onto the porch, wielding a double-barreled shotgun. Both hammers were eared back, and a long, shaky finger was on the triggers. "Hold it right there!" he snapped. "Get off my property, you filthy Yankees!"

"Sir," Buck said, "we've got a wounded man, here. He's—"

"I said get off my property! *Now!*"

"Sir," reasoned Brownell, "we mean you no harm. This man has a severed artery and a broken collarbone. I'm asking you to allow him a place to lie down while Private O'Dell, here, keeps a compress on the wound."

"I have a wife and granddaughter in the house, mister!" spat the old man. "Why should I trust any of you stinkin' Yankees not to harm *them*?"

"I give you my word, sir," said Buck. "The minute this wounded officer is comfortable, Captain Runyon and I will head back to the battle. Private O'Dell will not raise a finger toward the women."

"That's right, sir," put in O'Dell. "I won't even have a weapon, and even if I did, I wouldn't harm you or anyone else in the house. All I want to do is take care of my captain so he doesn't bleed to death. You can hold that scatter-gun on me the whole time if you want."

"We'll be back to pick them up once the battle is over, sir," said Runyon.

The old man still held the shotgun steadily on the Yankees. His jaw was stern, but it was evident he was giving it consideration. Suddenly a voice thundered from the corner of the shed, "Drop that gun, old man!"

Buck's head whipped around and he saw Jack Egan moving in with his revolver aimed at the farmer. A frightened woman whined just inside the door as the old man bristled. There was fire in his watery old eyes. Holding the shotgun steady, he rasped, "That does it! All of you get off my property this instant!"

"You can't get us all with that shotgun, you old fool!" blared Egan, staying clear of his line of fire. "You pull those triggers, you'll die where you stand. Now put the gun down! We're taking over this house whether you like it or not."

"Egan, get back where you belong," Buck shouted angrily. "This kind gentleman was about to let us use his house for Captain Merritt. You're interfering."

Egan regarded Brownell with a venomous glare, then looked

back toward the porch just as the farmer bellowed, "Get off my property! All of you! Right now!"

Egan swore and fired his revolver. The old man took the slug dead-center in the stomach. He buckled from the impact, and the shotgun flipped forward in his hands. One barrel discharged, sending the blast into the floor of the porch. As he fell, the women in the house screamed.

Buck railed, "Egan, you fool! You didn't have to shoot him!"

"Don't tell me what I didn't have to do, Brownell. The old buzzard was gonna shoot us!"

The farmer's wife and nineteen-year-old granddaughter ignored what danger they might face and crossed the porch to the old man, who lay face-down, sprawled over the edge of the first step. Both were sobbing and wailing.

"You're under arrest for murder, Egan!" Buck hissed. "Lieutenant Runyon, take his gun!"

Egan took a step backward and aimed his revolver at Runyon. "Nobody's taking my gun. Put the musket down, Lieutenant."

Runyon shifted his flustered gaze to Brownell, then back to Egan.

"Egan, you'll face a court-martial for this," warned Brownell.

"Not if I kill all three of you."

"Right," said Brownell. "Then it'll be a firing squad."

Private O'Dell was positioned on Brownell's right side at an angle that blocked Buck's holstered revolver from Egan's view.

Shaking his gun at Runyon, Egan spat, "I told you to put the musket down, Lieutenant! Do it!"

Buck felt the slight tug at his holster a split second before the loud report of his gun rocked the air. Egan died on his feet with a bullet through his heart. The gun in his hand slipped through lifeless fingers and clattered to the ground just before he fell on top of it.

With the smoking revolver in his hand, the young private said to Brownell, "I'm sorry, sir, but when he spoke of killing us, I didn't know what else to do."

"You did the right thing," Buck said, glancing at Egan's crumpled form. "Now, let's see about the old man and get Captain Merritt inside."

At Matthews' Hill, General Hunter was carried from the field of battle. Colonel Burnside took charge and rode his horse back and forth along the slope, shouting at the men to take the hill. Intense Rebel fire from the woods above them mauled the Yankees. Bullets and cannon shells were dropping them all across the broad sweep of the hillside. Suddenly Burnside's horse fell beneath him, a bullet in its head. The colonel was able to leap from the saddle before the animal flopped hard to the ground.

Colonel Andrew Porter was close by on foot. He dashed to Burnside and helped him to his feet. Together they urged their troops upward, adjusting the lines as they sought to make their way to the Confederate stronghold. Both Union officers were surprised when Rebel infantrymen suddenly burst from the protection of the trees and swarmed down the hill toward them.

Atop the hill, Colonel Evans peered through the heavy brush and watched his musketeers exact their toll. Yankees were dropping along the front line, but no matter how many fell, more came up behind them. Little by little, they were gaining ground.

Moving to Major Wheat, who stood a few feet away, Evans said, "Major, we're outnumbered. We need reinforcements, and it won't be long till we'll be low on ammunition. I'm going to send a runner to General Beauregard. He's got to give us more men and ammunition."

"I agree, sir, but that'll take time. The way those Yankees are comin', I'm not sure but what they'll be on us before we can get help."

Holding his voice above the roar of the battle, Evans said, "I'll send a man on my horse. He can go off the back side of the hill." Evans moved among the trees and called a corporal from the firing line.

Major Wheat watched as Evans gave instructions, then the corporal ran to the colonel's horse and rode away.

When Evans returned, Wheat said, "It's still gonna take time to get help, sir. I've got an idea that'll buy us some time. I'll take my five hundred Tigers and rush 'em."

Evans raised his eyebrows and frowned. "You mean, just go running at them?"

"Well, runnin' and shootin' at the same time. We've got bayonets on our muskets and Bowie knives on our hips. We can cut a big hole in 'em, Colonel."

"Who am I to argue with a tough old veteran like you, Major?" smiled Evans. "Just let me know when you're ready."

Ten minutes later the Yankees were shocked to see five hundred red-shirted Louisiana Tigers swarming down the hill, yelling their bloodcurdling Rebel yell.

CHAPTER SEVENTEEN

★

Two hours before dawn that same morning, Private Mike Durbin hurried by the Henry house and climbed the hill to his own house, a half-mile to the south. He couldn't pass the opportunity to spend a few minutes with his wife before going into battle with the Yankees. Durbin had been assigned to General Barnard E. Bee's Third Brigade in the Army of the Shenandoah, and had not seen Jo-Beth for over two months.

The stars were twinkling overhead like diamonds against a black velvet sky. The old two-story house Mike had bought when he married Jo-Beth two years previously was a welcome sight as he topped the hill. He could make out that the upstairs bedroom windows were open. It was a warm night.

Mike planned to move up just under Jo-Beth's window and call to her. He knew that Orville, her fifteen-year-old brother, would be asleep in a bedroom on the other side of the house. He hoped he could stir his wife without awaking Orville. Pal would no doubt be sleeping in Orville's bedroom. If both bedroom doors were shut, Mike might be able to get by without disturbing the big Newfoundland.

Mike was within fifty feet of the house when he heard the deep-throated bark of his dog. His sensitive ears had picked up Mike's soft footfalls on the grass. It was only seconds until Pal's big broad head appeared at Jo-Beth's window above. The dog was barking and snarling as if to warn the intruder against coming any closer. Moving up under the window, Mike said, "Hey, boy! Don't you know me?" Pal's demeanor changed instantly. Releasing a whine, he yapped a note of recognition and hoisted himself onto the window sill. He was so excited to see his master, he was going to leap down to him.

"No, boy!" shouted Mike. "No! Not from up th—"

Pal's one-hundred-sixty-pound bulk landed on Mike, knocking him down. Neither master nor pet were hurt, but before Mike could get to a sitting position, Pal was drowning him with long-tongued kisses. Mike hugged him and said, "I'm glad to see you, too, boy!"

"Mike!" came Jo-Beth's shriek of joy from the upstairs window. She was holding a lantern out the window, letting its orange glow cast a circle of light on the scene below.

Still lying on the ground with Pal all over him, the Confederate soldier looked up and said, "Hi, honey!"

But the lantern's light was back inside the room, and Jo-Beth had disappeared. Mike worked his way out from under Pal and headed for the front porch as he heard the door come open. By the dim light of the stars overhead, husband and wife were in each other's arms on the porch steps.

Jo-Beth was in her robe, her long blond hair showering over her shoulders. She kissed Mike several times, then settled into one long, tender kiss. Pal's whines for attention were momentarily ignored.

Jo-Beth gripped her husband's upper arms, looked up into his face, and asked, "How did this happen? Why did you get to come home? Are you hurt?"

"No, honey, I'm not hurt. Did you get my letters?"

"I got five. The last I heard, you were at the camp near Winchester."

"Well, I wrote another one a few days ago, telling you that we were coming this way to fight the Yankees over at Manassas Junction. We arrived at the Junction at noon yesterday."

"Oh," said Jo-Beth, gripping him harder. "I heard rumors about a pending battle. I didn't realize you'd be in it."

"I wanted to come sooner, but General Bee said I had to stay with my company. No one could leave the camp. Well, since there's no question the battle's going to start this morning, and since the general saw that I wasn't asleep an hour ago, he told me to come see you real quick, but to be back before dawn."

Jo-Beth began to weep. Embracing him, she sobbed, "Oh, Mike! I don't want you to have to face those Yankee guns!"

"I know, honey, but I have to. It's my duty. We're thinking that if we whip up good on those smart-aleck Yankees today, maybe this whole thing will be over. Maybe they'll go back home and let us Southerners live our lives in peace. That's the way I see it, and that's what I'll be fighting for."

Orville stepped through the door onto the porch, rubbing his eyes. "Hello, Mike," he said sleepily. "I didn't know you'd be home so soon."

Letting go of Jo-Beth with one arm to embrace Orville with it, Mike said, "I didn't either. And I can't stay but just a couple minutes. I have to get back to camp. We're going to have it out with the Yankees over by Manassas Junction today."

The dim light showed Orville's eyes wide. "You're gonna shoot Yankees *today?*"

"Yep."

"Good. I hope you kill all of 'em."

"Maybe we won't have to do that. Maybe we can just kill enough of them to send them running. I want this war business over with so I can come home."

Pal wagged his big bushy tail and barked.

Mike bent over and patted the dog's head. "You too, eh?"

Pal barked again.

"I guess he's missed me, huh?" Mike said to Jo-Beth.

"Has he ever! Every morning he goes all over the house, searching every room. He lies right next to your chair during breakfast, lunch, and supper. I've seen him out at the barn and over at the tool shed a dozen times a day, scratching at the doors, thinking you're in there."

"Yeah," interjected Orville. "Several times I've gone out and let him in both buildings, so he could see you weren't."

Smiling down at the soft-eyed animal, Mike rubbed Pal's ears and said, "You were well-named, weren't you, boy?"

Pal whined and licked his master's hand.

"He hasn't missed you as much as *I* have," Jo-Beth said, leaning her head on Mike's shoulder.

"That's for sure!" spoke up Orville. "She's been doin' a lot of cryin'. I mean...morning, noon, and—"

"That's enough, little brother! You don't have to tell everything you know."

Orville laughed, then hugged his brother-in-law and said since Mike couldn't stay, he would go back to bed so Mike and Jo-Beth could have some time alone. When Orville was gone, Mike and Jo-Beth kissed again, then sat on the porch swing together, with Pal at their feet. They exchanged words of love and talked of the future for a few minutes. Then Mike said, reluctantly, "Well, sweetheart, I have to go."

When they had kissed good-bye on the steps for the third time, Mike said, "Take Pal inside with you and close the windows far enough that he can't get through them...or you know what he'll do."

Eyeing the massive black dog with tenderness, Jo-Beth nodded. "Yes. He'll be going along to fight Yankees with you."

Mike stepped back inside the house and petted his dog while Jo-Beth made sure all the windows were lowered sufficiently.

Jo-Beth was weeping again when she kissed Mike at the door, then stood on the porch and watched him walk away. Inside the house, Pal whined and scratched at the door. When the darkness swallowed Mike, Jo-Beth slipped inside and closed the door. Pal was rushing through the house, checking every window and door to find a way of escape.

Heavy-hearted, Jo-Beth walked into the parlor, dropped onto an overstuffed chair, and broke into heavy sobs. She could still hear Pal pacing the house when she awakened. The sun was up, and she heard a sound like thunder in the distance. Making her way out onto the porch, she looked northward. The fighting was underway, she thought, somewhere near Stone Bridge on Bull Run Creek. Thick clouds of blue-white smoke rose toward the morning sky.

After feeding Orville his breakfast, Jo-Beth warned the youth to be careful going in and out of the house. He must not let Pal get out. When she tried to feed the dog, he ignored the food. Pal had pined for his master for weeks while he was gone. Now that he had seen Mike again, there was only one thing on his mind. He wanted to go to wherever his master was and be at his side.

As the morning wore on, the battle sounds never let up. Pal ran up and down the stairs continually, stopping at each window for a moment, then scratching at a door. When he had made the rounds of the house, he started all over again. Jo-Beth occupied herself by cleaning and recleaning every room, the incessant thunder of cannons and the rattle of muskets assaulting her ears. Orville sat on an old wooden box in the yard, in the shade of a huge oak tree, his eyes never straying from drifting clouds of powder smoke to the north.

It was high noon when Orville heard Pal's whine, and turned to see the determined dog using his bulk and strength to force the dining room window upward on its track. Somehow Pal had been able to work the gap of the partially open window wider with his head until he could get his neck under it. He soon had the opening wide enough to slip through. Like a black streak, the Newfoundland bounded down the hill, heading north.

Orville ran to the house, calling loudly to his sister. When Jo-Beth appeared on the porch, Orville shouted, "Pal got out! Pal got out!"

"How?"

"He managed to get the dining room window open enough to get out," panted the youth. "He's gone! He headed right for where Mike's fighting the Yankees!"

Colonel Evans looked on electrified from his position atop Matthews' Hill as Major Wheat led his five hundred Louisiana Tigers into a violent clash with the Yankees. Although the Tigers were vastly outnumbered, their wild charge had the exact effect Major Wheat had intended. Such daring and hardy warfare threw the Federals into confusion, and that was what Evans desperately needed. The confusion would buy time for General Beauregard to dispatch reinforcements to Matthews' Hill.

The sun climbed toward its peak as the battle raged. While Confederate guns continued to blast away, Colonel Evans's runner returned with the news that General Beauregard was sending reinforcements. If he could do it, Beauregard would send more help later. Colonel Evans's momentary elation was dampened, though, when the runner also informed him that Captain Alexander had sent General Beauregard a flag message that another column of Yankees was coming south past Sudley Springs.

Evans told the runner to get back on the firing line, then smacked a fist into a palm and swore. He belted down a swig of whiskey, then turned back to the battle on the hillside below. The gallant Louisiana Tigers fought hard in the suppressing heat, and though many were falling, they showed no sign of retreat. Face to face with overwhelming odds, they battled on.

The Confederates atop Matthews' Hill continued to hold the Federals at bay. Muskets popped and howitzers roared. Colonel Evans moved amongst them, checking on their ammunition supply. It was running dangerously low. It was about twelve-thirty when he returned to his regular position at the edge of the trees. His heart quickened pace when he saw General Barnard Bee and his two companies come rushing up to his left, guns blazing. The surprised Yankees turned to meet them, which took pressure off Evans's troops atop the hill.

The colonel's elation grew when he saw Colonel F.S. Bartow and his two companies coming on directly behind Bee. They quickly waded into the battle alongside Major Wheat and his troops. Evans's elation grew even more when he spotted a Confederate ammunition wagon riding the wake of Bartow's troops. The wagon broke through the lines, and the driver popped the reins, bawling hoarsely at the team, sending them charging up the hill toward Evans.

Colonel Evans's mind then went to the new column of Yankees that were coming by way of Sudley Springs. The whole Southern contingent on the hill was still outnumbered by the enemy, and a new arrival of Union troops would make it worse. Evans appreciated that General Beauregard would send more help if possible. But Evans needed more than that. He had to have more reinforcements, and he had to have them soon. Returning to his runner on the firing line, he sent him hurrying back to Beauregard with the message, "Without sufficiently more help, our men at Matthews' Hill are doomed."

Down on the hillside, the battle was fierce. Bee's and Bartow's men had marched six miles in the broiling heat to get to Matthews' Hill. Their canteens were dry. They were thirsty and a bit weary. There had been no time to rest, nor to stop and refill their canteens. The thrill of battle made them forget their thirst, and the adrenaline that flowed through their bodies soon erased the weariness.

It was nearly one o'clock when Colonel Evans saw the column of Yankees coming at a trot out of the northwest. He estimated there were about two thousand men in the column. There was only one thing to do. Evans would have to send his troops down the slopes. His brigade could do more good down amongst the other Rebels, especially now that they had plenty of ammunition.

Within minutes Evans had his infantry charging down the broad hillside. Some filled in among the ranks of Rebels firing across sixty or seventy yards of slope at the enemy. Others joined the Louisiana Tigers as they met the Yankees head-on with bayonets and Bowie knives.

The battle at Matthews' Hill had become larger and more fierce than any of the other battles along Bull Run Creek, even the one at Stone Bridge.

The column of Yankees that forged into the battle were led by Brigadier General S.P. Heintzelman. Bartow's troops were on the northwest side of the hill and took the brunt of their fire. They drew back into a thicket, and from the wooded protection, rained hot lead on the Yankees. When the Yankees dug in and returned fire, it was a hurricane of bullets going both directions.

While Bartow's companies were battling at the thicket, Bee's troops pushed up a bald slope leading to Burnside's position. The sound of battle was deafening. As Bee's A Company crawled toward Burnside's position, some sixty yards across the open slope, Private Mike Durbin inched his way alongside Ozzie Zeller, a boyhood friend. They had to weave amongst lifeless bodies strewn on the ground.

Pausing, Durbin took aim at a Yankee lieutenant who stood erect—as if to blatantly defy Rebel bullets—barking orders at his men. Ozzie, head low, was ramrodding a ball into the barrel of his musket and watching Mike line his weapon on the enemy officer.

"Betcha can't hit him," Ozzie said above the roar of the battle.

"Just watch," retorted Mike. Holding his breath, he squeezed the trigger. The musket barked and the Yankee lieutenant went down.

"Hey, you got him!"

"You expected something else?" asked Durbin, who still had his head high enough so he could see if the Yankee lieutenant stayed down. Suddenly his attention was drawn to a furry black object moving up behind the Yankee lines. His breath caught in his chest and his heart froze.

"Oh, no!" he gasped.

"What's the matter?" Ozzie asked.

"It's my dog! He followed me here, and he's looking for me."

Bullets were dropping Yankees and chewing up sod where the big Newfoundland was heading. If Pal stayed on the course he was traveling, he would soon be in the open space between the firing lines. Durbin's mind was racing. Uncertain what to do, he could only gape at the scene.

"Keep your head down, Mike!" Ozzie shouted. "Don't let him see you! If he starts across that open field, he'll get killed."

"He'll come this way anyhow. He's got an uncanny sense about things. His big ol' heart must be telling him where I am."

Pal was almost to the front edge of the Union line and headed straight for Mike.

The relationship Mike Durbin had with his dog had been a special one since Pal was just a puppy. He loved the animal deeply. The awful knowledge that Pal was in imminent danger clouded Durbin's reason. Concern for his own safety was lost. From somewhere deep within him there erupted a sudden surge of panic, impelling him to his feet.

"No, Mike!" wailed Ozzie. "Get down! Get down!"

Mike was deaf to Ozzie's voice, to the din of battle, and to the angry bullets flying all around him. Screaming at the top of his voice, he waved the dog away. "Pal! Get outta here! Get outta here! Go home!"

The Newfoundland's sharp eyes focused on his master. Unable to hear Mike's words, Pal barked and darted for him.

"No! Go back! Go back!"

Pal was a black streak on the body-strewn slope. He had come to find his master, and now had found him. The dog was halfway across the open field when a bullet struck him in a back leg. Ejecting a yelp, he hit the ground, rolling. He came up on all fours and started toward his master, but the wounded leg gave way. Gallantly he attempted to go forward. A bullet seared across his broad back, and he fell to his belly.

Mike was running toward him, his eyes wild. His cap flew off just before he reached Pal and fell to his knees. "You big, wonderful pup!" he gasped, reaching underneath him. "You should've stayed home!"

Pal whined and licked his master's face as Mike stood up, cradling him in his arms. Just as Mike wheeled around to carry his beloved friend to safety, a bullet struck him in the lower back, severing his spine. Man and dog fell to the earth. A bullet hissed past Pal's head and plowed sod a few feet in front of them.

Mike Durbin felt as though his lower body had just dropped off. There was no feeling below his waist. Another bullet tore across his left shoulder, burning like fire. With his legs immobile and Pal seriously wounded, Mike knew he and his dog would not make it. Pal whined as Mike hugged him close and said, "Well, old buddy, I guess you and I are gonna go out togeth—"

Two slugs hit Mike simultaneously. When he went limp, Pal wriggled himself loose from Mike's arms and crawled painfully on top of him in an attempt to provide protection from the awful objects buzzing all around them. He was licking his master's face when another Yankee bullet struck him in the side, ripping through his valorous heart. Pal breathed out his last breath and slumped against the body of the man he loved so faithfully.

General Bee had seen the touching drama played out on the grassy slope by Private Durbin and his dog, but his attention was quickly drawn away to the desperate situation he and his men were in. General Bartow's troops had been driven away from Bee's right flank, and Colonel Evans's Demi-Brigade had been forced from his left, leaving both of Bee's flanks exposed to enemy fire. And the Yankees were coming on strong.

Another half hour of fighting found more Union forces moving in. Colonel Evans faced the cold hard fact that Matthews' Hill had at last become untenable. He signaled the retreat to both Bee and Bartow and began a hurried withdrawal back over Matthews' Hill southward toward Young's Branch. Bartow soon followed.

General Bee's troops began their withdrawal under heavy fire and suffered fearful casualties. As they hastened down the south slope of Matthews' Hill, they saw a new swarm of Yankees coming toward them. The fresh troops were Colonel Sherman's Second Wisconsin Battalion.

The Wisconsin Battalion had been resting north of Stone Bridge for over two hours. When General McDowell learned of the vehement Confederate resistance at Matthews' Hill, he ordered the Second Wisconsin that direction and told Sherman to leave the rest of his Third Brigade with subordinate officers.

Bee and his men met the oncoming horde with stiff resistance, carefully working their way to Young's Branch, where they would rejoin Evans and Bartow. Within twenty minutes, they had done so, but found that even with the combined units, they were grossly out-numbered.

Together, the Confederate troops fell back over Young's Branch. As the Federals closed in on them, panic set in. Many Rebel soldiers abandoned the line and raced across the Warrenton Turnpike and up the north slope of Henry House Hill. Bee, Bartow, and Evans found it impossible to stop them, in spite of shouting threats that they would face a firing squad for desertion.

Thankful that the majority of their men stayed to fight, the three Confederate officers regrouped and continued to offer courageous resistance. However, it soon became evident that the Rebels were about to be engulfed by an overwhelming tide of Yankees. General Bee called for them to withdraw toward Henry House Hill. They must find protection and keep fighting until General Beauregard sent reinforcements.

As the Rebels retreated southward, Sherman joined Burnside and Porter near the Matthews house on the newly won hill. Field commander McDowell and Third Division leader Heintzelman also joined them, feeling confidence rising. Together they watched as the Confederates fell back in full-scale retreat.

General McDowell ordered Sherman's fresh troops, along with Heintzelman, Burnside, and Porter's battle-weary units, to pursue the retreating Confederates. Sitting astride his horse, McDowell watched the troops march toward Henry House Hill. He smiled to himself. Despite heavy casualties, McDowell's army had the enemy on the run.

Things were going well. Once the Federals captured Stone Bridge and wiped out or captured the Rebels along Bull Run and those on Henry House Hill, they had to push only a little over three miles south to reach the tracks of the Manassas Gap Railroad. There they would be in position to cut off Confederate reinforcements coming in by rail from the Shenandoah Valley and could advance unimpeded to Manassas Junction. From there it would be a simple matter of putting his troops on railroad cars and running them down the tracks of the Orange and Alexandria Railroad to Richmond. Capture Richmond, bring the Rebels to their knees, and the Civil War would be over. The name of General Irvin McDowell would be on the lips of Northerners and Southerners alike.

The success that was at his fingertips flushed McDowell with excitement. Gouging his horse's flanks with his heels, he put it into a gallop and soon caught up with his marching men. Riding jubilantly along the blue-clad columns, he stood in his stirrups, waved his hat, and shouted, "Victory! Victory! The day is ours!"

CHAPTER EIGHTEEN

✦

John Henry stood on the porch of his mother's house and watched the frightened Confederate soldiers run up the side of the hill. When they neared the house, they were panting hard for breath. There were about forty in all, and terror showed on their faces.

They paused to catch their breath. One of them looked at John and gasped, "Better...better get outta here, mister! The Yankees are beatin' us down. They...they'll kill you! If you...you got any family in the house...better take 'em...and run!"

The terrified Rebel soldier did not wait to see if his words took effect on the farmer. He took off, and the others soon followed. John watched them disappear over the back side of the hill, then hurried into the house.

Mounting the stairs three at a time, John hastened down the hall and entered his mother's bedroom. His wife, Louise, and sister, Mary Sue, sat beside the bed. Judith Henry lay with just a sheet over her as she lifted her dull, sunken eyes to her son and said weakly, "John, the Yankees are comin', aren't they?"

"Yes, Mama," he replied, moving to the open window and parting the sheer curtains. "Those Rebels who just ran through the yard said they're coming."

"They wouldn't harm us, would they?"

"I can't say, Mama. One of the Rebels seemed to think so."

Fear was mirrored in Mary Sue's eyes. Looking at her brother's back, she asked with a tremor in her voice, "Why would Yankee soldiers want to hurt us? We're no threat to them."

"Maybe just because we're Southerners," Louise said, rising from her chair and moving beside her husband.

Mary Sue was holding her invalid mother's hand. "What should we do, Johnny?"

Louise followed John's gaze and saw the Negro neighbors near the bottom of the hill. James and Hattie Robinson had their four children in the family wagon and were pulling out of the yard. "I wish we could do what the Robinsons are doing," she said.

"I wonder where they'll go," John said, releasing the curtains to look at his mother and sister. "Seems to me the Yankees have taken over the whole valley. I hope they head south, at least."

The elderly woman looked at the others and said, "If there's really a threat of danger, why don't you youngins jump in the wagon and go? I'll be all right. Them Yankees wouldn't harm a crippled old woman."

Louise returned to the bed, patted her mother-in-law's wrinkled hand, and said softly, "Mama, John and Mary Sue and I wouldn't think of leaving you. We'll just stay here and pray to the Lord that the Yankees won't bother us."

"That's right, Mama," said John, turning back to the window. "We'll just stay here and let God watch over us. If it's time for us to leave this world, it's in His hands."

The younger women comforted aged Judith Henry as John studied the landscape to the north. After a few moments, he said, "Looks like we're gonna have company pretty soon."

"Yankees already?" asked Louise, rushing to the window.

"No, but there are thousands of Confederate soldiers coming this way. And the way they're hoofing it, I'd say the Yankees aren't far behind. Could be we're going to see what a battle looks like real close up."

Colonel Erasmus D. Keyes's First Brigade was still battling it out with Confederates along the Warrenton Turnpike some two miles north of Stone Bridge. The Yankees had lost ground, however, and had been forced to pull back some five hundred yards from their original position close to the road.

When General Irvin McDowell pulled William T. Sherman and the Second Wisconsin Battalion from the Turnpike battle to help reinforce the troops at Matthews' Hill, the Confederates took advantage of it and mounted a charge. There was a fierce hand-to-hand fight that lasted until General McDowell realized his mistake and sent four companies of cavalry under Major I.N. Palmer to the rescue. At the arrival of the cavalry, the Confederates had fallen back to their ditches and gullies near the road, and commenced musket fire and cannonade.

Captain Buck Brownell and his company of Zouaves were in a four-feet-deep ditch that ran across the field in almost a straight line for over two hundred yards. Rebel cannons had taken their toll on the Union cavalry horses, and Major Palmer finally had ordered his men to dismount and fight from the gullies and ditches. Some four hundred cavalrymen were strung out in the front-line ditch intermingled with Brownell and his Zouaves.

The afternoon's heat settled over the battlefield and sucked dry the men in the ditches and gullies. Trying to ignore his thirst, his canteen empty, Buck blasted away at the enemy and longed for beautiful Jenny. "Dear God," he prayed, "please let me live through this war and let us be husband and wife. She's all that matters, Lord, and—"

Buck's heartfelt prayer was cut off as he saw one of his Zouaves fall a few feet down the line. Shouting toward the men next to the fallen soldier, he said, "Heflin! Domire! Check on Spalding. See where he's hit."

"He isn't hit, Captain," Gifford Domire called back. "He passed out from the heat...and the lack of water. We've got some other men up the line here who've passed out. If we don't get some water, it's gonna get worse!"

Buck knew there was a small branch off of Bull Run that trickled across the field some three hundred yards behind the line. Calling above the roar to Domire, he said, "Pass the word along! Tell the men to send their canteens this way. I'll take as many as I can carry and fill them."

"I'll go, Captain," Domire replied. "The men need you here."

"I'll help him, Captain!" volunteered Lyle Heflin. "That way, we can fill twice as many canteens."

Buck granted permission for both men to go. The morale of the men in the long ditch seemed to pick up with the promise of water. They gladly passed their canteens down the line. When Domire and Heflin had their arms full, they told Brownell they would do the same for the men up the line the other direction when they got back. Buck hoped the other Yankees would see what Domire and Heflin were doing and send men from their own ditches for water.

Some 150 yards from the front line of battle, Colonel Keyes and Major Palmer sat on their horses in the shade of a stand of trees and studied the fierce conflict before them. As they discussed what to do if the Confederates brought in more reinforcements, they spotted the two Zouaves bent low and zigzagging their way across the battlefield in their direction, carrying the empty canteens. As they drew near, Palmer dismounted and walked out to meet them. Keyes followed, hurrying along at Palmer's heels. Palmer was by far the younger of the two.

"Is everyone up there out of water?" queried Palmer.

"Can't speak for those in other lines, sir," replied Corporal Domire, "but they sure are in ours. We've got men passing out from the heat. We're about to rectify that."

Both officers commended the two for what they were doing and allowed them to proceed. From the shade of the trees, they watched them reach the branch, fill the canteens, and head back. Weighted down with their load, they hurried to deliver the water to their comrades.

Suddenly, one of them went down. The other frantically tried to help him, but was hit, too. Now both men were on the ground, and neither was moving.

Palmer sucked in his breath as if a shaft of pain had hit his vitals. "Oh, God bless 'em! Those two boys are hit!" Wheeling about, Palmer ran to his horse and leaped into the saddle.

"Wait a minute, Major!" gasped Keyes. "Where are you going?"

"I'm going after those canteens—to distribute them to our men."

"No you're not! It's too dangerous! Let some of the men out there take care of it."

"They're too busy, Colonel. Now, please excuse me."

"Major!" rasped Keyes. "Get down off that horse! That's an *order!*"

Palmer looked at the older man and said, "Don't do this to me, Colonel. My men need water and so do yours. They can't keep fighting in this heat without water. I must take it to them...even if you maintain that order."

Keyes had been in the military since he was eighteen years old. He knew a real soldier when he saw one. Wiping a palm across his face, he sighed, "I'm probably sending you to your death, Major, but I withdraw the order. Go do what you must."

Palmer lashed his horse with the reins and put it into an immediate gallop. They soon reached the rear lines and came into musket range. Palmer's horse managed to keep a steady canter as it threaded among the corpses on the battlefield. It skidded to a halt when Palmer jerked rein and vaulted from the saddle, and stood there, ears laid back and snorting, as bullets tore sod all around and cannonballs exploded close by.

The major found that both men were dead, and water was bubbling out of three canteens that had been punctured with bullets. He wrapped the leather straps of the two dozen or more undamaged canteens around his neck, slung them over his arms and shoulders, and with effort, mounted his horse. Bending low over the animal's back, he prodded it forward toward the front line, then veered off to the right and headed for the end of the line. When he reached it, he rode along the ditch, dropping a canteen every few yards and shouting, "Drinks are on the house, boys!"

A Zouave fighting beside Captain Brownell elbowed him and pointed up the line at Palmer. "What's the major doing delivering water?" Buck gasped.

"Something must've happened to Domire and Heflin, sir."

Palmer was within a hundred feet of Buck when a cannon shell struck a few feet to his left. Shrapnel tore into the horse, and it dropped hard on its side, pinning Major Palmer's left leg. Another shell blew several men close by into eternity. Shrapnel ripped into the dead horse, which kept it from hitting the major.

Shouting for his men to keep firing, Buck leaped from the ditch and, bending low, darted along the line toward the trapped major. Buck reached the spot and slid on the grass to a prostrate position. Major Palmer had a couple of small bloody spots on his face, but otherwise was untouched. He looked at the Zouave officer levelly and said, "Captain, you have no business out here. Get back in that ditch!"

"I have as much business out here as you did, sir. Now, let's get you out from under your horse."

"It's too dangerous. The Rebel artillery has found the range. Another shell could hit right on this spot any second. I'm ordering you to get back in that ditch!"

"Sorry, sir, but all this noise has my ears ringing. I can't hear what you're saying. Just be ready to inch your way out when I heave on this horse."

Shells exploded on every side as Buck strained to free Major Palmer. Some twenty minutes of effort saw the major free and clear of his horse and in the ditch with Buck.

Water was distributed along the line, and Union soldiers were refreshed. While the battle continued, Major Palmer took a drink for himself, then handed the canteen to the Zouave officer who had insisted that the major drink first. While Buck was drinking, a cannonball whistled down and struck Palmer's horse.

The major shook his head, wiped sweat, and said, "Captain, I owe you my life. What's your name?"

"It really doesn't matter, sir. What's important is that our cavalry still has its leader."

"I appreciate that," smiled Palmer, "but I want to know your name."

Before Buck could speak, the Zouave next to him spoke up. "It's Brownell, Major Palmer. Captain Buck Brownell. Far as I'm concerned, it should be General Brownell."

Palmer smiled again. "I don't think I can pull that one off, soldier, but if I have anything to say about it, he'll soon be Major Brownell!"

General Bee and Colonels Bartow and Evans led their troops up the north slope of Henry House Hill with the Federals in pursuit. They were almost to the crest where the house stood when beyond the house, they saw a Confederate flag waving in the breeze. The flag could barely be seen above the top of the hill, but it was moving toward them.

Evans pointed to it and said, "That flag can only mean one thing. Reinforcements are coming!"

The Rebel soldiers who followed the officers ejected a wild whoop. Coming over the hill were five regiments of the First Brigade of the Army of the Shenandoah, led by Brigadier General Thomas J. Jackson. There was elation at the welcome sight, and the gallant men who had fought so hard on Matthews' Hill were ready to turn around and meet the oncoming Union troops head-on.

Leaving Bartow and Evans with the troops, Bee put his horse to a gallop and raced to meet Jackson. As he drew up, he smiled, raised a hand in greeting, and said, "General Jackson! Am I ever glad to see you!"

Smiling in return, Jackson said, "General Beauregard thought you just might be." Looking past Bee and the Confederate soldiers, he focused on the massive force of Federals crossing Young's Branch in the distance. "We'd best get fortified. We're still outnumbered, and those blue-bellies will be here in twenty minutes."

While the Confederates joined forces and prepared to meet the oncoming enemy with artillery and infantry, Jackson, Bee, Bartow, and Evans held a quick strategy meeting.

They had not noticed the faces in the windows of the Henry house, and were surprised when they saw a man emerge from the back door and head toward them. Jackson left the others to meet him. "Good afternoon, sir. I'm Brigadier General Thomas Jackson. Are you Mr. Henry?"

"Probably not the one you have in mind, General. My father is dead. My mother still lives here. I'm taking care of the place, along with my wife and sister. I'm John Henry."

As the two men shook hands, Jackson asked, "The women are in the house now?"

"Yes, sir."

"That's not good. There's going to be some heavy fighting here real soon." Swinging his gaze toward the barn, he said, "I see you have horses and a wagon. Best thing for you to do is harness up the team as fast as you can, load the women in the wagon, and hightail it out of here."

John rubbed the back of his neck and replied, "Can't do that, General. My mother's an invalid. She can't be moved."

"Then get inside and keep the women away from the window."

"Do you think the Yankees will want to take the house, sir?"

"I don't know. But we're going to do our best to see to it that they don't even get near the house. Now, you get back inside." Jackson wheeled and headed back toward the other officers.

He had taken only a few steps when John called after him, "General Jackson...!"

Pausing, the stalwart Confederate officer made a half-turn. "Yes?"

"God bless you, sir."

Jackson smiled. "He does, Mr. Henry. In spite of all my shortcomings, He does."

John returned the smile and turned toward the house.

The Confederates made ready quickly, positioning howitzers on both sides of Henry house, aiming their deadly bores down the gentle green slope. Infantrymen flattened out on the crest, cocking the hammers of their muskets and waiting for the Union forces. When the Yankees drew within cannon range, the big Rebel guns cut loose. Within a half-minute, Union cannons were answering back while their footmen came on like a swarm of hornets.

On the hills overlooking the smoke-filled battlefield, the civilian spectators ate their picnic lunches and drank warm lemonade, tea, and water in the oppressive heat. Though it was difficult for them to tell just how the battle was going, they endured the discomfort because they were certain of a Union victory and wanted to be on hand to observe it.

Governess Patricia Winters sat on the ground in the shade of Rose Greenhow's surrey and chatted with Jenny Jordan. Both Jenny and Patricia had given up the idea of trying to spot the men they loved. The distance was too great, and there were so many men in the battle.

When Tad and Willie had finished their lunches—having taken them to the big rock to eat, along with some other boys—Tad approached his governess and asked, "Miss Patricia, could me and Willie go a little farther down the hill? There are some trees and bushes down there a little ways. We could see the battle better down there. Could we, please?"

Patricia started to correct Tad's grammar but decided to let it go. Rising to her feet, she said, "Show me what trees and bushes you're talking about. I don't want you getting much closer to the battle."

Tad took her hand, looked up with a winsome smile, and said, "C'mon."

Five minutes later, Patricia returned, sighed, and sat down once again beside Jenny.

Jenny dabbed at the perspiration on her face with a hanky and asked, "So did Mr. Tad Lincoln persuade you to let them go farther down the hill?"

"Mm-hmm," smiled Patricia. "It's still a long way from the bottom, and plenty of distance from the battle. They'll be all right there."

Letting her gaze drift back to the scene of the conflict in the valley below, Jenny bit down hard on her lower lip. Somewhere amid the fire and smoke was Captain Buck Brownell. Again, she breathed a prayer for his safety.

General McDowell was positioned at the Robinson house, where he observed his troops slowly making their way up the gentle slope toward Henry house where the Confederates had dug in to make their stand. He was short of artillery and had sent for two batteries under the command of Captains James B. Ricketts and Charles Griffin, who were waiting in reserve at Centreville. As he paced back and forth on the safe side of the Robinson house, he nervously looked up the Warrenton Turnpike to catch sight of them.

There was still heavy fighting at Stone Bridge and beyond the bridge along the Turnpike. McDowell hoped the captains would make a wide circle around the two hot spots so as to arrive intact at Robinson house. From the looks of things, he was going to need their cannons to insure the capture of Henry House Hill.

Along the Turnpike between Centreville and Stone Bridge, Colonel Duryee's Zouaves and Major Palmer's cavalrymen were still battling it out with General Beauregard's Rebel forces. Bodies—in blue and gray—lay scattered over the fields, in the ditches, and even on the Turnpike.

Situated in an abandoned farm house high on a hill a mile east of Henry House Hill, and about a mile-and-a-half south of Stone Bridge, Generals Beauregard and Johnston were in conference. Beauregard had anticipated that McDowell would send troops from Centreville due south to Mitchell's Ford and had placed brigades there to meet them. As the fighting centered farther north and west, Beauregard decided to pull these two brigades to the Turnpike. Johnston agreed, and the two brigades were now on their way.

To fortify the Confederate position on Henry House Hill, Beauregard sent three companies from Captain William Smith's Forty-ninth Virginia and Colonel Jeb Stuart's First Virginia Cavalry. The Confederates still faced a foe that greatly outnumbered them, and Beauregard knew it. Together, he and Johnston made further plans to shift troops as fast as possible to Henry House Hill.

CHAPTER NINETEEN

★

At the Turnpike where Colonel Duryee's Zouaves and Major Palmer's cavalrymen fought hard against the Confederates, Captain Brownell was bent low in the ditch, doing what he could to help a wounded Zouave captain. Shells were exploding all around, sending their death-dealing shrapnel in every direction. Suddenly Buck looked up to see Colonel Duryee roll into the ditch a few feet away, landing on a dead Zouave private.

Duryee crawled toward Buck. He had lost his hat, and his face was smeared and caked with grimy sweat. The colonel looked at the fallen captain, then eyed Buck and asked, "How bad is it?"

"He's dead, sir. Just breathed his last."

Duryee shook his head. "Captain, there are three cannons out there that we've got to dispose of. They're cutting us to pieces. I know about your expertise in handling such problems. Do you think you can take a few men and wipe out those cannon crews?"

"It won't be easy, sir, but I believe we can handle it."

"Good! The quicker, the better."

In less than five minutes, Brownell had six Zouaves crawling on their bellies behind him toward the enemy howitzers. Colonel Duryee peered over the edge of the ditch and watched with keen interest. Beside him now were Zouave captains Dane Saltzer and Howard Beery. Both had given word to their companies to give as much fire cover to Brownell and his small group as possible.

The din of the battle remained steady as Brownell and his men slowly made their way to the first howitzer. The crew was cut down as Union guns barked from a nearby cluster of bushes. Within twenty minutes, all three howitzer crews were dead, and the Rebels were scurrying about, trying to find others who could man them. Buck and his men were racing back to their ditch. Just as they arrived and were being congratulated for a job well done, Zouave lieutenant Dean Frizzell came running across the field and dived into the ditch where Duryee and Brownell were crouched.

"Colonel!" Frizzell gasped. "They're coming up behind us!"

Duryee jerked around and peered over the edge of the ditch toward the southeast. Bonham's and Early's brigades were coming in a huge wave of gray. The threat behind was greater than the one at the Turnpike. By this time, Major Palmer found his way to where Colonel Duryee and his three captains were assembled in the ditch.

Quickly the colonel and the major turned two-thirds of their men and cannons toward the oncoming horde. Within minutes, the new battle was in violent progress.

The Yankees fought back furiously, but General Beauregard's tactical move had a devastating effect. Zouaves and cavalrymen were dropping along the lines, filling the ditches with corpses and wounded men. Buck saw Captains Saltzer and Beery die within two minutes of each other. Lieutenant Frizzell took orders from Colonel Duryee and began crawling back to his men. Before he reached them, Rebel bullets took his life.

Colonel Duryee shouldered a musket next to Brownell and fired. He rolled onto his back to reload and shouted at Buck, "Captain, where'd all those Rebs come from?"

Buck fired his musket, dropped down, flipped onto his back, and began reloading. "Looks like the Frenchman had them hidden somewhere, sir," he replied.

"I don't understand it," said the colonel, packing his powder and ball tight. "You'd think the Rebels knew we were coming and when."

"I think they did, sir. They were just too well prepared."

"Spies?" suggested Duryee, rolling back onto his belly, ready for the next shot.

"What else?"

"Guess that's what it had to be," said the colonel, raising up to sight and fire.

Suddenly a bullet slammed the colonel, making him howl. He fell, cursing the Rebels.

Buck leaned over him and asked, "Where you hit, sir?"

"Right shoulder," replied Duryee through clenched teeth. "I...I think the slug went on through."

Buck scrutinized the wound and found that the slug had exited the back side. "You're right, Colonel. Let me see what I can do to stop the blood flow."

Buck ripped up the shirt of a dead Zouave in the ditch and used it as a compress and bandage on the wound.

In evident pain, the colonel looked up at Buck and said, "Captain Brownell, you're the only Zouave officer left in this whole line. You'll have to take charge."

"Yes, sir," nodded Buck. "You just stay right here and hold on, Colonel. I'll regroup the men and lead a counter charge."

"There's not an officer in this entire outfit more qualified to lead it, son. It's in your hands. Go to it!"

General Thomas Jackson studied the oncoming Federal troops from the crest of Henry House Hill. He saw the Ricketts and Griffin batteries come wheeling their cannons and driving their ammunition wagons across Young's Branch. He knew that General McDowell was sending the fresh artillery to try to blow him and his army off the hill.

Sending a runner to Beauregard, Jackson described the artillery that was on the way. He asked for more artillery to offset it. The messenger returned, telling Jackson that the general was sending in a South Carolina militia unit known as the Palmetto Guard. They had ten howitzers and were good with them.

Jackson smiled. The Palmetto Guard was indeed good. One of their cannoneers was the "Father of Secession," Edmund Ruffin. Ruffin had been the man to fire the first shot at Fort Sumter.

The units of General Bee, Colonel Bartow, and Colonel Evans were spread out over the crest of Henry House Hill on both sides of General Jackson and his brigade. While cannons roared and muskets barked, Jackson stood tall and erect, shouting commands. Periodically, he stole a glance over his shoulder to see if the Palmetto Guard was coming up the backside of the hill.

A half hour had passed since the runner had brought the encouraging message, and in his mind, Jackson was trying to hurry them. The Yankees were making progress up the hill in spite of all the Rebels were throwing at them. The two new Union artillery batteries were getting closer.

Bee's brigade was being torn apart along the hill's southwest side. McDowell's artillery was pounding them hard. Soon Bee ran up the side of the hill and approached Jackson, saying breathlessly, "General Jackson, they're giving my unit a terrible pounding! If they wipe us out, they'll charge right over our bodies and wipe out every unit on the hill!"

"We've got artillery reinforcements on the way," replied Jackson. "General Beauregard is sending the Palmetto Guard up here. I'm expecting them just any time. When they get here, I'll have them concentrate on the Yankee guns that are blasting you. That'll take the heat off."

"I appreciate that, General," said Bee. He paused a moment, then added, "Seems to me both sides will be running out of powder pretty soon."

"No doubt," nodded Jackson, keeping his gaze on the lusty battle below. "When that happens, we'll give them the bayonet!"

General Bee hurried back down the hill to give his men the good news that the Palmetto Guard was on its way. Using a rifle himself, he shouted words of encouragement to his men.

The battle was fierce. At one point, General Bee looked up to see the rough and rugged Jackson repositioning some of his cannons to give Bee and his men relief from the artillery onslaught. The Palmetto Guard had not yet arrived, and Jackson was taking alternative action.

"God bless him!" shouted Bee, pointing up the hill for his men to see what was happening. General Jackson stood like a statue, barking orders, while enemy fire whistled all around him. His concern for Bee's unit made him oblivious to his own danger.

Bee waved his hat and shouted to his men, "There's Jackson, standing like a stone wall. Rally behind him, men! Rally behind him!"

One of Bee's men shouted, "That's what he is, General Bee. He's a stone wall—Stonewall Jackson!"

A Yankee shell whistled down shrilly and exploded, ripping General Bee's body with deadly shrapnel. When the smoke had cleared, the gallant general lay dead.

The day wore on and the tumultuous conflict continued. On Henry House Hill, in the woods, on the open fields, at Stone Bridge, and along the banks of Bull Run Creek was the constant thunderous roaring of the big guns, the sharp sound of the rifled cannons, the crack of Minie rifles and muskets, and the fiery burst of shells.

At the old farmhouse, Generals Beauregard and Johnston waited eagerly for the arrival of the eight-hundred-man Palmetto Guard under the command of Colonel Bertrand Waverly. Beauregard had them bivouacked some five miles south of Manassas Junction in reserve. They would be fresh and ready to fight.

Beauregard had called in two other units that had been held in reserve along Aquia Creek on the lower Potomac: a brigade of three hundred men led by Brigadier General Theophilus H. Holmes and the six-hundred-man Hampton Legion, commanded by Colonel Wade Hampton. The colonel was a dynamic, wealthy South Carolina plantation owner and politician, and had put together, fed, clothed, and armed the legion at his own expense. They had their own infantry, artillery, and cavalry.

At 3:15, the Palmetto Guard arrived and was sent immediately to Henry House Hill to bolster the troops there. It was just past 3:30 when Holmes and Hampton brought their units in from the east. Beauregard and Johnston mounted their horses and rode like the wind to greet the two units. Beauregard sent Johnston back to the old farmhouse to keep an eye on the rest of the conflict, and personally led Holmes and Hampton to Henry House Hill. General "Stonewall" Jackson was very happy to see the two fresh units, and immediately spread them out on the crest of the hill to counter the new strength added to the enemy lines by the arrival of the Ricketts and Griffin batteries.

The Confederate lines stabilized with the additional troops and guns. General Beauregard had salvaged a defense out of what had seemed to be certain disaster just an hour before. Now fully in command of the situation, he rode his horse along the lines on Henry House Hill, urging his men to fight on.

Inside the Henry house, John and the two younger women moved from window to window on the lower floor, watching General Beauregard. Above the roar of the battle, they could hear him shouting to the men, telling them that the fight was turning toward their favor and that they must contend harder than ever to see it through to victory.

John Henry embraced Louise joyfully, saying, "Honey, it sounds to me like the South is going to win this thing!" Tears filmed Louise's eyes.

Mary Sue hugged them both, then exclaimed, "Let's go upstairs and tell Mama!"

While John, his wife, and sister were heading for the stairs, disaster was brewing at the bottom of the hill. Captain James Ricketts and his artillery battery had taken a position some three hundred yards from the Confederate line at the top of the hill. While Ricketts was getting his guns ready for action, the Confederate reinforcements located near the house began a rain of lead on the battery.

Ricketts saw his men and horses falling all around him. He peered through the dust and smoke and concluded that the shots were coming from inside the Henry house. He commanded his gunners to turn their cannons on the house.

John, Louise, and Mary Sue were halfway up the stairs when they heard a shell hit on the second floor. They halted, gripping the banister. Another shell tore through the west wall and exploded in the kitchen on the bottom floor. The women wailed in terror. John hastily ushered them to the cellar, telling them to stay put while he ran to check on his mother. Clinging to each other while sitting on the cellar floor, they both sobbed and begged John to be careful.

Ricketts had stopped shelling the house by the time John was climbing over rubble in an effort to enter his mother's bedroom. There were two huge holes in the wall, and the room was a shambles. Mrs. Judith Henry lay on the mattress of her collapsed bed. Shrapnel had torn into her body. One large fragment had torn off her left foot.

To John's amazement, his mother was still breathing. He made a hasty tourniquet for her ankle, then hoisted her frail body into his arms, carried her to Mary Sue's bedroom, and laid her on the bed. He was about to call his wife and sister for help when the elderly woman stopped breathing. Weeping, John pressed his ear to his mother's breast to listen for a heartbeat. The roar of the conflict outside was too great.

When he couldn't find a pulse with his fingertips, John knew his mother was dead. Something seemed to explode inside him. Leaving his mother's lifeless form on the bed, he charged down the stairs and through the front door. Standing on the porch, he shook his fists at the Yankee forces and wailed, "You killed my mother! You foul beasts! You killed my poor, innocent mother!"

By four o'clock, the tide in the Bull Run battle began to swiftly go against the North. General Stonewall Jackson unleashed the newly arrived artillery on the batteries of Ricketts and Griffin, and soon wiped them out. Then the big guns were turned on the other Yankee units all over the hillside. Clouds of dust, mingled with puffs of gun smoke, floated on the hot breeze over the valley. The acrid smell of burnt gunpowder stung the eyes and nostrils of Yankees and Rebels alike. Lifeless bodies were everywhere, and among them were wounded and bleeding men.

When General McDowell saw the tide turning against him at Henry House Hill, he sent for the Zouaves, who had beaten back the Rebel troops along the Warrenton Turnpike. While Colonel Duryee lay wounded in a ditch, Buck Brownell led the Zouaves to Henry House Hill. At the same time, McDowell had also dispatched what was left of a U.S. Marine battalion to the hill.

The Zouaves charged in, blasting away, but Buck could tell it was useless. Too many men in blue were dead. Multitudes of others had collapsed from heat exhaustion and dehydration. Many were dead of sunstroke.

The feisty Rebels had known that McDowell's forces were coming; they had been ready for them. In spite of the heat and other adverse elements, General Beauregard's troops were showing real grit and determination.

The Union troops fought doggedly, but they were being whipped. From time to time, Buck saw General McDowell riding to and fro along the fighting front, rallying his men. It was all academic. All over the valley, Federal regiments were becoming a jumble of fragmented, confused soldiers. Whatever semblance of organization that remained was on the verge of disintegrating.

At 4:45, McDowell committed the last fresh reserves to the battle: three regiments from Maine and one from Vermont, commanded by Colonel Oliver Howard. Howard's troops were not truly fresh, though they had yet to see combat. They had made the long march from Centreville over sun-burned hills and through waterless, heat-packed valleys with heavy field packs and empty canteens. They were at the point of exhaustion.

Though they gave it their best effort to obey McDowell's order to deploy at a run, at least a third collapsed before they reached the firing lines. When the other two-thirds reached the point of battle, they were unnerved to see bloodied Union soldiers throwing down their muskets and fleeing in terror.

Howard's first line was badly mauled by blasts from atop Henry House Hill. With dead men lying all around him—many from other units—Colonel Howard shouted orders for his second line to move up. But when he turned to observe them, they were drawing back, eyes bulging with horror. Howard had no alternative but to order all his men to retreat. They broke and fled, dashing for Young's Branch. When they reached the shallow stream, they threw themselves flat and slaked their thirst. On their feet again, they ran to the Turnpike and headed northeast, noticing that their comrades had forsaken the battle at Stone Bridge and were sprinting toward Washington.

While thousands of Union soldiers continued to fight at Henry House Hill, still other thousands were heading for the hills where the civilians had been watching the battle. Cavalrymen goaded their horses into a gallop. Ammunition wagons threw up dust as their drivers snapped the reins and aimed them toward the capital city.

General McDowell and his officers were alarmed at the signs of panic. They rode back and forth, desperately trying to keep any more men from fleeing. When men did make a break for it, the Union officers did their best to re-form the frightened, scattering soldiers.

Union horsemen were the first to reach the hills to the north and east. Eyes wild, they shouted at the hundreds of civilian spectators to run. Dozens of Union wagons bounded over the fields toward the hills at top speed. More cavalrymen were coming in waves on galloping steeds toward the alarmed and frightened Washingtonians. Stunned at the sudden unexpected turn of events and shocked to see their men retreating like scared rabbits, the civilians hastened to load their families in the horse-drawn vehicles and escape the Rebels. From what the soldiers were saying, Beauregard's troops were coming, and would shoot everybody.

Children had been allowed to play together in small groups. Parents and guardians were scurrying about, trying to collect them so they could get away.

As Rose Greenhow and her girls were piling in the surrey behind the hired driver, Rose turned to Jenny and whispered, "Looks like our little espionage effort has paid off. However, I hope your Captain is all right."

"Yes," nodded Jenny, "so do I."

Patricia Winters was chatting with a couple she had known in Illinois when the first wave of horsemen rode up, yelling for everybody to get off the hill. Patricia began looking for Tad, who had been playing near a clump of bushes some distance down the slope. Earlier, Willie had abandoned his little brother and was playing "war" nearby with several boys. Willie came running up out of breath, and cried, "Miss Patricia! We gotta get Tad!"

Expecting that the youngest Lincoln son would now be nearly to the crest of the hill, the governess ran that direction. Willie stayed beside her. When Patricia reached the crest and could not see Tad anywhere, she gasped, "Willie, I don't see him, do you?"

"Yes, ma'am," replied the boy, pointing. "Tad wanted to get closer to the battle, so he went down to those trees. See him? He's running this way."

The governess stared in disbelief. Tad had been in the shade of the trees a moment before, but now she could see him running up the hill for all he was worth. He was more than a hundred yards away, and a swarm of bounding wagons and galloping horses was moving up behind him at a distance of no more than five hundred yards.

Patricia stood rooted to the spot, her heart hammering. Tad was in the open now, and there was no way he could outrun the charging wheels and hooves.

Suddenly Jenny was beside Patricia, whose terror had her unable to move. Following the eyes of the governess and Willie, Jenny spied Tad and quickly understood his predicament. Before anyone could speak, Jenny had her skirt hoisted calf-high and was bolting down the slope toward the frightened boy.

As Patricia stood transfixed, her eyes glued on the scene below, she felt a hand grip her shoulder. Turning, she recognized Senator Charles Sumner. The senator also had a hand on Willie's shoulder.

"I couldn't help but notice," said Sumner levelly. "Isn't that Colonel Jordan's daughter?"

"Yes," stammered Patricia. "I...I don't know why Tad went all the way down there without asking my permission."

"They'll both be trampled to death. Come on. Let's get in the safety of these trees."

The senator ushered Patricia and Willie to a stand of trees a few yards away, where the three of them watched the scene below with grim fascination. In the safety of their surreys, buggies, and carriages, many others observed, also.

While Jenny plunged down the hill, she noticed a deep cleft in the ground just ahead of Tad. If the two of them could drop down in the cleft, the hooves and wheels might possibly pass over them. But could they make it? The deathly swarm was closing in fast.

Tad's face was sheet-white as he ran up the slope, looking back every few seconds to check the progress of the oncoming horde. Unaware of the cleft ahead of him, he set his eyes on Jenny, raising his arms and reaching for her.

When Tad circled around the cleft, Jenny shouted, "Tad! Jump in the hole! Jump in the hole!"

But the roar was too loud; he couldn't hear her. Certain death was on his heels. Running like a frightened fox before a pack of vicious hounds, he wailed in terror, reaching...reaching...

The front line of horses and wagons was no more than fifty yards behind the boy. Jenny, with sharp, cold needles prickling her face and neck, was closing in. Only a few more steps...a few more steps...

When Jenny and Tad came together, the impact knocked them both off their feet. Gasping for breath, Jenny snatched the president's son in her arms and dashed to the cleft. Diving in, she covered Tad's body with her own. It sounded like the whole earth was caving in on them as the pounding hooves and spinning wheels passed over harmlessly.

It seemed like an eternity for the galloping escapees to pass, but finally they were gone. Covered with dirt, her hair disheveled, Jenny raised up and looked down at the terrified boy. "You all right, Tad?"

Trembling, he nodded. "Yes, ma'am."

Glancing to the fields below, Jenny saw some stragglers, but the initial swarm was gone. Standing, she helped the boy to his feet. "Come on, Tad. Let's get out of here."

They had barely begun to climb the gentle slope when they saw a cluster of people hurrying toward them from the crest. Senator Sumner was in the lead. Directly behind him were Willie and a weeping Patricia Winters.

CHAPTER TWENTY

✦

By 5:30 dark clouds were moving across the sky from the west, adding to the gloom that General Irvin McDowell felt in his soul. The Confederates, without a doubt, had been fed information that put them on the alert and enabled them to prepare for this morning's attack. Now they were hammering the Union troops unmercifully and beating them back.

McDowell saw some of his men fall under heavy fire, while others were fleeing across the fields, discarding their gear as they went. Those who were running away seemed to infect those they came in contact with. There was nothing to do but command a retreat and get his army out of the valley before they were annihilated. The general signaled his officers to lead their men in retreat and head for Washington.

At the time the retreat was sounded, Buck Brownell and some seventy-five of his Zouaves had a handful of Rebels cornered in the woods at the eastern base of Henry House Hill. Knowing he had to obey the retreat order, Buck led his men to rush the Rebels, guns blazing. They would get in one last good punch before heading north.

Though the Rebels in the woods were outnumbered, they

fought back gallantly as the Zouaves closed in. However, when they saw their comrades falling all around them, they realized it was surrender or die. A Rebel sergeant began waving his white handkerchief and shouting at the Zouaves to stop firing. When the guns went silent, thirteen Rebels were still alive in the woods. Captain Brownell took them captive and herded them at gunpoint as he and his men began their retreat.

All over the valley, the Union retreat became a rout, then degenerated into a full-scale panic. Yankees, crazed with fear, stampeded up the Warrenton Turnpike toward Centreville. Some who stumbled and fell from exhaustion were picked up and dragged by their fellow soldiers. The best McDowell could do was attempt to cover the hasty withdrawal against enemy pursuit. He sent a battalion of hard-bitten Regular Army infantry to protect the vulnerable rear ranks of the fleeing Yankees.

General Pierre G.T. Beauregard sent one unit after another in pursuit of the enemy. Hundreds of Yankees were collapsing. Having thrown down their guns, they were quickly taken captive by the shouting, whooping Rebels.

While several of his units were chasing Union troops across Young's Branch, General Beauregard heard a rumor that there were Yankee units heading southeastward for Union Mills. Fearing they might regroup and try another attack, he sent the bulk of his troops toward Union Mills. By the time they returned to tell him it was a false alarm, the Union troops heading north were out of sight. Beauregard looked at his weary, bedraggled men and decided they were too exhausted to chase the Yankees. He officially called off the pursuit shortly after seven o'clock. Heavy clouds were now filling the sky, and daylight was beginning to fade.

Beauregard collected his troops on the banks of Bull Run just south of Stone Bridge to congratulate them on their hard-fought victory and to check on the wounded. They would bury the dead tomorrow.

As the Rebels were patting each other on the back and joyfully kidding General Jackson about his new nickname, a soldier rushed up to Beauregard and said, "Sir, I don't know where it came from, but there's a Union wagon sneakin' across the bridge."

Beauregard looked toward the bridge, squinting against the gathering gloom. "Well, look at that, will you? There's a straggling Yankee ammunition wagon. We can't let that get away."

The general had noticed only moments earlier that a howitzer stood close by. Running his gaze over the multitude of dirty faces, he asked, "Who's cannon is this?"

Colonel Bertrand Waverly of the Palmetto Guard moved forward and said, "It's ours, sir. And it's loaded."

Looking back at the Union wagon, moving slowly across the bridge, Beauregard said, "Looks like they're overloaded, Colonel. Blast the stinking blue-bellies."

Waverly motioned to a wrinkle-faced man in Palmetto uniform. As the old man responded, threading his way amongst the Rebel soldiers, Waverly turned back to Beauregard and said, "Sir, you remember who fired the first shot at Fort Sumter, don't you?"

"Certainly. Who could forget Edmund Ruffin?"

"Well, sir, he's here. Since he fired the first shot at Sumter, how about letting him fire the last shot at the Battle of Bull Run?"

Beauregard made a sweeping motion toward the howitzer and said, "Quite fitting, I would say."

Seconds later, as the Union wagon was just about to leave Stone Bridge, Edmund Ruffin—his long, silver hair dangling on his shoulders—fired off the cannon. The shell struck the wagon dead-center. There was a horrendous explosion, followed by a series of others as the wagon became a huge ball of fire, killing team and crew. The Rebels lifted a rousing cheer for Ruffin's accuracy.

Darkness fell with the smell of rain in the air, and the Bull Run battle was over.

* * * * *

Driving in haste, most of the civilian spectators arrived back in Washington before dark. They were in a state of shock over the Union defeat, but thankful that the blood-hungry Confederates had not followed them.

Jenny alighted from Rose's surrey and headed up the walk toward the house. She glanced at the sky. Black, ominous clouds told her a storm was on the way. Biting her lip, she entered the unoccupied house, aware that her father was still at the Capitol. Because she did not know if the man she loved was dead or alive, she sank onto a parlor chair and wept.

Patricia Winters was in a terrible mental state when she and the Lincoln boys arrived at the White House. Anguish registered all the way to her marrow as they alighted from the carriage and crossed the portico. She dreaded having to face Mrs. Lincoln. She had no choice but to confess that her negligence at the battle site could have gotten young Tad killed. If she was fired from her job, it would be only just.

The maid met them at the door, and Patricia asked how Mrs. Lincoln was. Upon learning that she was better and was sitting up in a chair in her bedroom, the governess hastened through the mansion, taking Willie and Tad with her.

When they entered the room, Mary opened her arms to the boys and embraced them. The president had already sent a message to his wife, informing her of the Union defeat at Bull Run, and she was happy to see that her sons were unharmed.

While Mrs. Lincoln clung to the boys, Patricia admitted her mistake in taking the boys to the battle site, then told the story of her negligence and Tad's brush with death. She gave full credit to Jenny Jordan for saving Tad's life at the risk of her own. The governess asked Mrs. Lincoln to forgive her and begged not to be fired.

Leaving her chair, Mary embraced Patricia, telling her she was forgiven and that she still had her job. Willie and Tad jumped for joy, hugged their governess, and thanked their mother for not firing her.

Mary told Patricia she was too good a governess to lose, then said she wanted to tell the president about Jenny Jordan risking her life to save Tad. She was sure Mr. Lincoln would want to thank Jenny for her heroic and unselfish deed. But that would have to wait. His mind was wrapped up in the rout at Bull Run. He had been at the Capitol all day and had sent word that he would be there all night.

Mrs. Lincoln would decide when to tell her husband about Jenny's deed. In the meantime, she would send a note to Jenny, expressing her appreciation. She then gave Tad a good scolding for his part in the near-tragedy.

On a dreary Monday morning, July 22, 1861, a light but steady rain was falling on Washington. Down-hearted citizens were at their windows and on their porches to view the beleaguered Union troops as they moved without any semblance of order up Pennsylvania Avenue toward the Capitol. They were covered with mud, soaked through with rain, and inching their way along the street.

The line of wagons, riders, and groping foot-soldiers was strung out for over ten miles. Observers along the avenue could not believe the change that had come over their army since they had seen them marching along the same thoroughfare on Saturday. Then there had been a look of confidence on their faces as flags waved and bands played. Now there were no bands. There wasn't a flag but that clung, limp and ashamed, to its staff. The look of confidence had been replaced with consternation, uncertainty, helplessness, and disappointment. Fearfully worn, they were hungry, thirsty, and haggard.

One frustrated male citizen shouted at the soldiers, "Bull Run was *your* work! If you were one-tenth the men we thought you were, this wouldn't have happened!"

Others—men and women—joined with him, casting the shameful defeat in their teeth. Not one soldier even glanced at them. Other Washingtonians brought food and hot coffee from their homes and shops, showing compassion for their whipped army. When the soldiers received the refreshment with weak smiles and faint words of appreciation, many of their benefactors wept.

It was a bitter, bitter hour for the United States. The vaunted Union thought to be so strong, so impregnable, seemed crushed beyond repair.

By midmorning, the last of the dispirited soldiers joined their comrades in front of the Capitol. General McDowell moved among them, speaking words of comfort and encouragement. President Lincoln appeared on the Capitol steps, along with his Cabinet, the Senate Military Committee, and General Winfield Scott. Each man carried his own umbrella, except for the president. His secretary, John Hay, held the umbrella that protected him from the rain.

High up in the Capitol, Jenny observed the heartrending scene from a rain-splattered window near her desk. The sky seemed to be weeping along with the Washingtonians. The steady rain made it impossible for Lincoln to speak to the soldiers, but he lifted a hand and smiled to show he had not lost faith in them.

The president called for an aide and told him to carry a message to General McDowell, who had remained among his downtrodden men. The general was to send the troops on to their camps. Clara Barton was overseeing makeshift tent hospitals at each camp to care for the wounded. Lincoln wanted to meet with McDowell and his division leaders in the Senate Military Committee chambers at eleven A.M.

While Jenny studied the throng of drenched, muddy soldiers, Lola Morrow—a part-time file clerk at the U.S. Patent Office—drew up beside her. Jenny glanced at her, then focused once again on the scene below.

"Seen any Zouaves?" asked Lola, knowing what was on Jenny's mind.

"Just caught a glimpse of some. They're hard to distinguish from the others because they're all so mud-caked." Pointing with a forefinger, she showed Lola a patch of dirty-red and said, "Right down there. See them?"

"Mm-hmm. Are you going down?"

Jenny turned and set weary, sleepless eyes on Lola. "I have to. I'm so afraid, Lola...afraid that those Zouaves will tell me Buck was killed yesterday."

"I understand, honey. You stay here. I'll go down and see what I can find out."

"No! I have to go down myself. Thank you, but this is something I can't shirk off on you or anyone else. If...if Buck is dead, I want to hear it from his men."

"All right. But I'll go with you."

"Thank you," Jenny said, gripping Lola's hand.

The scattered units were attempting to cluster together for their short journey to the camps. Jenny and Lola reached the street and threaded their way amongst them toward the rain-drenched Zouaves.

A young Zouave sergeant blinked against the rain, moved up to them, and said, "May I help you, ladies?"

"I hope so," half-choked Jenny, the rain dripping off her nose. "I'm...looking for Captain Buck Brownell. Is he—?"

"He's somewhere over that way, ma'am," replied the sergeant, pointing, "talking to our commander, Colonel Keyes. If you'd like, I'll go tell the captain you're looking for him."

"I don't want to bother him if he's busy," said Jenny, feeling a wave of relief wash over her. Buck was alive and apparently unscathed. She silently breathed a prayer of thanks.

"I assume the captain knows you well, ma'am?"

"Yes. Quite well," Jenny said, brushing rain from her face.

"You stay here. I'll be right back." He started to turn away, then asked, "May I tell him your name, ma'am?"

"Just tell him it's Jenny."

"Be back in a minute," he said, and was gone.

Lola took hold of Jenny's hand. "He's alive, honey. I'm glad for you."

Squeezing hard on Lola's fingers, Jenny said with trembling lips, "Yes! Thank the Lord, he's alive."

Lola looked around to see if anyone was within earshot. Deciding the rumble of voices and the patter of the rain would keep their conversation private, she said, "Jenny, I guess we don't dare hope that this whipping our Rebels gave the Yankees will be enough to bring the war to a halt."

"I don't think so. From what I hear around the Senate chamber, Mr. Lincoln is going to regroup and go after the Rebels again."

"Well, for your sake, I wish it was over. You and Buck deserve to be together."

There was a note of despair in Jenny's voice. "Lola, I love Buck with all my heart, but...how can we ever have a life together even if he lives through this war? Buck's love would turn to bitter hatred the moment he learned my father and I were spying for the South."

"Not if it's the real thing," Lola said calmly.

"Even true love has it's limits," Jenny said with a quiver in her voice. "There would be no way I could conceal from Buck what Daddy and I had been. And once he found out, he'd—" Jenny's words were cut off as she spotted the young sergeant coming with the rain-soaked captain beside him.

Buck's eyes met Jenny's, and he dashed toward her. Jenny breathed his name and met him, weeping. "Oh, darling," she cried. "I'm so glad you're all right!" They locked in a tight embrace and their lips blended in an urgent kiss.

Holding her close, Buck breathed into her ear, "I thought of you all during the battle, Jenny. Hoping...praying that I could live to hold you in my arms again."

"Oh, Buck, I wish Mr. Lincoln would call the war to a halt. Just...just let the Southerners have their own states and live life the way they want. He's going to pull the army together and invade the South again. I just know it."

Keeping her in a tight embrace, Buck said, "I'm sure the war's far from over, honey. We got royally whipped out there, but I know our president and military leaders are not about to quit. But...when this thing *is* finally over, I want us to be together."

Lola was standing close enough to hear. When Jenny did not reply to Buck's words, Lola understood why. Butting in, she said, "Jenny, you haven't introduced me to your handsome fella."

Buck smiled at Lola as Jenny eased back in his arms and said, "Darling, this is my good friend, Lola Morrow. Lola works in the Patent Office."

Lola extended her hand, and Buck let go of Jenny to shake it. "Happy to meet you, Miss—it is Miss Morrow?"

"Yes," sighed Lola. "Much to my dismay, I still haven't found a handsome, dashing man to marry."

Buck was hoping Jenny would say something like, "Well, Lola, you can't have this one. He's all mine." But the words did not come.

Lola sensed Buck's thoughts, and feeling the awkwardness of the moment, saved it by saying, "Captain, I think you should know something that Jenny did yesterday."

Before Jenny could stop her, Lola was telling Buck the story of her daring rescue of Tad Lincoln. When she finished, Buck squeezed Jenny's hand and said, "That was a very brave thing to do."

"I didn't think about it being a brave thing," Jenny said shyly. "I just saw that sweet little boy running for his life...and I knew he wasn't going to make it on his own."

"Does Mr. Lincoln know about it?" queried Buck.

Jenny shrugged. "I don't know."

Buck folded her in his arms once more. "Well, I'm sure when he finds out about it, you'll hear from him."

By this time, women were converging on the weary, battered troops, looking for husbands, sons, and sweethearts. There were tears of joy upon finding men alive...and tears of sorrow upon learning that the bodies of their loved ones were lying in the fields and on the hills surrounding Manassas Junction. Some women were offered hope when it could not be verified that their men were dead. Hundreds of Yankees had been taken as prisoners of war.

Buck was still holding Jenny in his arms when a Zouave corporal told him Colonel Duryee was about to be moved to the Zouave camp in an ambulance and wanted Buck to accompany him. Reluctantly Buck kissed Jenny good-bye, then left to rejoin his commander. His heart ached. Somehow he would show Lieutenant Colonel Jeffrey Jordan he was worthy to take Jenny for his wife.

At eleven o'clock, President Lincoln held his meeting in the Senate chambers. He did not upbraid General McDowell and the other officers present for losing the battle, but shared his conviction that Confederate spies had gained access to classified information and carried it to Lee and Beauregard. There was no other way they could have been so well prepared. McDowell and the other officers agreed.

After three hours of discussion, Lincoln adjourned the meeting, asking Generals Scott and McDowell to remain. In private, the president told the generals the leak had to be right there in the Capitol where the classified information was passed out and kept. He was going to hire Allan Pinkerton and his detective agency to ferret out the spy or spies. Lincoln wanted that information kept between himself and the two generals, and Scott and McDowell assured him they would keep his secret. They wanted the guilty party caught and executed as soon as possible.

Lincoln emerged from the meeting room and found John Hay

chatting with Senator Charles Sumner of Massachusetts. Stepping away from the senator, Hay approached Lincoln and said, "Mr. President, I have three letters that you need to sign so I can post them...and Senator Sumner wants to see you for a moment."

Lincoln nodded, then looked at Sumner and said, "I'm headed for a meeting at the White House, Senator. What can I do for you?"

"I have an appointment to keep myself, sir," Sumner replied, extending an envelope. "I'd like for you to take this. It's a letter from me pertaining to a valiant and brave thing I saw a young woman do at Bull Run when our troops were fleeing from the Confederates. You no doubt already know of the incident, since it involves your son, but I wanted to make an official statement about it. I believe her deed is worthy of a presidential commendation."

Lincoln's heavy brows arched. "My son? I—"

"Mr. President!" cut in Senator Henry Wilson, chairman of the Senate Military Committee, hurrying down the hallway, "I need to see you before you go to the White House. It's very important!"

Lincoln looked toward Wilson, then back to Sumner. Accepting the envelope, he said, "I'll give it my attention later, Senator. Thank you."

Sumner nodded, smiled, and walked away. Lincoln shoved Sumner's envelope into his valise, then followed his secretary to a desk and sat down to sign the letters. Senator Wilson waited patiently for his moment with the chief executive.

Forty minutes later, Lincoln was in a private meeting in the Oval Office with Allan Pinkerton. The famous detective assured the president that his agency would catch the spy or spies. His plan was to have the president secretly hire a Pinkerton agent to be John F. Calhoun's assistant. The agent would go by the name of Chester White. Working in Calhoun's office, White would be in a perfect position to observe clerical workers and members of the Senate Military Committee.

Lincoln was optimistic of success and happy to know that White would report for work the next morning.

On Wednesday, July 24, President Lincoln had a private meeting in the Oval Office with his general-in-chief, seventy-five-year-old Winfield Scott, to discuss the shameful defeat at Bull Run. The shattered Federal army had to be pieced back together as quickly as possible. Both men agreed that it must be done under a new field commander. Though the loss could not be blamed on General McDowell, it happened under his command; the men had lost faith in him. It would take fresh blood to raise the troops' morale and make them ready for war again. Lincoln was adamant that it be done quickly. The Secessionists *must* be punished for breaking federal law and forsaking the Union.

General Scott suggested to Lincoln that General George B. McClellan, who did a brilliant job in leading the Union to victory at Rich Mountain, be appointed in McDowell's place. The president was favorable to the suggestion. He ordered Scott to relieve McDowell of his command immediately and to appoint McClellan field commander of the Union forces at Washington.

On Friday morning, Lincoln, looking weary and haggard, returned to the Oval Office at ten-thirty. He had been in a meeting with Generals Scott and McClellan, along with the Senate Military Committee, since seven o'clock, discussing the next military moves to be made against the Confederacy. Before another major battle could be fought, the Union would have to establish military strongholds in several key places across the Potomac in Virginia. Lincoln left it to the Committee, Jeffrey Jordan, and Generals Scott and McClellan to plan the offensive moves.

As the chief executive sank into the chair behind his desk, John Hay entered through a side door, carrying some papers. Lincoln rubbed his eyes and massaged his temples as he said, "Good morning, John."

Taking a seat in front of the desk, Hay responded, "Good morning, Mr. President. Are you all right?"

Easing back in the chair, Lincoln said softly, "Just tired, John. I have hardly slept since Sunday. Haven't seen my boys since last Friday, I think, and I've barely had a word with Mrs. Lincoln." Rubbing his eyes again, and blinking, he looked at the papers his secretary held in his hands. "Something important?"

"Yes, sir. I wouldn't bother you at this time if it wasn't. I have two letters, here. One from Major I.N. Palmer of the Union Cavalry, and the other from Colonel Abram Duryee of the Fifth New York Zouaves. Both have written concerning Captain Buck Brownell."

The president's face relaxed and a smile tugged at the corners of his mouth. "Ah, yes. Brownell. The man who shot Colonel Ellsworth's killer. Fine man. What about him?"

"Well, sir, everything else in this morning's mail I have either already taken care of or passed on to someone else to handle. However, these two letters demand your personal attention." As he spoke, Hay laid the letters in front of Lincoln.

The weary president donned a pair of half-moon spectacles and began to read the letter from Major Palmer. The major told how Buck Brownell had rescued him from under his fallen horse while cannon shells were exploding all around. Palmer felt the young Zouave officer deserved a presidential commendation for his bravery, and he also suggested that Brownell be promoted to the rank of major.

Smiling as he laid aside the first letter, Lincoln took up the second. Colonel Duryee explained in his letter how Captain Brownell had taken charge of the Zouave regiment when Duryee was shot and put out of commission. Brownell had led the regiment gallantly and had taken an impressive toll on the enemy. He had also captured thirteen Rebels, which were now incarcerated at one of the Union army camps. Duryee had been in conversation with Major Palmer and was aware that Palmer was suggesting Brownell be promoted to major. Duryee felt that since Brownell had performed so well in the battle, taking the place of a colonel, he should be promoted to that rank.

As the president laid the letter down, Hay said, "Some kind of soldier, this Buck Brownell."

"That he is," nodded Lincoln. "And I'm going to take Colonel Duryee's suggestion. We're going to need sharp young colonels like Buck Brownell in the battles ahead."

CHAPTER TWENTY-ONE

✦

On Monday, July 29, Buck Brownell was cleaning and oiling his revolver in his private tent when a corporal stuck his head past the flap and said, "Captain, sir. General Scott would like to see you at his tent in ten minutes."

Rising from the cot he was sitting on, Buck smiled, "Tell him I'll be there."

Buck wiped the excess oil from his gun, loaded it, and slipped it in his holster. After checking himself over and wiping dust from his boots, he stepped into the stark sunlight and headed down the long row of canvas shelters toward the general's tent. As he drew near, he noticed several officers gathered with General Scott, including Major I.N. Palmer.

The officers greeted Brownell warmly, then General Scott said, "Captain, I have been instructed by the president to make a presentation to you on his behalf, in the presence of these men. Colonel Duryee expressed his desire to be here for this occasion, but as you know, he is currently laid up."

"Yes, sir," nodded Brownell, running his curious gaze over the smiling faces of the officers.

Scott then explained to Brownell that the president had received letters from Major Palmer and Colonel Duryee recommending a presidential commendation for the courage he displayed on the Bull Run battlefield and recommending a promotion in rank. While the men applauded, Scott handed Brownell an official-looking paper. The formal commendation was written on White House stationery and signed by the president.

Scott then said, "Captain Brownell, it is my honor as general-in-chief to advise you that you have been promoted to the rank of colonel."

The officers—who also included newly appointed field commander, General George B. McClellan—applauded and voiced their approval.

Scott handed an overwhelmed Brownell a pair of colonel's insignias to go on his uniform, shook his hand, and said in a lusty tone, "Congratulations, Colonel Brownell!"

After each officer had shaken the new colonel's hand, General Scott informed Buck that he was being assigned to do special training of the troops in all the camps around Washington. It would be Brownell's job to help lift the spirits of the men during the training sessions and get them ready to do battle with the Confederate army.

Late that afternoon, after a particularly strenuous training session with the troops at the main camp, Colonel Brownell bathed in a nearby creek. He had finished dressing and was combing his hair before a crude mirror in his tent when a voice called from outside, "Colonel Brownell."

"Yes?" he replied, moving to the flap and pulling it open. He recognized one of the sentries.

"Excuse me, sir, but there's a young lady at the gate who is asking to see you. I told her you were about to go to supper. She said it would only take a minute or two."

Grinning, Buck asked, "Is this young lady devastatingly beautiful, with hair like midnight and sparkling dark-brown eyes?"

"I'd say that's a pretty good description of her, sir," chuckled the sentry.

"Well," sighed Buck, reaching for his hat, "I'd gladly miss supper for a minute or two with her!"

Moments later, Buck approached the gate to see a smiling Jenny waiting beside her horse. Moving past the sentries, he took both of her hands in his and asked, "To what do I owe this pleasure, lovely lady?"

Jenny eyed the colonel's insignias on his shoulders and collar and replied, "I heard about your promotion."

"Now, how'd you hear about that?" he asked, smiling broadly.

"I'll never tell," she giggled. "I...ah...just have some friends in high places, and they keep me informed about such things." She paused, then added, "I wanted to come out and congratulate you. I think it's wonderful."

Buck folded her in his arms. "Thank you, Jenny. Do you suppose maybe my being made a colonel will put me in a different light with your father? I mean...am I now high enough on the social scale that he might give his consent for me to marry his daughter?"

Buck felt Jenny tense up. "I...I don't know what will go through Daddy's mind when I tell him. I hope he'll be pleased. But...since there's still a war on...and your a soldier—"

Buck drew his lips into a thin line. "I guess it's just wait until the war's over, huh?"

There was a lump in Jenny's throat. When the war was over, what then? How would Buck feel toward her when he found out both she and her father had been enemy spies? All she could say was, "I hate this war."

Buck ignored the watching sentries and planted a brief kiss on Jenny's lips. "Okay, I'll wait. War time is a bad time to start a marriage, anyhow."

Jenny was fighting tears as she told Buck she must head for home and prepare supper for her father. He helped her into the saddle, and told her he loved her.

"I love you, too, Buck," she said softly, and put the horse to a trot.

Jenny looked over her shoulder twice before the camp passed from view. Both times, Buck was standing where she had left him, watching. Tears wet her cheeks as she aimed her horse toward Washington. Her heart was torn asunder. Her attachment to the South stood between her and Buck, and threatened to keep them from each other.

Her father was the very center of a Confederate spy ring, and she must protect him at all costs. She must never be in a position where one slip of the tongue to Buck could expose Jeffrey Jordan. And now, since the war would go on, Jenny would be called upon by Rose Greenhow to carry messages to Confederate military leaders.

If Jenny gave in and told Buck that one day she would marry him, she would be living a lie. She had no doubt he would despise her the day he found out she had deceived him. *Whenever* he found out about it—now or after the war was over—what Buck felt toward her would die. To give him hope for the future would be inexcusable. There was no way she could do it. Even now she was eaten up with guilt that she had allowed the relationship between them to develop thus far.

In the weeks that followed, there were no major battles between the North and South. There were skirmishes and minor battles, however, along the Potomac as the Union attempted to establish military strongholds just across the river in Virginia. Each attempt was met with failure; the Confederates knew the Federal plans ahead of time and were there to meet them with sufficient fire power.

This was a direct result of classified information being pipelined from John Calhoun and Jeffrey Jordan to Rose Greenhow, then carried to the Confederates by Rose's girls. Rose had not yet pressured Jenny to carry messages for fear that Buck might be involved in one of the skirmishes and be killed.

On Tuesday, August 13, John Hay ushered Allan Pinkerton into the Oval Office. President Lincoln rose from his desk, shook the detective's hand, and said to Hay, "John, I do not want to be disturbed. When Mr. Pinkerton and I are finished, I will advise you."

"Yes, sir," nodded Hay, moving through the door and closing it behind him.

Lincoln sat behind his desk and the beefy man settled into a chair in front of him. "So you have something important to tell me?" said Lincoln.

"Yes, sir," said Pinkerton, wiping a hand across his heavy mustache. "I don't have enough evidence to make an arrest yet, but we're on the trail of your spies."

"*Spies*...plural?"

"Yes. Two at this point, and you're going to be shocked at one of them. There are others involved, but all I have for you right now are two names—John Calhoun and Jeffrey Jordan."

Deep lines etched themselves in the president's brow and there was horrified amazement in his eyes. "Jordan! Why, it can't be!"

"I'm afraid it is, sir. The man we're calling Chester White began to pick up on subversive things going on between Calhoun and Jordan. When he overheard them plan a meeting in the office after hours, White hid in the closet. Thinking they were alone, Calhoun and Jordan discussed how their spy work had contributed to the Confederate victory at Bull Run."

Lincoln looked ill. His face was rigid and grim. "When was this?"

"Friday night. I didn't come to you when White told me about it Saturday because I wanted him to work another day. Yesterday White overheard Calhoun and Jordan talking about a woman who was helping them in their espionage, but they only said 'she.' No name. Apparently they're still at it. That's why your army is having such stiff opposition along the Potomac every time they try to set up an installation. The Rebs know they're coming before they get there. Like I said, there's not enough evidence to make an arrest yet, but once we can get our hands on something on paper, we'll move in. I knew you'd want to be filled in on at least this much, though."

"Yes," Lincoln nodded, staring vacantly. Then focusing on Pinkerton, he said, "I just can't believe it. Calhoun is shock enough, but Jordan. *Jordan*. I even questioned him about his loyalties before I made him military adviser. He convinced me his allegiance was to the Union." Tugging at his beard, he added, "I guess you can never know a person for sure, can you?"

"Well, at least not in every case, sir."

"Tell your man to keep a close watch on them. I want concrete evidence as soon as possible. Once we get it, Jordan, Calhoun, and the woman—whoever she is—will face a firing squad."

"I have an idea more people are in on it with them. Seems like they'd need more than just one woman to carry those messages past our lines. For sure Calhoun and Jordan aren't involved in that part of it."

"Whoever is involved, we've got to root out every last treacherous one of them."

Pinkerton lifted his bulk off the chair. "You can count on it, Mr. President. I'll be in touch."

On Thursday morning, Jeffrey Jordan entered the kitchen with his mouth watering. The sweet aroma of bacon and eggs had filled the house and stimulated his appetite. Jenny was at the stove with her back to him, filling his plate from a steaming skillet.

"Good morning," he said cheerfully, taking his place at the table. "What's Daddy's little girl going to do on her day off today?"

There was a hot cup of coffee at his place-setting. Lifting the cup to his lips, he blew on it and took a sip. Then he noticed there was no place-setting for Jenny and that she had not responded to his greeting. He looked her direction just as she turned with the plate of hot food in her hands. Her eyes were red and swollen.

Jordan frowned as his daughter set the plate before him. "What is it, honey? Aren't you going to eat any breakfast?"

"I'm not hungry, Daddy," she said softly, her voice quavering.

He took hold of her hand. "Jenny, what is it?"

Tears began to spill down her cheeks and her lower lip trembled.

Pushing his chair back and rising to his feet, Jordan cupped Jenny's face in his hands, looked deep into her tear-filled eyes, and said, "It's Buck, isn't it?"

Sniffing, she nodded.

"You told me you saw him Monday. Have you seen him again?"

"No, but I'd spend every day of my life with him if I could. Oh, Daddy, I love him so much!"

As she spoke, Jenny broke into uncontrollable sobs. Jordan took her into his arms and held her close, saying nothing for a long moment. When her sobbing subsided, she clung to him and drew tiny shuddering breaths. Finally, he said, "Honey, I've thought a lot about this situation. I...I can't put reins on your heart and tell you who you can or cannot love. Buck loves you as much as you love him, doesn't he?"

"Yes," she said, sniffling. "He wants me to marry him. When the war is over, I mean."

"And that's what you want, isn't it? To marry Buck?"

"Yes. More than anything in all the world, that's what I want."

Looking deep into her eyes, Jordan said, "Jenny, I'm sorry. I was wrong to stand between you and Buck. I didn't want you to fall in love with a soldier because I didn't want you to have your heart torn out if he got killed. But...what I did was wrong. Please forgive me for overstepping my bounds."

Jenny stood on her tiptoes, kissed her father's cheek, then hugged him tight. "There's really nothing to forgive, Daddy. You meant well. You were, in your own way, trying to protect me, and I love you for that." She sniffed, then said, "I didn't tell you what Buck said when I went out to the camp to congratulate him on his promotion. He asked if maybe you would look at him in a different light now that he is a colonel...if he might be high enough on the social scale that you would consent to his marrying your daughter."

Jordan was quiet for a moment, then said, "I did understand you correctly—that Buck wouldn't want the two of you to be married until after the war is over?"

"Yes. We both know that would be best."

"Good. Then this North and South thing won't be a point of contention. It'll be a thing of the past."

A sick feeling washed over Jenny. There was still the spy situation. She was living a lie before Buck, and the awful dread of the moment he learned of it was haunting her. It would help if she could talk to her father about it, but that would have to wait. He was due at the Capitol shortly. At least he had put his blessing on her marrying Buck when the war was over. She breathed a prayer of thanks for that.

Easing back in her father's arms, Jenny said, "Well, Lieutenant Colonel Jeffrey Jordan, you'd better eat your breakfast before it gets cold."

Kissing her forehead, he said, "You're right. I'll have to hustle. The Committee is meeting with Lincoln at seven-thirty."

Ten minutes later, Jordan donned his hat and headed for the front door with his valise in hand. Jenny was at the door and pulled it open, warming him with a smile. "Now, that's more like it," he said. "I'm glad to see that smile again."

"I love you, Daddy," she said, tiptoeing to kiss his cheek.

"I love you, too, sweetheart." He kissed her forehead again, and was gone.

At nine-thirty that morning, Pinkerton detective Chester White was at his desk across the room from John Calhoun when the sound of male voices came through the open office door, echoing down the hallway.

White glanced at Calhoun. "Sounds like the Committee meeting is over."

"I'm surprised," remarked Calhoun. "I figured it'd go on all morning."

Seconds later, Jeffrey Jordan appeared at the door, glanced at White, then said to Calhoun, "John, I need to talk to you in private for a moment."

White rose to his feet. "I can leave, if you wish," he said politely.

"That won't be necessary," spoke up Calhoun, pushing his chair back and standing up. "The colonel and I can take a little walk and have our talk. By the way, Colonel, have you met our newest employee?"

"Haven't had the pleasure," smiled Jordan.

Calhoun introduced the two men, then leaving White in the office, walked with Jordan down the hall. Neither man was aware that the new "employee" was at the office door, watching them.

When they were out of earshot from everyone else, Jordan pulled a slip of paper from his pocket. Looking around to make sure none of the senators milling about in the hall were looking, he handed it to Calhoun and said, "Get this to Rose right away. McClellan is sending cavalry out of Porter's brigade across the Potomac due west of Hagerstown. Once Hagerstown is secure, they'll send in the infantry to hold it. All the details are on that paper."

Slipping the paper into the pocket of his suit coat, Calhoun said, "Rose will have it within the hour."

"Good. I've got to get back to the meeting room. We're only on a fifteen-minute break. Additional plans for Union aggression will be made in our next session. I'll probably have more for you to send to Rose before the morning's over."

"If you do, I'll have Lola take it to Rose. I'll tell Chester I've got an errand to run, and carry this one to Rose, myself, right now."

"Good."

Jenny was mopping the kitchen floor when she heard the knock at the front door. Placing the mop in the bucket of hot soapy water and leaning the handle against the cupboard, she hurried to open the door.

Rose O'Neal Greenhow smiled and said, "Hello, Jenny. May I come in?"

"Of course," Jenny nodded, noticing Rose's carriage and driver on the street.

Closing the door, Jenny followed the socialite to the dining room. Halting at the table, Rose asked, "Can we sit down? I have something very urgent and important to discuss with you."

"Certainly." Jenny pulled a chair out for Rose to sit on.

Rose sat down and pulled Jeffrey Jordan's paper from her purse. Handing it to Jenny, she said, "You'll recognize your father's handwriting. I need you to deliver this to General Stonewall Jackson *today*. My other girls' are becoming a bit too familiar along the Union lines. Read it, then we'll talk about it."

Jenny read it, then set her dark eyes on Rose. "Who will be going with me?"

"No one. I'll have to send you by yourself. Like I said, my other girls are becoming too well-known by the Union sentries. They're willing to take risks, but I thought you wouldn't mind carrying this one because it involves only the cavalry, and Buck wouldn't be in on it."

Jenny swallowed hard. "All right. I'm a little frightened, but...I'll do it. It's my duty."

"Good!" exclaimed Rose. "I knew I could count on you. Now the safest thing is for you to fix your hair in an upsweep, fold this paper as small as you can, and hide it in the folds of your hair. If for some reason you should be searched, they'll never think to look there."

Jenny nodded. "Okay."

"You'll note the circled 'R' in the corner. This will tell General Jackson that the message is genuine."

"And where do I find him?"

"You know the bridge over the Potomac that leads to Fairfax Courthouse?"

"Yes."

"You take Constitution Avenue out of town west. You're in the country for about three miles, then you come to the bridge. There's a Union army camp right there on the river, and they've got sentries on the bridge. Just charm them with your good looks, honey. Tell them you're going to Fairfax Courthouse to visit your sick aunt."

Jenny's mouth tightened. "I hate to lie, Rose."

"No choice. Our soldiers don't like to kill, either, but war's war. Spies have to lie."

Jenny nodded, thinking of how she was living a lie before Buck.

"You go straight west on that same road for about two miles," Rose continued. "You'll find the Rebel camp right there. Just tell them you have a message for General Jackson. When he sees the circled 'R' on this paper, he'll know it's from me. Don't give it to anyone but General Jackson. Understand?"

"Yes."

"All right, honey," said Rose, rising to her feet. "I'll be going. How soon can you ride?"

"It'll take me about a half-hour to fix my hair and change clothes."

"Good. That'll put you in Jackson's camp by three-thirty...maybe a little before."

Chester White watched Jordan and Calhoun move down the hall, but soon they vanished from his view. He had not seen anything pass between them. However, when Calhoun returned to say he was going on an errand, White wondered if he was carrying a message to a partner in the spy ring. The woman they had mentioned, possibly? He wanted to follow Calhoun, but the man had given him some work that required immediate attention. He could not risk detection by failing to have it done when Calhoun returned.

White was working at his desk when Calhoun came back. White looked at the old clock on the wall, noting that it was almost noon. Calhoun had returned to the office at about eleven-fifteen and seemed a bit on edge.

Or is it just my imagination? White asked himself. *He keeps looking toward the wall, like he's expecting someone. Jordan, maybe? Is the colonel gathering information now, in the Committee meeting, that he'll pass on to Calhoun?*

Suddenly the hall was alive with committeemen, and their voices filled the place. "Lunch break, eh, John?" White asked.

Calhoun looked at him. "Yes. They'll take about two hours. Since it's noon, why don't you go on down to the lunch room yourself, Chester?"

"That's all right. You go ahead. I'll eat when you get back."

"I've got some work here that's quite urgent. You go on."

"Okay," sighed White, standing and stretching. "See you in an hour."

Picking up his lunch box, the Pinkerton man moved into the hall and weaved his way among the committeemen who were knotted in small groups and talking excitedly. White went as far as he could down the hall and still keep Calhoun's office door in sight. He casually leaned against the wall as if waiting for someone. It wasn't long before he saw Jeffrey Jordan hasten from the meeting room and enter Calhoun's office.

Calhoun set his anxious gaze on Jordan as he came through the door. "More?" he asked.

"Yes," nodded Jordan, closing the door. "Where's the new man?"

"He just went to lunch."

"Good," said Jordan, sitting down in the chair in front of Calhoun's desk. "Here's an urgent one."

Calhoun looked at the paper in Jordan's hand. "How urgent?"

"Has to be delivered to Rose immediately. The Committee just approved a plan of McClellan's to make a quick move on Virginia at a spot south of Washington where the Potomac and Rappahannock draw close together. McClellan convinced the Committee that that piece of land will be strategic for the Union in the days to come. Those rivers could become quite vital, and he wants the Union to control who sails them."

"So when's this move to take place?"

"At dawn tomorrow."

Calhoun's eyebrows arched. "Whooee! We've got to move fast."

"Real fast."

"Wouldn't look good for me to leave the building again," said Calhoun. "I'll take it down to Lola like I said earlier. She can fake a headache or something and rush it to Rose."

"Perfect," smiled Jordan.

The lieutenant colonel had already disappeared from the hall when Calhoun left his office with the vital paper in his suit coat pocket. He hurried down the broad staircase to the ground floor and made his way down a long hall to the U.S. Patent Office. He approached the receptionist's desk and asked, "Shirley, is Lola busy?"

"She's back at her desk, but I think she's about to head for the lunch room."

"Thanks," he said with a weak smile and moved toward the back room where huge file cabinets lined the walls. He spotted Lola at her desk, talking to another young woman.

Lola saw him, smiled, and gave a little wave. She quickly finished the conversation, and when the other woman walked away, John drew up. Looking around to make sure no one was within earshot, he said in a subdued voice, "I've got an urgent message that must be in Rose's hands immediately. Can you come down with a headache?"

"Strange that you should ask that. It hasn't been more than an hour since I developed one. My supervisor saw me taking some powders and asked if I wasn't feeling well. I told him I had a headache. He's at lunch, so I'll just tell Shirley that the powders didn't help, and I'm going home. She can pass it on to him when he gets back. No problem."

"Good," said Calhoun, pulling the paper from his pocket. "Take it and run."

Both Calhoun and Lola were startled when they heard Chester White's sharp words, "Run where?"

Behind the detective stood Shirley, eyes bulging. White was holding a cocked revolver on the startled pair. "I'll take that paper, John," he said, reaching for it.

"This paper is official government business, Chester. What on earth are you doing with that gun?"

"I'm holding it on you and your accomplice. I want that paper."

"I told you this is official government business!" Calhoun blared, clutching the paper. "You have no right to take it from me."

"Oh, but I do," White chuckled, snatching the paper from Calhoun's fingers. "Tell him, Shirley."

The owl-eyed receptionist moved closer, gulped, and said, "His name is Leonard Mansfield, John. He showed me his credentials. He's a detective with the Allan Pinkerton Agency."

"Pinkerton!" gasped Calhoun. He and Lola exchanged fearful glances.

"The president hired us to ferret out the spies who've been feeding information to the Rebel army," said the detective, shaking the paper at the guilty duo. "And here's all the evidence we need. Shirley, send for the police."

As the receptionist hurried away, bitter bile welled up in John Calhoun's throat. He knew the penalty for being caught as an enemy spy. Lola was white with shock. Fully aware that she would face a Union firing squad, her hands quivered and her knees turned to jelly.

CHAPTER TWENTY-TWO

Just after breakfast on Thursday morning, August 15, Colonel Buck Brownell crossed the grounds of the main Union camp, speaking to soldiers as he went, and drew up to General George McClellan's tent. An adjutant lieutenant stood at the opening, smiled at Brownell, and said, "Good morning, Colonel."

Buck still had not adjusted to his new rank. *Colonel* sounded strange when applied to him. "Good morning," he replied, returning the smile. "I'm here at General McClellan's request."

"Yes, sir, he's expecting you," said the lieutenant, then turned and spoke into the tent, telling McClellan that Colonel Brownell had arrived.

"Send him in," came the general's reply.

McClellan shook Brownell's hand and invited him to sit in front of his desk. The general eased himself onto the straight-backed chair behind his desk and wasted no time getting down to business. "Colonel, I have sought permission from General Scott to transfer you from the Zouaves into the regular army. I might say that he enthusiastically granted the request."

"Yes, sir," nodded Buck, wondering what was coming next.

"You've done a marvelous job in training the men, Colonel," McClellan proceeded, "but I've got a new job for you, which will carry a great deal more responsibility. You will get a change of uniform immediately. I think you'll look good in regular blues." Leaning forward, he said, "To tell you the truth, I've never cared for those gaudy uniforms of the Zouaves. Especially those baggy pants."

"Yes, sir," nodded Brownell. He hadn't cared for the Zouave uniforms, either, but had never voiced it to anyone.

Leaning back again, McClellan said, "With General Scott's consent, I am putting you in charge of the First Brigade of First Division, Colonel. You will replace Colonel Erasmus Keyes. As you know, he was wounded at Bull Run and is getting a medical discharge."

"I didn't know about the discharge, sir. I'm sorry to hear that his career has to end this way."

"Me, too. But since it's happened, I'm glad that I've got a man of your caliber to put in his place. You know, then, that you'll be under the command of General Daniel Tyler, commander of First Division."

"Yes, sir. I've only met General Tyler on a couple of occasions, and I like him very much. We'll get along well together."

"I have no doubt of that. You also know that First Brigade is camped about a mile-and-a-half south of here where the bridge crosses the Potomac just east of Fairfax Courthouse?"

"Yes, sir."

"That bridge is First Brigade's responsibility. Your men know they are to screen any and all civilians who come and go across the bridge. As commander of First Brigade, you must see to it that they never become lax in their screening. We've got spy activity going on, and it must be stopped."

"That's for sure," agreed Brownell. "Aside from what happened at Bull Run, we've had too many experiences of late where we've tried to move into Virginia and found the Rebs waiting for us. Has to be Confederate espionage."

"Well, it's going to come to a halt. One of these days we're going to catch those Rebel spies red-handed. When we execute a few of them, maybe the rest will find something else to do. Anyway...you've been at First Brigade camp, so you know Major Donald Sparks. He's in charge over there at the moment and will be your right-hand man."

"That's fine with me. He and I get along real well."

"You are aware, also, that First Brigade camp has a guard house where Union soldiers on detention from all the camps are confined?"

"Yes, sir, I've seen it. It's a big old barn where compartments have been built to form cells."

"Right. At present, only two or three soldiers are confined there...for drunkenness. I assume, then, you also know about the two sheds where your thirteen Confederate prisoners are being kept."

"Yes, sir."

"Both the incarcerated Union soldiers and the Rebel prisoners are now your responsibility."

"I understand, sir."

"Good," nodded McClellan, reaching into a desk drawer and drawing out a folder. Handing it to Brownell, he said, "Should any of the soldiers in the guard house cause trouble, here's the manual with discipline regulations. Such discipline will be at your discretion within the lines drawn by the Senate Military Committee."

"I'll stick strictly to the book, sir."

"I'm sure you will," grinned McClellan. "Also in the manual are regulations concerning spies. You are to oversee the execution of any spies caught within ten miles either direction on the river from your camp. Study them, Colonel. I have a feeling we're going to catch some Rebel spies at their game."

"Yes, sir. I hope we do. And again...I'll stick strictly to the book."

"All right," said McClellan, rising. "Of course, if you have any questions later, take them to General Tyler. I understand you already have some training sessions lined up for this camp today, so I want you to proceed with them after you get into your new uniform. You can work with the men until late afternoon, then ride on down to your camp. Major Sparks knows to keep an eye on things until you arrive and assume command."

As Buck left McClellan's tent to claim his new uniform, he saw General Tyler riding toward him from the rope corral. As Tyler drew near, he smiled, leaned from the saddle, and extended his hand. "Haven't had the opportunity to congratulate you on the promotion, yet, Brownell," he said as they shook hands. "I'm glad for you. No one deserved it any more than you."

"Thank you, sir," smiled Buck.

"General McClellan told me you're training the men here the rest of the day, then heading for your new post this evening."

"That's right, sir."

"I'm riding into Washington right now. I'll probably be back before you head down river. Maybe we'll have a few minutes to talk about some plans I have in mind for your camp."

"Fine, sir. I'll see you then."

Buck hurried to the supply shack and was given his blue uniform. He took it to his tent and changed clothes. Emerging into the brilliant sunshine, he headed for the spot where the training sessions would take place. He liked his new uniform; it made him look more distinguished than the uniform he wore as a Zouave. He told himself that Jenny would like him in blue, too.

It was almost three o'clock that afternoon when a nervous Jenny Jordan rode along the edge of the Union camp and headed for the bridge that spanned the Potomac. A small group of soldiers huddled at the bridge. Jenny eyed the camp with its long rows of tents and noted the old barn and the two sheds that stood in their midst. She figured there once must have been a farmhouse on the site.

The sun danced on the rippling waters of the Potomac as Jenny approached the bridge. Soldiers who milled about stopped to look at her. She wore her black riding boots, a black split skirt, and a ruffled white blouse. On her head was a small black hat, topping off the upsweep of her thick, dark hair. A sergeant left the group and strode toward her.

Jenny's heart skipped a beat as she drew rein. Struggling to mask her fear, she painted on a warm smile.

"Good afternoon, Miss," said the sergeant, touching his bat brim and smiling in return. "It isn't often we see a young lady traveling alone. Are you a Northerner or a Southerner?"

"Half-and-half," she replied, maintaining the forced smile. "I live in Washington, but I was born in Virginia. I'm on my way to visit an ailing aunt in Fairfax Courthouse."

"You'll be returning yet today, I assume, since you're carrying no luggage."

"That's right, Sergeant. I'm only planning to stay an hour or so."

"Well, ma'am, I hate to detain you, but with all the spy activity of late, you'll have to be searched."

Fear formed and settled in Jenny's stomach. "Searched? Do I look like a spy, Sergeant?"

Scratching at an ear, the sergeant replied, "Well, ma'am, I wouldn't take you for one, but I'm really not sure what a spy looks like. All I know is, somebody's been carrying classified information to the Confederate army. General McClellan has laid down strict orders to search everybody who crosses from the Union to the Confederate side. No exceptions."

Jenny's face blanched. She ran her gaze over the men who stood around and said loudly, "Well, just who is going to make this search, sergeant?"

The sergeant blushed. Shaking his head, he said, "Oh, I'm sorry, ma'am. We have a farmer's wife just over that hill behind you who searches the women for us."

Jenny saw an officer detach himself from the nearby group and move toward her and the sergeant. Running his gaze between the two, he asked, "Is there a problem, here, Wilkins? The lady sounds upset."

"It's my fault, sir," said Wilkins. "I told her she would have to be searched, but I forgot to explain that Mrs. Harrison would do the searching."

Smiling up at Jenny, the officer touched his hat brim and said, "I'm Major Donald Sparks, Miss—"

"Jenny Jordan. My father is Lieutenant Colonel Jeffrey Jordan." Jenny hoped possibly this would spare her the search.

"I've long been an admirer of your father, Miss Jordan," said Sparks. "He made quite a name for himself in the Mexican War. I was pleased when President Lincoln made him military adviser for the Senate Military Committee."

"Thank you, Major," she nodded. "May I be allowed to resume my journey now? As I told the sergeant, I'm on my way to visit my sick aunt in Fairfax Courthouse."

"As soon as Mrs. Harrison searches you, ma'am. I'm sorry for this delay, but I'm under strict orders. Everyone who crosses this bridge must be searched. General McClellan made it clear that there are to be no exceptions."

Jenny had no choice but to submit to the search. If she told them she had changed her mind about visiting her aunt, they would immediately suspect her. If she wheeled her horse and galloped away, she would not get far. There were horses in the camp. They would ride her down. Besides...they knew who she was now. If she ran for it, they would soon have her in custody. She could only hope that the farmer's wife would not think to look in her hair.

The farmer's wife was summoned. Jenny was taken into the old barn, and in a private cell, she allowed Mrs. Harrison to search beneath her skirt and blouse.

When nothing was found there, Mrs. Harrison said, "I'll have to ask you to remove your boots, honey."

When the boots were cleared, the woman asked Jenny to remove her hat. While Mrs. Harrison ran her nimble fingers beneath the brim on the inside of the hat, Jenny felt a trickle of cold sweat run down her back.

Mrs. Harrison smiled and handed the hat back. "Okay, honey, you're cleared. Sorry to put you through this, but you understand."

"Of course," nodded Jenny, inwardly breathing a sigh of relief. "We must do all we can to stop this Confederate espionage."

As Jenny raised the hat to her head, Mrs. Harrison gazed at the thick folds of carefully upswept hair. "Just a minute, Miss Jordan," she said. "I just realized I didn't do as thorough a job as I should have. I'll have to ask you to let your hair down."

Jenny's nerves were suddenly taut and screaming. She was caught.

With shaky hands, she unpinned her hair. When the folded slip of paper fell out, Mrs. Harrison grabbed it. Jenny let out a tiny whine of mounting dread as the woman quickly read it and called for the soldiers.

Sergeant Wilkins and Major Sparks entered the small cubicle to find Jenny with her hair undone and her hands covering her face. She whimpered fearfully as Sparks read the message intended for General Thomas J. Jackson, grunted disgustedly, and handed it to Wilkins to read. Sparks turned to Jenny and said, "If you are really Jeffrey Jordan's daughter, Miss, this is going to bring great shame to him. His own daughter a Confederate spy."

Jenny's heartbeats felt like club blows in her chest. She could hardly breathe. Her mind was racing. Would this lead to her father's capture? What would Buck think of her? Jenny knew the president's edict concerning spies. She would face a firing squad and die without ever knowing the answers to these questions.

Excusing Mrs. Harrison, Major Sparks said, "Young lady, according to Federal law you must be executed within twenty-four hours. Nothing can alter that, but you could at least die with a clear conscience. How about telling me who the other spies are?"

Jenny lifted her tear-stained face and looked Sparks in the eye. She thought not only of her father, but of John Calhoun, Rose Greenhow, and Rose's girls. There was no way she would turn the Yankees on them. Moving her head slowly back and forth, she released a shaky, "Never."

"I thought so," Sparks sighed. "You will be locked in this compartment, ma'am. I'll see that you have water. It's really a shame, you know, for a beautiful young woman like you to have to face a firing squad. I'm sure glad your execution won't be on my shoulders. Our new commander will be here about supper time, and it'll be up to him to set the exact time of your execution."

Sparks and Wilkins left the cubicle and secured the door with a steel bolt. Jenny sat on the small cot in the gloomy cell. The terror that gripped her seemed to steal her breath, which was coming in short, painful gasps. She feared for her father's life, wishing somehow she could let him know she had been caught. Her mind then turned to Buck. Breaking down completely, she buried her face in her hands and sobbed Buck's name.

Jenny's weeping was interrupted by a young soldier who brought her a bucket of water and a tin cup. She said nothing, but stared at him while he set the bucket on a crude table, placed the cup beside it, and moved back to the door. Pausing, he looked at her with compassion and said softly, "I wish Mr. Lincoln hadn't set such a hard-and-fast rule about Rebel spies. It ain't gonna be easy to find men in the camp who will want to be part of the firing squad."

Jenny continued to stare at him, but said nothing.

"Well," the soldier said, "my prayers will be with you, ma'am."

When the steel bolt was shot home and the place was quiet, Jenny clenched her fists and said in a shaky voice, "Lord, You know I've hated living deceitfully before Buck. I didn't want to. I didn't ask for this awful war, and I didn't ask to be a Southerner living in the North. I...I don't want to die, Lord. Please let me live! And please, please don't let Buck hate me! I want to live...and to be his wife. Oh, God, please don't let them kill me!" Jenny broke down again, sobbing.

Word spread quickly through the camp that a Confederate spy had been caught at the bridge, carrying classified military information to General Jackson, and that the spy was a beautiful young woman. Major Sparks had told Mrs. Harrison and Sergeant Wilkins not to tell anyone that the spy was Jeffrey Jordan's daughter. He wanted to keep that kind of information confidential until Colonel Brownell arrived and decided what to do about it.

Some of the men-in-blue gathered around Major Sparks, concerned that they were going to have to execute a woman. Sparks ran his gaze over their faces and said, "Gentlemen, I admit this has me mighty shaky, myself. But this is war. Nobody is forced into becoming a spy. The lady knew what she was doing when she rode in here carrying that message for Jackson. We all know the army regulations about the fate of spies. The responsibility for the execution lies on the shoulders of First Brigade's commander. And I don't mind telling you, I'm glad I'm not in Colonel Brownell's boots. Putting a woman to death—especially one as pretty as she is—will wrench his insides, I'll guarantee you."

"Major," said one of the soldiers, "how will the colonel choose his firing squad?"

"He won't get any volunteers, that's for sure. He'll have to choose them, making it an order."

"Is it true, sir," asked another, "that the execution has to be done within twenty-four hours of the time she was caught?"

"That's right. When the president sanctioned the rule, he meant for the execution to be swift and without mercy. The rule is known far and wide, even in the South. Mr. Lincoln made it so to discourage enemy personnel from becoming spies."

Another soldier spoke up. "Major, I guess if Colonel Brownell chose me for the firing squad and I refused, I'd be in trouble, wouldn't I?"

Every eye was on Sparks as he nodded slowly and said, "You sure would, Corporal. Then you might be facing a firing squad. Not a man of us would volunteer to kill this woman, but the law says it must be done. Some kind of welcome for our new commander, eh?"

Inside the large shed adjacent to the barn, nine of the thirteen Confederate prisoners were making plans to escape. They had been working on a plan previously, but when they heard about the female spy who was to be executed within twenty-four hours, they accelerated those plans. When supper was brought to them, they would overpower the guards, seize their weapons, and take them as hostages. They would demand the release of their four comrades in the other shed, and the release of the woman spy.

They would then head deep into Rebel country, taking the woman and the guards with them. The Yankees would be warned that if they pursued them, the guards would die. If there was no pursuit, the guards would be held as prisoners of war.

As the sun was lowering toward the western horizon, Buck Brownell saddled his horse for the ride down the river bank to his new command. From the corner of his eye, he saw General McClellan coming his way. Grinning to himself, he made as if he was having trouble with the cinch.

Drawing up, McClellan frowned and asked, "Got a problem, Colonel?"

"Yes, sir. It's this weird saddle. Whoever designed it must've been half-asleep at the time."

The general's brows knitted together and his mouth pulled tight. "I'll have you know, Colonel, I designed that saddle!"

Feigning ignorance, Buck said, "Oh, no! Is that why they call it a McClellan saddle, sir?"

The general saw that Buck was joshing him. He broke into a hearty laugh and said, "You just about had yourself a court-martial!"

The two officers laughed together, then McClellan said, "I want to thank you for a job well-done, Colonel. You've really sharpened up the troops with your training. Next time they face the Rebels, they'll be ready for them."

As the general spoke, he looked past Buck to see General Tyler riding in, accompanied by a pair of adjutant lieutenants. Spotting McClellan and Brownell, Tyler excused the lieutenants and beelined for them. "Gentleman, I've got some mighty good news!"

As Tyler was dismounting, McClellan said, "I'm sure we can use some of that kind of news, General. What is it?"

"Unbeknownst to everyone except Generals Scott and McDowell, the president hired Allan Pinkerton and his agency to hunt down the Rebel spies he suspected were working within the Capitol. It paid off. Three Rebel spies were caught and arrested today. One of them was a genuine shock to Mr. Lincoln."

"Someone in high places?" queried McClellan.

Tyler hitched up his pants by the belt. "You might say that. Lieutenant Colonel Jeffrey Jordan."

The name hit Buck Brownell like the kick of a mule. His scalp tingled, and his mouth went dry. "*Jordan?*" The word left his lips before he was aware he had spoken it. "*Jeffrey Jordan?*"

"I'm afraid so," said Tyler. "You sound like you might know him personally."

"I do, sir. It...it just doesn't seem possible. Jeffrey Jordan a Rebel spy. This is going to hit his daughter awfully hard."

"Who were the other ones?" asked McClellan.

"John Calhoun, a clerical worker in the Senate Chamber, and a woman named Lola Morrow who is employed in the U.S. Patent Office. Or I should say *was* employed there."

"How'd they catch them?"

"Lincoln hired a Pinkerton detective to work undercover as assistant to Calhoun. He saw Calhoun acting suspicious with Jordan, whom we all know was military adviser to the Committee. Following his suspicions, the detective caught Calhoun passing a slip of paper to the Morrow woman and confiscated it at gunpoint. It was a message to Confederate military leaders, divulging classified information about an upcoming Union move on Rebel territory. The handwriting was Jordan's."

Buck was feeling sick all over for Jenny.

"So," proceeded Tyler, "the three of them are to die the moment the sun goes down. General Scott is overseeing the execution, and he told me that Pinkerton says there are definitely more spies in the ring...but all three refuse to name them."

Buck's mind was racing. He wanted to be by Jenny's side, though it was too late to get to her before the execution. What an awful thing for her to have to endure alone.

Looking at his superior officers, Buck said, "General McClellan...General Tyler...I need to ask something of you. I said a moment ago that I know Jordan. Actually, I know his daughter better. The fact is, I'm in love with her, and she feels the same way about me. This has to be an awful ordeal for her. I would like permission to ride into Washington immediately and be there to comfort her."

Tyler looked at McClellan. The field commander shook his head. "I'm sorry, Colonel, but you must be at your post down river as scheduled. For the young lady's sake, I wish I could let you go, but you are in charge of the camp down there, and you must go immediately."

"Yes, sir," Buck replied, trying not to show his disappointment.

"I'm on my way now."

Buck rode south along the bank of the Potomac and watched the sun go down. Jeffrey Jordan and his two espionage companions were now dead. Buck vowed to go to Jenny as soon as possible. She would understand why he could not come to her immediately. Another thought came to mind. At least one good thing could come of this dreadful situation. With Jenny's father gone, they could have each other. Once she was over her grief, he would propose. He had no doubt she would accept the proposal.

Twilight was hovering over the camp when Buck rode in. Major Sparks was there to meet him when he moved past the sentries.

"Good evening, Colonel," said Sparks as Buck dismounted. "I was getting a bit worried about you."

"Had a slight delay in getting away," Buck replied.

"I have your tent ready, sir. It is the same one that Colonel Keyes occupied."

"Fine. Have the men had their evening meal yet?"

"No, sir. Ordinarily we would have, but we had some excitement around here. We're about ready to eat now, though."

"I would like to meet with you and the rest of the officers right after supper, then," said Brownell. "What was the excitement?"

"You remember when you brought the thirteen Rebel prisoners in, we put nine of them in that larger shed over there, and the other four in the small one."

"Yes."

"Well, sir, the nine in the large shed made an escape attempt about a half hour ago. They grabbed a couple guards to use as hostages and demanded to take the other four with them, along with a woman spy we caught this afternoon. Our marksmen went into action and took out all nine. The guards didn't get a scratch."

Buck's eyebrows arched. "A *woman* spy?"

"Yes, sir. She was carrying classified information to General Jackson. I'm sure you know what the regulation manual says about spies."

Buck felt a hot spot in his stomach knowing he would have to oversee the execution of a woman. "Yes, Major, I am fully aware of my responsibility. Executions are to take place at sunrise or sunset, but within twenty-four hours of the time the spy is caught. Executing a woman—even an enemy spy—is a distasteful thing, but it must be done. The execution will be at sunrise in the morning."

"Yes, sir."

"Major, I want you to pick out seven of our best marksmen for the firing squad. I have some news to tell you about captured spies, too, but it'll wait until later this evening when I meet with you and the other officers. Right now, I want to talk to this woman and see if I can get her to tell me more about the spy ring."

"All right, sir. I'll take you to her."

Sparks led his commanding officer through the big barn door, past several cubicles, and halted at one in a corner. Lantern light glowed through the cracks between the boards. "We've already given her supper, sir. I didn't want her to have to sit in the dark, so we brought in a lantern."

"Good gesture," nodded Brownell.

Sliding the bolt, Sparks said, "She's a pretty one, Colonel. You'll see that for yourself."

Buck waited for the major to pull the door open and step in ahead of him. Sparks moved inside the cubicle with Buck on his heels. "Miss Jordan, this is our camp commander, Colonel Brownell."

Buck saw Jenny sitting on the cot at the same instant he heard Sparks call her "Miss Jordan."

Their eyes met.

Jenny was stunned, but the horror that slammed into Buck was so powerful, it knocked the breath from him. A roaring began in his ears, red spots danced madly before his eyes, his flesh crawled. The cubicle seemed to swirl and heave around him.

CHAPTER TWENTY-THREE

✦

Buck Brownell felt like he was in a wild nightmare from which he could not escape. Jenny's misty eyes were riveted on Buck with ill-concealed shame rising in their depths. Major Sparks could tell the two of them knew each other.

Buck was finally able to find his voice and gasped, "Jenny! I...I can't believe this. What—? I—"

"You know this woman well, sir?" cut in Sparks.

Keeping his stunned gaze on Jenny, who remained on the cot, Buck replied, "Yes. I've...been in love with her for several months."

"Then you know she's Jeffrey Jordan's daughter?"

"Yes. I know." It had been hard enough for Buck to accept that Jordan was an enemy spy, but his shock at finding out the same thing about the woman he loved was like nothing he had ever experienced before. His flesh crawled as he faced the burning realization that he must direct her execution.

Buck's mouth was dry as sand as he said shakily, "Major, I'd like to talk to Jenny alone. You go ahead and do what I told you."

"Yes, sir."

When the major was gone and the door shut, Buck stood over Jenny, trembling. His chest rose and fell irregularly. His voice was strained and his words ran breathlessly together as he said, "Jenny, I don't care what you've done...I still love you as much as ever."

Jenny had lowered her eyes and was staring at the dirt floor. Buck's words sank in slowly. When they registered, she lifted her graceful chin and met his gaze. Her lower lip trembled. For a long, unbelieving moment, she explored his face, reading him with a careful scrutiny. Her eyes filled with tears.

"You...still love me? Even when you know I've lived a lie before you?"

Buck fought the lump in his throat. "You weren't lying when you told me you loved me. I know you weren't."

Jenny released a piteous wail and flew from the cot into his arms. He felt the tremor of her body as he held her tight. Jenny had her arms around him and her head against his chest. "Oh, Buck," she sobbed, "I'm so sorry for deceiving you! I was eaten up with guilt. But I wasn't lying when I said I loved you. I love you with all my heart!"

Their lips came together. The kiss was long and full of desperation.

Once again Jenny laid her head against Buck's chest. As they held each other, she wept and said, "Buck, I need to explain something to you."

"No, Jenny, you don't owe me any explana—"

"Please, darling, let me get it out." Jenny paused to compose herself, then continued. "I've been under such pressure to do this spy thing. I ask you not to make me divulge where the pressure was coming from—I just can't do that—but let me explain this...I have been under constant pressure to carry messages since just before the Bull Run battle. I refused, because I knew you would be involved, and I just couldn't do it."

Jenny's words touched Buck deeply. He remained silent as she continued.

"You've got to believe me, darling...this is the only one I've had anything to do with!"

Laying a palm next to her face and pressing her head tighter against his chest, Buck said softly, "If you say that's the way it was, Jenny, I believe you." Knowing it was going to fall on him to tell Jenny about her father's capture and execution, he took a deep breath, held it for a moment, then said, "Honey, I know where this pressure you speak of was coming from."

Jenny pulled her head up and looked him in the eye. "You do?"

"Yes. Your father."

Jenny had been thinking more of Rose Greenhow than her father, but she blinked and asked, "How did you know that?"

"I think you'd better sit down. I've got something to tell you."

Sitting beside Jenny on the cot, Buck held her hand and told her of the capture and execution of her father, John Calhoun, and Lola Morrow that very day. Overwhelmed with grief, Jenny clung to Buck and wept a long time. When she regained control of her emotions, she held onto his hand and said, "Buck, there's something more I need to explain to you. It was Daddy's role as a spy—and the fact that I was as responsible as he since I didn't turn him in—that kept me from making any promises to you about the future. Daddy's attitude toward you, I could have overcome because I love you so much. But I had no choice but to let you think it was his attitude that was keeping me from making any commitment as to our lives together after the war.

"I hated deceiving you, Buck. There never should be any deceit between two people who love each other, but I was between a rock and a hard place, as they say."

Buck kissed her tenderly. "I love you more than ever, Jenny. And now...now..."

Squeezing his hand, she said dolefully, "Now it's your duty to carry out my execution."

It was a moment of dismay. Stroking her cheeks lovingly with both hands, Buck said with tremulous voice, "I have an idea, honey. It's a long shot, but it's the only chance we've got to spare your life."

"Run away?" she asked, fear evident on her face.

"Wouldn't work," he said, shaking his head. "We could make a break for it, but they'd track us down. As I see it, there's only one chance, and that's what I'm going to do."

"What?"

"You risked your life to save Tad Lincoln, didn't you?"

"Yes," she said weakly.

"Tad's still alive because of you, isn't he?"

"Well...yes."

"Did you ever hear from Mr. Lincoln about it?"

"No. I received a letter from Mrs. Lincoln. She thanked me for it in a very nice way."

"Certainly the president knows by now. Maybe your brave deed will be enough to persuade him to give you a stay of execution."

"But...but I'm a spy," she said in a despairing tone.

"But you only carried one message, and that under pressure from your father. He's got to weigh that against the fact that you could have been killed trying to rescue Tad. It's all we've got, honey. If I can get him to reduce the sentence to imprisonment rather than execution, we can still be together. This war can't last too long. When it's over, all prisoners of war will be set free."

Jenny wrapped her arms around his neck and squeezed tight, "Oh, I asked the Lord to perform a miracle. I prayed that He would somehow spare my life and let us be married. Maybe this will be His way. I can take being locked up if it means that eventually I can be your wife."

Buck kissed her soundly and said, "Okay, sweetheart, the execution is due to take place at sunrise. I've got to ride to the White House immediately. You sit tight and keep praying. I'll be back as soon as I can."

They kissed again, and Buck pushed the door open. Major Sparks was coming in the barn with a lantern in his hand. Beside him was army chaplain Glenn Harding. Buck had met him on a few occasions.

The two men drew up, and Sparks said, "I thought with what your lady was facing, Colonel, she might want to talk to Chaplain Harding."

"I appreciate that, and I thank you for coming, Chaplain. Let me explain something to both of you, then I've got to ride for town."

Quickly, Buck told Sparks and Harding what he was going to try to accomplish by going to the president. Both men understood and wished him their best. Jenny observed it all from the cubicle. She set loving eyes on Buck as he said to Harding, "Please stay with her, Chaplain. Her daddy was executed today. Do what you can to comfort her. Read to her from that Bible in your hand, and pray that Mr. Lincoln will give her a stay of execution."

Hurrying back to Jenny, Buck kissed her once more and dashed out of the barn with Major Sparks on his heels. "Colonel, what am I supposed to do if somehow you don't return by sunrise?"

"I will, Major," breathed Buck. *I will.*

"But...but what if something unexpected happens and you don't?"

They reached Buck's horse. As he swung into the saddle, he said, "I'll stop at the main camp upriver and tell General McClellan what I'm doing. If I'm not back here by the break of dawn, you ride to the camp and get your orders from him."

"All right, sir," said Sparks. "Go with God."

Colonel Brownell galloped hard along the bank of the Potomac by the light of a half-moon rising in the eastern sky. Moments later he arrived at the main camp to find that General McClellan had gone into Washington for the night and would not return until noon tomorrow.

Buck explained the situation to General Tyler, who was in charge. Tyler understood but told Buck that if he was not back by dawn, it would be Tyler's duty to ride to the camp and see to it that the execution was carried out at sunrise. Army regulations must be obeyed to the letter. Buck told Tyler he understood, but assured him he would be back in time. With that, he spurred his horse into a gallop and rode toward Washington.

It was exactly nine o'clock when the desperate rider reached the White House. After being delayed by White House personnel for nearly an hour, he finally learned that President Lincoln was not at home. He had gone to Baltimore, where he had a meeting scheduled early in the morning with some wealthy men from Europe who wanted to talk to the president about giving financial aid to the Union cause. Fearful of possible Confederate attack on Washington, they had asked Lincoln to meet them in Baltimore.

Learning that Lincoln was at the Baltimore Arms Hotel, Buck rode hard across the Maryland countryside in the pale moonlight. It was nearly forty miles to Baltimore, and his horse was showing signs of fatigue when he dismounted in front of the hotel and tied it to a hitching post.

Buck entered the lobby and hastened to the desk where he found a young clerk asleep in a chair. The place was dimly lit with a couple of low-burning lanterns. When the clerk did not stir at Buck's approach, he circled the counter, gripped his shoulder, shook it lightly, and said, "Pardon me."

The clerk awakened with a start, snorted, and looked up at the colonel. Sleepily, he said, "Umm...what can I do for you, General?"

"I understand President Lincoln is staying here. I must see him immediately. It's an emergency. What room is he in?"

The clerk rubbed his eyes and focused on a clock that hung on the wall above him. "Sir, it's one o'clock in the morning. Can't you wait until the president awakens at his regular time?"

"No, I can't! I told you. It's an emergency!"

"All right, General. Mr. Lincoln is on the third floor, room 360."

Buck bolted for the fancy winding staircase that led upstairs. Reaching the third floor, he hurried down the dimly lit hall toward room 360. As he drew close, he saw two well-dressed men sitting on straight-backed chairs, one on either side of the door. Both men rose to their feet, noted his rank, and eyed him warily.

"I'm Colonel Buck Brownell, gentlemen," he said, a bit out of breath. "I need to see the president immediately. I realize it's the middle of the night, but this is an extreme emergency...a matter of life and death."

The men explained that they were Pinkerton detectives, and that they had strict orders to see that Mr. Lincoln was not disturbed. The colonel would have to wait till morning.

Buck was on the verge of panic. Speaking fast, he explained the situation, and the men agreed to awaken the president. One of them ushered the nervous colonel into the first room of the presidential suite and stayed with him, while the other went to the bedroom. Buck prayed silently, *Oh, Lord, please...move on Mr. Lincoln's heart. He must give Jenny a stay of execution. I beg of You, please spare her life.*

The detective returned from the bedroom after a few minutes and said, "The president is dressing, Colonel. When I told him your name, he did not hesitate to say he would see you. Please sit down. He will be with you shortly."

"Thank you," sighed Buck, but preferred to stay on his feet.

The detectives returned to the hall, closing the door. Buck paced the floor, praying. No more than four minutes had passed when Abraham Lincoln emerged from the bedroom. He had put on his slippers and trousers, but showed his long underwear from the waist up. Running his fingers through his coarse, tousled hair, he said sleepily, "Good morning, Colonel. I understand you have an emergency."

"Yes, sir," nodded Buck, his voice showing the strain he was under. "I'm sorry to disturb you like this, Mr. President, but it is a matter of extreme urgency."

Buck told Lincoln he was aware of Jeffrey Jordan's arrest and execution. He quickly explained Jenny's dire situation and reminded the president of her heroic deed. He explained that she had gone on only one spy mission for the Confederates, and that under duress.

Stunned that Jenny had also been in the spy ring, Lincoln scratched his head and said, "Colonel, I'm sorry, but I know nothing of your young lady saving Tad's life. I didn't even know he'd been at the Bull Run battle."

Buck's blood ran cold. "I don't understand why no one told you about it, sir. Mrs. Lincoln wrote a letter to Jenny, thanking her for what she had done. If nothing else, I'm surprised the governess hasn't told you."

Rubbing his tired eyes, Lincoln said, "Colonel, there's a reason I haven't heard it from them. I've been so busy ever since the Bull Run battle that I've barely seen them. And even when I've been home with them, my mind has been so preoccupied with this war, they probably didn't feel they could bring it up."

Buck could feel time slipping away like sand in an hourglass. "Believe me, sir," he said with urgency lining his voice, "what I've told you is the absolute truth."

"I'm not doubting you, Colonel, but as you well know, this spy problem is a big one. I've made a lot of it with my Cabinet, the Senate Military Committee, and even with the newspapers. Such a timely and important thing as this forces me to have someone else's word about Jenny saving Tad's life. With all due respect to you, if I don't handle this correctly, it could create some serious problems with handling enemy spies who are caught in the future."

Buck's hands were shaking. "Mr. President, could you at least write an order giving me the authority to delay the execution until you can hear testimony from the boys and their governess?"

Suddenly Lincoln's eyes lit up. Snapping his fingers, he said, "Wait a minute!" and crossed the room to a desk where his valise lay on top. Pawing through it, he found the sealed envelope that had been handed him by Senator Charles Sumner.

While the president was slitting the envelope open, Buck asked, "What is that, sir?"

"I just remembered that shortly after the Bull Run battle, Senator Sumner handed me an envelope and said something about a valiant young woman who had done a brave thing at Bull Run. It's sketchy, but seems like someone else made a passing remark about that same time concerning my son at Bull Run. It slipped my mind until now. Sumner also said something that day about the young woman being worthy of a presidential commendation."

While Buck looked on with bated breath, the president unfolded Sumner's letter and read in the senator's own handwriting how he had witnessed Jenny Jordan's brave deed at Bull Run. With no thought for her own life, she had saved the president's son from a sure and violent death under the hooves and wheels of charging horses and wagons.

The hand that held the letter trembled as Lincoln set his tear-filled eyes on Buck and said, "Colonel, only God knows how much I love that bright-eyed boy of mine. Senator Sumner saw the whole thing, and wrote it all down right here. If...if it weren't for your Jenny's courage and unselfishness, I couldn't go home and feel that dear boy's arms around my neck."

Buck's heart was in his throat.

"You feel confident that she is telling the truth when she says she went on only that one mission...the one that got her caught?"

"Absolutely, sir. Would a woman who so gallantly risked her life to save Tad be a liar?"

Lincoln shook his head. "Of course not. Forgive me for even asking. You understand, I'm a very tired man right now."

"Certainly, sir."

Pulling out the chair, the president sat down at the desk. Producing a slip of paper from a drawer, he picked up a pen, dipped it in the desk's inkwell, and said, "Colonel Brownell, I'm going to write Jenny Jordan a full pardon."

While the room was filled with the sounds of the pen scratching the paper, Buck brushed tears from his eyes and offered a silent prayer of gratitude to the Lord.

When the pardon was written, Lincoln hastened to the adjoining room and awakened his secretary. John Hay witnessed the president's signature on the document by signing his own. The pardon was now official and beyond alteration.

Placing the life-saving document in an envelope and handing it to Buck, Lincoln said, "Due to the nature of this situation, Colonel, it would be best for both you and Jenny to relocate immediately. After having three spies executed just yesterday—and one of them Jenny's father—it would be wise to remove her from the Washington area. Since you've been so deeply involved, it's best that you leave here, too. As you no doubt know, we have Union forces in Missouri, and it looks like there'll be fighting there soon. We need men like you on that front, Colonel. I'll put through an order tomorrow that you be transferred as soon as possible. Jenny's been a good receptionist at the Capitol. I hate to lose her. But take her and go to Missouri with my blessing."

Elation had Buck's heart drumming his ribs. "I will, sir. Jenny and I will get married before we head west."

"Wonderful. Congratulations."

With deep emotion, Buck thanked Lincoln for Jenny's pardon and soon was on his horse, galloping southward. It was just past two o'clock. The hour's rest had refreshed the animal, and it was running at full speed. Buck figured he could make it to the camp in a little over three hours if the horse could keep up the hard pace. It had to. Jenny's life depended on it. General Tyler had no choice but to go ahead with the execution if Buck was not back by sunrise.

Dawn came about five-thirty, and sunrise about six. All things

BATTLES OF DESTINY

328

going well, Buck would make it to the camp just at the break of dawn.

The gallant steed obeyed Buck's promptings and galloped hard. Saliva from its mouth flecked Buck's uniform and sometimes sprayed his face. It mattered not. The eager rider knew every rapid step took him closer to the camp...and closer to Jenny. Jenny, who was going to live and become his wife!

The moon had shifted to the west, but was still giving off enough light to illuminate the roads, hills, and fields as horse and rider flew like the wind. Recognizing certain landmarks along the way, Buck was just telling himself he was only about six miles from the camp when suddenly his horse stumbled and fell. Buck was thrown about twenty feet and hit the ground hard. He was in a grassy field when the horse went down, and a haystack stopped his roll. Buck was momentarily stunned, then he managed to struggle to his feet and stumble toward the fallen animal.

The horse's sides were heaving as it lay on its side, its eyes bulging. Then Buck saw the broken leg. The horse must have stepped in a hole. Buck knew he'd have to put the horse out of its misery. Standing over it, he wagged his head sadly. Just before he pulled the trigger, he said, "I'm sorry, boy. You did your best. You really did."

Looking past the haystack, Buck saw a farmhouse and outbuildings about three hundred yards to the south. Making sure he still had Lincoln's pardon in his pocket, he ran toward the farmhouse as fast as he could. He had to get another horse, and fast. The eastern horizon was showing a dull gray. It would soon be dawn, and he had six miles to go. Panic gripped him as he ran.

Buck's lungs felt like they would explode by the time he drew near the buildings. Three saddle horses and two Holstein cows stood together in the corral. He was headed for the house when he caught sight of a shadowy figure moving from the back porch toward the barn. The farmer was carrying a milk bucket. There was enough light from the sky for Buck to tell that the farmer was in his late thirties or early forties. The man hauled up, clutching the handle of the empty milk bucket, and eyed Buck's blue uniform in the gray gloom.

Gasping for breath, Buck said hoarsely, "There's no...time for an...explanation, sir...but I need to borrow...a horse...*fast*."

The farmer eyed Buck with disdain. "I ain't interested in helpin' no Yankee. I may live in Maryland, but my heart's below the Mason-Dixon Line. You ain't gettin' no horse from me."

The farmer's rude refusal riled Buck. "Mister, a woman's life is at stake. She'll die if I don't get to her before sunrise!"

Squinting, the farmer said with a sneer, "What kind of poppy-cock you tryin' to feed me, Yankee? Get off my property!"

The wild fury of the desperate moment ripped through Buck. He lunged at the man, striking him on the jaw with his fist. The farmer went down and lay still.

Buck dashed to the barn. It took him a few seconds to locate a bridle in the dark interior, but once he had one in his hand, he hurried into the corral, picked the fastest-looking horse, and bridled it. He wouldn't take the time to put on a saddle. Every second counted.

Leading the horse to the corral gate, he opened it, brought the animal out, then closed the gate. He was about to hop on its back when he heard from the shadows, "Hold it right there, Yankee!"

The farmer stood beneath a huge oak tree some twenty feet away. He was a bit unsteady on his feet, but he had produced a musket from somewhere and had its black, ominous muzzle leveled at Buck.

Buck had a mental picture of the seven men of the firing squad rising from their cots.

"Get away from the horse, Yankee! I want you off my property *now!* I don't hanker to kill you, but if you don't make tracks real quick-like, I will!"

Desperation was a living thing in Buck Brownell. Turning from the horse, he moved cautiously toward the farmer, opening his hands and saying, "Sir, I tried to explain that a woman's life is at stake—a

Southern woman, caught yesterday spying for the Confederacy. She is scheduled to be shot at sunrise, but I have a pardon in my pocket signed by President Lincoln."

Moving steadily toward the farmer, Buck continued. "As you can see, it won't be long till the sun comes up. I've got six miles to go to reach the camp. If I don't get there in time, they'll put her before a firing squad. You're in sympathy with the Confederacy; won't you even help save the life of a Southern woman?"

Buck was now eight or nine feet from the man. The muzzle was still trained on his chest.

Extending his free hand, the farmer said, "Let me see that there paper. I wanna know if you're tellin' the truth."

This was exactly what Buck was hoping the man would do. Stretching out his arm to place the envelope in the man's hand, Buck waited till it was almost there, then with the swiftness of a cougar, seized the barrel of the musket and thrust it upward. The hammer came down and the weapon discharged, sending the roar echoing across the surrounding fields. The envelope fluttered to the ground as Buck twisted the musket from the farmer's hand and used it as a club in one smooth motion. The stock cracked solidly against the Southern sympathizer's head, and he went down like a tree in a high wind.

Buck was aware of someone appearing on the front porch of the farmhouse as he vaulted onto the horse's back and galloped away. He didn't bother to look back and see who it was. The envelope was again safely in his coat pocket, and he was driving the animal as fast as it could go.

The eastern sky was coming alive with light. Buck's blood turned to ice as he pictured the men of the firing squad loading their guns. General Tyler would do his duty. He would see that Jenny was shot at sunrise if Buck was not there.

With the wind in his face, Buck pictured Jenny being led to the place of execution and Chaplain Harding flanking her. "Please, God," he prayed, "let me make it in time."

CHAPTER TWENTY-FOUR

✯

At the First Brigade camp, Chaplain Glenn Harding stood over Jenny Jordan as she sat on the cot in her cubicle. She was holding his Bible. She had slept little, and her eyes showed it.

Gripping the big black Book until her fingers turned white, Jenny looked up at Harding and said, "The Lord is going to do it, Chaplain. I just know He is."

Harding glanced at the cracks in the barn wall that were showing increasing light. He wanted to say, *He's going to have to hurry*, but instead, he said, "Miracles are God's business, Jenny. He can perform one any time He wishes."

Footsteps were heard outside the door. Jenny jumped up, holding the Bible to her breast and said, "It's Buck, Chaplain! He's back!"

The door came open. Jenny's countenance fell as Major Donald Sparks, looking dismal, said, "Miss Jordan, I'm sorry. It's time."

Harding asked, "Can't you give it a few more minutes, Major? I'm sure Colonel Brownell has got to be on his way."

"I wish I could, Chaplain, but it's sunrise. General Tyler is here. He gave the order for me to come and get her."

Harding turned to Jenny, gripped her shoulders, and said, "Don't give up yet. Buck could come riding in here any minute."

Jenny bit her lip and nodded.

A corporal moved in with a short length of rope in his hand. There was a black cloth stuffed in his hip pocket.

Harding eyed the rope, looked at Sparks, and asked, "What's the rope for, Major?"

"We have to tie her hands. I don't like it, but it's army regulation."

"Look," Harding argued, "this ordeal is bad enough for her, certainly you don't have to—"

"It's all right, Chaplain," Jenny cut in. "I don't mind." Turning toward Harding, she handed him the Bible. "Thank you for letting me read it," she said softly. "It was a real comfort."

The corporal's hands were trembling as he tied Jenny's wrists together behind her back.

Noting the black cloth, Harding asked, "And what's the cloth for?"

"It's a hood," replied the corporal. "Miss Jordan has her choice whether she wants it on when she faces the...faces the firing squad."

Jenny stared at the hood but said nothing.

Taking her arm gently, Major Sparks said, "We have to go now."

Sparks led Jenny outside, with Harding and the corporal following. The sun's upper rim was peeking over the eastern horizon. Jenny's line of sight ran across the open fields to the edge of the forest westward; soldiers stood at attention in a straight line at the edge of an open area. Each one held a musket by its barrel with the butt resting next to his leg on the ground.

Major Sparks led Jenny to a spot some forty feet in front of the firing squad, then halted. The sight of the seven muskets sent an icy chill down her spine and her knees buckled. Sparks steadied her as the morning breeze blew a long wisp of hair across her eyes. She couldn't brush it away with her hands tied behind her back. The chaplain saw it and brushed it away for her.

"Thank you," she said.

Harding nodded, then ran his gaze in a panorama and said to Sparks, "Where are all the soldiers? Camp looks empty."

"They didn't want to watch this," replied the major. "They've all gone into the woods."

Jenny looked toward Washington, but again there was no movement...no rider coming that way. Where was Buck? Had something happened to him? From the corner of her eye, she saw a man emerge from a tent and move her direction. She did not recognize him.

Nobody moved. The stately officer drew up and said, "Miss Jordan, I'm General Daniel Tyler. We were expecting Colonel Brownell back by now, but since he has not returned, it is my duty to conduct this...this execution in his absence."

Jenny raised her eyes to meet Tyler's then dropped them and nodded.

Tyler looked to the corporal who now held the black hood in his hand. "Have you offered Miss Jordan the hood, Corporal?"

"Not yet, sir." The corporal stepped to Jenny and asked, "Would you like to have this over your head, ma'am? It...makes it easier when you can't see."

Jenny's heart thudded wildly. The horror of what was about to happen rose in her throat, choking her, making her incapable of speech. Her cheeks twitched as she bit her lip and gave a jerky little nod.

The corporal raised the hood toward Jenny's head, but Harding gently seized his wrist and said, "Just a moment, Corporal."

The corporal looked to General Tyler, who indicated it was all right. He lowered the hood, and Harding let go of his wrist.

Positioning himself directly in front of the condemned woman, the chaplain said, "Jenny, I'm sorry. There is no way to know what's happened to Colonel Brownell...and no time to try to find out. The Lord doesn't always do things the way we think He should. His will is often far different than ours."

Her features pale, Jenny nodded. Then finding her voice, she said, "Chaplain...please tell Buck I know he did his best...and that I died loving him with all my heart."

It was Harding's turn to choke on a lump in his throat. He nodded, bent down and kissed her cheek, and stepped back. The corporal's hands trembled as he carefully dropped the hood over Jenny's head.

General Tyler made a gesture toward Sparks, Harding, and the corporal, directing them to move aside. When they were far enough away, Tyler stepped out of the line of fire, backed up a few more steps, and set his eyes on the firing squad. Taking a deep breath, he barked, "Ready!"

Seven muskets were brought into firing position and the hammers cocked in a staccato of dry clicks. Tyler glanced at the victim. Her entire body was shaking like a leaf in the autumn wind. He took another deep breath and barked, "Aim!"

The unwanted sun shafted its yellow light on Buck as he thundered toward the camp. He gritted his teeth and prayed as the camp came into view. He could make out the long rows of tents in the open areas, but a stand of trees blocked his view of the spot where the execution would take place. Lashing the horse with the tips of the reins, he bellowed, "Hyah! Hyah!"

He was some fifty yards from the center of camp, the trees still blocking his view, when above the rumble of the horse's galloping hooves he heard the unmistakable sound of rifles being fired in a short, crisp series of shots.

Buck's heart seemed to burst in his chest as he cried, "*No-o-o!*"

Seconds later, horse and rider burst into the clearing, and Buck wailed again as he saw Jenny lying on the ground. Her hands were tied behind her back, and there was a black hood over her head. She lay motionless in a crumpled heap.

The horse skidded to a halt in a cloud of dust as Buck sailed from its back and landed beside her. Kneeling, he sobbed, "No! No! Jenny! No!"

His shaky hands tore at the hood and slipped several times before he got it off. Her eyes were closed and her face sheet-white. But she was still breathing!

Buck looked for blood and bullet holes, but there were none. Puzzled but ecstatic, he realized that Jenny had simply fainted. She moved her head slowly back and forth, and moaned. Buck quickly removed the rope from Jenny's wrists and gathered her into his arms. She moaned again.

It was then that Buck realized there was no firing squad to be seen. There were no soldiers in view at all. Where was everybody? Jenny's third moan brought his attention back to her. Elated and thankful that she was unharmed, he kissed her, then stroked her cheek tenderly and said, "Jenny...Jenny..."

Her eyes rolled beneath the lids, then fluttered and came open. It took only seconds for her to focus on the face of the man she loved. "Buck!" she gasped. "I...I'm alive!" She flung her arms around his neck and wept, sobbing out words of thanks to the Lord for performing His miracle.

Buck held her tight, doing some praising of his own. Suddenly both were aware of a shadow falling over them. They looked up to see General Tyler above them, sided by Major Sparks and Chaplain Harding. The chaplain was thumbing tears from his cheeks.

Buck helped Jenny to her feet and stood holding her as he saw the seven-man firing squad coming toward them from the woods to the east, followed by hundreds of men in blue.

Buck reached in his pocket and handed General Tyler the envelope. "President Lincoln gave Jenny a full pardon, General. It's all there, spelled out word for word."

"Thank God!" breathed Harding.

Buck gave a quick explanation of what had delayed him, then squinted against the morning sun and asked, "What happened here, General?"

Tyler scrubbed a hand over his handsome face and explained that just as the firing squad was ready to fire, the four remaining Confederate prisoners hit the door of their small shed and burst out. Apparently they had planned their escape carefully. Watching from a window in the shed, they had meant to time it with the firing of the guns, so the noise of the smashing door would not be heard.

General Tyler, feeling sick at heart for having to order Jenny's death, paused extra long before giving the order to fire. The nervous prisoners jumped too soon. When they came piling through the door, Tyler and the firing squad saw them. While the seven Union soldiers swung their guns around, Tyler shouted for the prisoners to halt. When they kept running, he gave the command to fire. All four of the Confederates were cut down. It was this volley of shots that Buck had heard.

Everyone had rushed to the fallen escapees, including Chaplain Harding, but all four were dead. Their bodies were carried into the woods for burial. Tyler, Sparks, and Harding went along, then it suddenly dawned on them that in all the excitement, no one had stayed with Jenny.

Looking at Jenny, who was still in Buck's arms, Tyler said, "I saw you collapse, but the prisoners were my first concern. I'm sorry we neglected you, Miss Jordan."

"That's all right, sir," Jenny smiled. "I really didn't know I was being neglected. When I heard you tell the firing squad to aim, my head began to spin. I guess I didn't hear your command for the fleeing prisoners to halt. The last thing I remember was the sound of the rifles firing. Naturally, I thought it was the moment of my death...and I must have fainted."

All the camp personnel gathered close, happy to see Jenny still alive. Taking advantage of the moment, General Tyler read President Lincoln's pardon so everyone could hear. While the soldiers cheered, Jenny clung to Buck, weeping with relief and thanking God in her heart.

Buck turned to Tyler and said, "General, I need a few minutes alone with Jenny, then I would like to talk to you and Chaplain Harding."

When Tyler agreed, Buck led Jenny into the tent that had belonged to Colonel Erasmus Keyes. He dropped the flap, took her in his arms, and kissed her soundly. Then he held her at arm's length and said, "Honey, President Lincoln is going to issue an order immediately, transferring me to a post in Missouri. You're aware that things are heating up out there."

"Yes," she nodded, a quizzical look in her eyes.

Grinning, Buck added, "Not only that, but the president feels with all that has happened—you know, all this spy business with you and your father—it would be best for you to leave the Washington area. So he has ordered me to take you to Missouri with me."

A smile tugged at the corners of Jenny's mouth. "He has?"

"We can't disobey the president of the United States, can we?"

Jenny knew what was coming. The smile broadened. "No, of course not. Not your Commander-in-Chief, darling."

"Well-l-l, it really wouldn't be proper for us to travel all that distance together without—"

"Yes, I'll marry you!"

"Wonderful!" Buck exclaimed, and kissed her again.

They held each other in a long embrace, and Jenny said aloud, "Thank You, dear Lord in heaven. Thank You for giving me the miracle I asked You for."

"Amen and amen," breathed Buck.

Holding his wife-to-be at arm's length again, Buck said, "This is what I wanted to talk to Chaplain Harding about. I'm going to ask him if he'll perform the ceremony."

"Wonderful," she said. "And just where and when will this ceremony take place?"

"At my brother's house…tomorrow. Robert and Kady have a big front yard. We can hold the ceremony right there."

"Buck," she said, looking at him askance, "we can't just show up at your brother's house and announce that we're going to use his yard for our wedding ceremony. Besides, isn't tomorrow a bit soon?"

"Mr. Lincoln is putting my orders through right now, honey. We'll probably be leaving tomorrow. You don't think you can be ready by then?"

"Well…if I can get into Washington real soon, so I can make some arrangements for Daddy's burial, and for his house and furniture. I'll have to pack my belongings in a couple of trunks."

"All right, we'll head for town immediately. We'll go to Robert and Kady's first. They'll be very happy to meet you, and I'm sure they'll be glad to let us use their yard. They live at Sixth Street and Florida Avenue, which is only a few blocks from the railroad station."

"That puts them pretty close to the White House, then, doesn't it?"

"It does. The station's about halfway between Robert's place and the White House."

"Well, my love," Jenny said smiling, "we have a lot to do. We'd best get started."

After another long, sweet kiss, the couple emerged from the tent. Buck explained his pending transfer to General Tyler, and told him he and Jenny were getting married the next day. He then asked Chaplain Harding if he would perform the ceremony. Harding was happy to oblige, and the wedding was set for eleven o'clock the next day at the house of Robert and Kady Brownell. General Tyler congratulated them and wished them his best.

Buck drove Jenny to Washington in an army wagon. Robert and Kady were delighted to meet her and were more than happy to hold the wedding in their front yard. From there Buck and Jenny went to the Capitol, where Jenny learned that her father had already been buried. With mixed emotions, she made arrangements for the Jordan house and furniture, then packed her belongings in two trunks from the attic. She would spend the night in the house, and Buck would pick her up for the wedding in the morning.

During the afternoon, the president's order of transfer was delivered to General Tyler. There was a letter enclosed, which explained that John Hay had made arrangements for Buck and Jenny to catch the 2:00 P.M. train from Washington to Kansas City the next day.

At 10:45 the next morning, a dozen soldiers of First Brigade—invited by Buck—stood in the Robert Brownell yard, waiting for the ceremony to begin. An army wagon bearing Jenny's trunks and Buck's luggage waited in the street to carry the newlyweds to the railroad station. Colonel Abram Duryee sat in a wheelchair nearby, attended by a First Brigade corporal. General Tyler and Major Sparks stood close, in conversation with Robert and Kady Brownell.

The situation did not allow Jenny to wear a wedding gown, but she wore her nicest Sunday dress, and Buck was pleased at how beautiful she looked. The happy couple stood with Chaplain Harding, waiting to begin the ceremony. As they chatted, Buck and Jenny noticed that Harding kept looking westward down the street.

"By the way, Chaplain," Buck said to Harding, "I haven't even thought to ask you how much your fee is."

Harding pulled out his pocket watch, glanced down the street again, then flashed a sly grin and asked, "How much is she worth to you?"

Buck grinned and said, "There's not that much money in the world."

Harding chuckled. "Well, in that case, I guess there won't be any fee." As he spoke, he let his eyes stray down the street once more. A wide smile spread over his face.

Buck and Jenny followed his gaze and noticed two important-looking carriages approaching, one behind the other.

"Darling," said Jenny, "who would this be?"

"I can't tell yet, but I think Chaplain Hardy knows."

Hardy kept his eyes on the carriages and said, "You just wait and see."

A moment later, Jenny gasped when she recognized the people in the first carriage. President Lincoln wore his stove-pipe hat. Mrs. Lincoln sat next to him. Behind them were Willie and Tad, crowded next to Patricia Winters and Lieutenant John Hammond, his arm in a sling.

"Oh, Buck, look!" Jenny exclaimed.

"I see," responded Buck, smiling broadly.

In the second carriage were several armed men from the Pinkerton Detective Agency, who had come along as bodyguards at Allan Pinkerton's insistence.

While watching the carriages draw near, Harding said, "I contacted the president yesterday afternoon and told him about your wedding. I felt sure he would want to attend if possible. He canceled a couple of appointments to be here."

While soldiers and civilians looked on, the Lincolns alighted from their carriage, along with the governess and the wounded lieutenant. President Lincoln spoke to his sons, and they waited beside Patricia a few steps from the carriage.

The president and the first lady approached the bride and groom. Chaplain Harding greeted them, then retreated a step or two.

The tall, rawboned man smiled at the couple and said, "Mary, you know Jenny."

"Yes," smiled Mary. "Nice to see you Jenny. And…congratulations."

Then looking at Buck, the president said, "Mary, this is Colonel Brownell."

"Nice to meet you, Colonel. And congratulations to *you*. Jenny is a wonderful young lady."

"My pleasure, Mrs. Lincoln," said Buck, doing a slight bow. "And I couldn't agree with you more."

Lincoln towered over Jenny and said, "Young lady, I want to express my gratitude to you for saving my son's life. Such courage is highly commendable." Reaching inside his coat, he produced a large white envelope. Holding it in his hand, he spoke with quivering voice. "This is a presidential commendation for your brave and unselfish deed. I'll see that you have it in your hands after the ceremony."

"Thank you, Mr. President," replied the beautiful bride. "I will treasure it."

Lincoln cleared his throat. "Jenny, there is a boy back here who wants very much to hug the bride. Is it all right?"

Jenny glanced toward Tad Lincoln where he stood beside his brother and governess. "Of course," she smiled.

Looking back, the president said, "Okay, Tad."

The bright-eyed boy broke into a run and didn't stop until his arms were wrapped around Jenny. She kissed the top of his head and said, "I'm honored that you would come to my wedding, Tad."

"Thank you, Miss Jenny," he replied, "I love you."

"I love you, too," she said softly.

Tad stepped back at his father's word, and Mrs. Lincoln embraced Jenny, followed by young Willie. When Willie backed away, the president looked at the bride with tired eyes and asked, "May I?"

"Of course," she smiled.

Buck looked on with pride as Abraham Lincoln discreetly embraced his bride.

The ceremony was performed, and after congratulations were

offered all around, the president gave Jenny the envelope containing the presidential commendation.

Robert and Kady welcomed Jenny into the family with hugs and kisses, then said good-bye to the bride and groom. Buck and Jenny thanked them for the use of their yard. Good-byes were said to the other guests, then Colonel and Mrs. Francis E. Brownell boarded the army wagon and hurried off in the direction of the railroad station to catch the westbound train.

Standing with his arm around Mrs. Lincoln, the president watched with tears in his eyes as the wagon rolled up the street. When the bride and groom were seen kissing, the soldiers whooped and whistled. Abraham Lincoln leaned over and planted a kiss on Mary's forehead.

When the wagon turned a corner and passed from view, the great man sighed and said, "Well, Mrs. Lincoln, we must be on our way, too. I've got a country to run...and a war to win."

EPILOGUE

✦

Though the Confederate army decisively routed the Federals in the first battle at Bull Run, it was done at a high cost. Of General Pierre G.T. Beauregard's 32,500 men, 387 were killed, 1,582 wounded, and 13 captured. Of General Irvin McDowell's 35,000 men, 460 were killed, 1,124 were wounded, and 1,312 came up missing. It is estimated that about a thousand of the "missing" were deserters who had experienced all the war they wanted under the Confederate guns at Bull Run.

In early fall of 1861, Allan Pinkerton's continual pursuit of enemy spies led him to the door of Rose O'Neal Greenhow. A search of her house produced proof of her espionage for the Confederacy. She was placed under arrest and jailed. The Union had quickly lost its taste for executing female spies. Rose was given a stiff prison sentence, but because there was no place for women in the Federal prisons, she was incarcerated in her own home under heavy guard. The house became known as "Fort Greenhow."

For the next few months, Rose was somehow able to communicate with the Confederacy, right under the noses of her guards. In

January 1862, Major General John E. Wool telegraphed the Senate Military Committee from a distant army post, advising them that someone in Washington was obtaining "all the information necessary for those who command the Rebel army. They know much better than I do what is going on in Washington."

Rose was then transferred to the Old Capitol Prison. Her fellow inmates were Rebel soldiers, Union deserters, and escaped slaves who had no means of supporting themselves. Because of squalor and disease in the prison, Rose was released on "parole" by the end of March 1862 and transported beyond the Union lines in Virginia with a solemn warning not to come back North for the duration of the War.

Rose O'Neal Greenhow never crossed the Mason-Dixon Line again. She drowned in a boating accident in the Cape Fear River near Fort Fisher, North Carolina, on September 1, 1862.

Clara Barton, a clerk in the U.S. Patent Office, had no formal nurse's training, but she labored unselfishly during the entire Civil War, soliciting and distributing medical supplies and caring for wounded Union soldiers. Oftentimes, she also found herself administering medicine and medical help to wounded and ailing Rebel prisoners.

In 1881, because of her love for helping others, Clara left her job at the Patent Office to become the first president of the American Red Cross. She spent herself caring for the injured, sick, and dying until her own health failed and she died in 1912 at the age of ninety-one.

A HEART DIVIDED

✴

If you enjoyed the love story of Buck Brownell and Jenny Jordan, you'll also want to read A Heart Divided. The following excerpt begins as Ryan McGraw unexpectedly encounters Victoria Coffield, the wife who deserted him years earlier.

Receptionist-secretary Rebecca Worley was working on a stack of papers at her desk, enjoying the slight breeze coming through the open window. The early afternoon sun had just gone behind a bank of clouds, easing the summer heat a little.

Rebecca allowed herself a moment to watch the dozen or so recuperating Confederate soldiers as they sat in the shade a few yards away. She wondered how many more Southern men would be brought in to Mobile's hospital before the horrible war came to an end. She had seen several hundred come and go...some to the local cemetery. Many had returned home missing arms and legs. Others had left blind or maimed. Still others had walked past her desk and out the door to return to combat.

Rebecca's heart was heavy as she beheld one young soldier with bandages over his eyes, walking across the hospital grounds, being led by a nurse. Suddenly her attention was drawn to a young mother plunging through the door, carrying a small boy in her arms. There was a bloody makeshift bandage on the child's right arm and a look of apprehension on the mother's pale features.

Rebecca stood up and stepped around the desk to meet the woman. As she drew up, Rebecca said, "Looks bad, ma'am. Is the cut deep?"

"Yes," she gasped. "Can a doctor see him right away?"

"Of course. Follow me."

The bleeding boy immediately had the attention of nurses in the examining room, and a doctor was summoned. While the worried mother stood close, the nurses removed the bandage and examined the four-inch gash on the child's upper arm.

The boy's eyes showed fear, and in an attempt to calm him, one of the nurses said, "Don't you worry, little fellow, the doctor will be here shortly and get you all fixed up. What's your name?"

"Tommy," came the reply, riding a whimper.

"How did you get this cut, Tommy?"

"Fell out of a tree and hit the picket fence."

"He sure did," spoke up another nurse. "I can see some tiny splinters in the cut."

"Oh, I thought I'd gotten them all out," the mother said shakily.

"It's all right, ma'am," said the nurse. "Dr. Bentley will do a thorough job on it." She looked toward Rebecca, who stood near the door. "Rebecca, I'm sure you need to get some information from this lady. Why don't you take her to your desk?"

"Right," nodded Rebecca. "Please come with me, ma'am. Tommy is in good hands."

Brow furrowed, the mother moved close to the table and said, "Tommy, you'll have to be Mommy's big brave boy now. Okay?"

Lips pulled tight, the boy nodded.

"I'll be just down the hall, honey. When the doctor gets you all fixed up, these nice nurses will let me know, and I'll take you home."

A bit frightened but wanting to show his mother that he was made of brave material, Tommy nodded, but showed no inclination to cry.

As they walked together down the hall, Rebecca said, "That's a fine boy you have there, ma'am."

"Thank you."

Rebecca, who was rather plain and had mouse-brown hair, looked on the attractive woman with envy as she gestured for her to sit down on a chair in front of the desk. The woman wore a pale yellow dress that held her tightly at waist and breast, and her glossy black hair dropped in a long fall behind her stately head. Her eyes were like ebony bits of marble, giving a hint that they could spark with anger or mesmerize a man with innate power. Her features were clear and exquisitely formed.

Taking a printed form from a drawer, Rebecca picked up a pencil and said, "Okay, I need to get some information from you."

The woman told Rebecca her name was Victoria Manning Coffield, that Tommy was her son, and that she was the wife of Captain Lex Coffield of Fort Morgan. The Coffields had a house in Mobile so the captain could be close to his family.

While telling the receptionist that Tommy was five years old and giving his birth date, Victoria glanced anxiously toward the closed door down the hall where her son was being treated.

Rebecca noted it and said, "Mrs. Coffield, I understand that you are concerned about Tommy, but really you needn't worry. He'll be fine. Dr. George Bentley is one of the very best."

Victoria smiled and replied, "I'm sure of that, Miss—" her eyes dropped to the small name plate on the desk—"Miss Worley. It's just that I've been upset about some other things lately, and...well, this sort of came at the wrong time. I'm afraid I'm not handling it very well."

"I'm sorry, ma'am. I hate to bother you with all of these questions, but it's routine, you know."

"I understand."

At that instant, Victoria's attention was drawn to the front door of the hospital as two Confederate officers entered, looking sharp in their gray uniforms. Her mouth fell open when the officers removed their campaign hats, and she recognized the tall, handsome man with the sand-colored hair.

Rising to her feet as the captain and the lieutenant drew near, Victoria Coffield felt her heart thundering in her breast. It took the captain only an instant to find her familiar face. Shock registered in his eyes. He stopped quickly, his face slightly losing color.

Ryan McGraw had not seen his ex-wife for over six years. She was twenty-one when she walked out of his life, and had matured a great deal. She was still beautiful, and her maturity somehow made her beauty more clearly defined.

Victoria's hands shook as she said with dry mouth, "Hello, Ryan."

The captain felt a tremor run through his body. He struggled to control his emotions. He thought he had his ex-wife out of his system, but even though she had torn his heart out six years ago, he found something deep within him responding to her presence. Forcing a calm into his voice, he said, "Hello, Tori. You're...you're looking well."

"You...you, too," she responded, looking him up and down. "You really do a lot for that uniform. And...you're a captain, I see."

"Army's desperate," he said shyly, looking uncomfortable.

Judd Rawlings, who knew the story on Victoria, took a step closer, and said, "Captain, if you need a little time to talk, I'll go on and visit the men."

Pulling his gaze from his ex-wife, Ryan set it on Judd and replied, "Sure. Do that. I'll be along shortly."

As Judd walked away, Victoria cast another anxious glance toward the door down the hall.

Rebecca realized an awkward situation had befallen the distraught mother. Rising to her feet, she said, "Mrs. Coffield, if you and the captain need to talk privately, there's a waiting room two doors down the hall to your left. It is unoccupied at the moment. We can finish up with these details on Tommy when you're through."

The name "Coffield" rang a hard bell in Ryan's mind. Was Victoria married to this Captain Lex Coffield who was in Tuscaloosa gathering torpedoes?

Setting expressive black eyes on her ex-husband, Victoria asked, "Would you like to talk for a few minutes, Ryan?"

"I guess maybe we should."

"If there is any word from the doctor before you're through,

I'll let you know, ma'am," spoke up Rebecca.

Victoria thanked her and walked slowly down the hall with Ryan. When they entered the room, Ryan closed the door and pointed to a couch, telling her to sit down. As she dropped onto the couch, he took a straight-backed wooden chair and sat down facing her.

"Tommy..." said Ryan. "Is that your son?"

"Yes," nodded Victoria, clasping her shaky hands. "He...he fell out of a tree and cut his arm. I've told him a thousand times to stay out of that tree, but you know how boys are."

"Yes. I used to be one. Trees just seem to beckon to a boy. Not much he can do if he's all boy but give in."

"I suppose," she said, relieved that he was not unleashing a tirade of scorn upon her. "Tommy's that, all right."

"I heard the receptionist call you Mrs. Coffield. Your husband happen to be Captain Lex Coffield?"

"Yes," she replied, looking surprised. "You know him?"

"No. My men and I just arrived at Fort Morgan yesterday, and General Page told us about him. I understand he's up in Tuscaloosa right now, collecting torpedoes for the upcoming naval battle in the bay."

"Yes. I...figured you'd be in the army, with the war and all, but I never dreamed you'd be a captain. Lex is a graduate of West Point, and that's as high as he has gone. You've done all right for yourself."

Ryan shrugged his wide shoulders. "Like I said, the army's desperate."

"You lead a unit of men?"

"B Company. First Alabama Sharpshooters. You heard of us?"

"No," she replied, wringing her hands. "I don't pay much attention to the war. Are you at Fort Morgan because of Admiral Farragut's gathering fleet? I know about him because Lex talks a lot about him being out there in the gulf."

"Yes. We're here to bolster the defenses. Some of my men got shot up in a Yankee ambush while we were traveling to Mobile from Montgomery. We left them here at the hospital yesterday. My lieutenant and I decided to ride up and check on them."

"I see," Victoria said, brushing at a lock of hair that had fallen on her forehead.

There was a heavy, blank silence. Victoria could hardly breathe.

Ryan's memory was torturing him. He was picturing the raven-haired beauty in her exquisite white wedding dress and remembering how utterly happy he had been the day she became his bride.

Feeling the pressure to break the silence, Victoria said, "Ryan, I know I was wrong to just leave a note when I ran off with Lex. At least I should have told you face-to-face that I was leaving you. It's just that...well, I did it in that sudden manner, feeling it was best to make it quick and clean."

Fixing her with ice in his pale blue eyes, Ryan said acidly, "Leaving the note wasn't where you were wrong, Tori. It was leaving me. You stood at the altar the day of our wedding and vowed before God and man that you would keep yourself only unto me as long as we both lived. You broke your vows."

Victoria avoided his gaze.

"So you married him at Fort Payne, eh?" pressed Ryan. "That's where the divorce papers came from."

"Yes," she replied, staring at the floor. "That's where he was stationed when we happened to meet in Hattiesburg. Do you want to know how we met?"

"No. I don't care."

A pained look pinched her face. Still avoiding his gaze, she said, "The reason we're here is because when the war broke out, Lex declared his loyalty to the South. He was immediately assigned to Fort Morgan. We've maintained a home here in Mobile so Tommy and I could be close by."

"I guess that's as it should be."

Raising her eyes to meet his, Victoria said, "This will sound inane, Ryan, but I'm going to say it anyway. It's good to see you...and I'm glad to know you're at the fort. It will be nice having you so close."

Ryan wanted to hate her, but he couldn't. Memories of their sweet times together were racing through his mind. Part of him felt the desire to lash out at her for daring to say it would be nice to have him so close, but another part wanted to show her kindness. He was reading something in her eyes...something that told him she was under a heavy strain.

"Tori, are you happy?"

Tears surfaced and her anguish etched itself on her face. Her lower lip quivered as she replied, "Not that you should even care, but I am very unhappy. Lex is not at all what I thought he was."

Leaving the couch, Victoria fell to her knees at her ex-husband's feet. Tears were now spilling down her cheeks as she laid a hand on his forearm and said with breaking voice, "Oh, Ryan, the last several months I have thought of you constantly. I have relived so many wonderful memories. I...I made such an awful mistake! You're right. The worst thing I did was break my vows. I deserve anything bad that happens to me. You have a right to hate me."

Breaking into sobs, Victoria pulled a hanky from the sleeve of her dress and dabbed at her eyes. Struggling to gain control of herself, she looked up at Ryan from her kneeling position and said, "Oh, darling, you don't hate me, do you?"

Victoria's use of the word darling tore at Ryan McGraw's heart. He was wishing their paths had not crossed in the hospital. Barely moving his lips, he said, "No, Tori, I don't hate you."

Swallowing hard, she closed her eyes and willed herself calm. Speaking with level voice, she said, "Ryan...?"

"Yes?"

Victoria was looking into his eyes searchingly. "Have you remarried?"

"No," he replied flatly, rising to his feet and towering over her. "I'm not married, but you are. I had best be going."

Jumping up, she clutched both his arms. "Ryan, I need your help!"

"You've gotten along without my help for six years, Tori."

"Please!" she begged. "Living with Lex is unbearable! He's

hot-tempered brute! He mistreats Tommy. He's mean and selfish. He wants everything his own way."

Ryan looked at her blandly. "That was your problem, too, Tori. At least it was the last year we were married. You changed from what you were when I married you. Suddenly everything had to go your way, or you threw tantrums and pouted like a spoiled brat. Remember?"

Victoria did not reply. She just stood there gripping his arms and looking at him through a wall of tears.

"I suppose that's why you left me for this Lex Coffield," continued Ryan. "You thought he would give you your way all the time. I can see why you're miserable. Two selfish, self-centered people in a marriage can put a strain on things. There's nothing I can do to help, Tori. You made your bed, now you'll have to lie in it."

Shaking her head and struggling to keep from losing control of herself, the troubled brunette sniffed and said, "I deserve anything you say to me, darling, but you can't just walk away and leave me. I need your help!"

"You're asking the impossible, Tori. I can't butt into your marriage."

Abruptly, Victoria wrapped her arms around him, laid her head against his muscular chest, and said with trembling voice, "It will help me immensely if we can just see each other now and then."

Ryan was about to say that they could not see each other when there was a knock at the door. Pulling away from his ex-wife, he went to the door and opened it.

Rebecca Worley said, "Excuse me, Captain. Dr. Bentley is about finished with Tommy. He wants to speak with Mrs. Coffield."

Dabbing at her eyes with the wet hanky, Victoria moved up ide Ryan and said, "Thank you, Miss Worley. Tell the doctor I'll ight there."

Rebecca nodded and walked away.

Turning to Ryan, Victoria said, "I want you to meet Tommy."

'Maybe some time later, Tori. Right now, I need to look in on my wounded men."

Laying a hand on his arm, she gave him a certain tender look that had been something special to Ryan when they first fell in love. "Do you still feel something for me?"

"Tori, I must get to my men," said Ryan, and moved into the corridor. "I hope your son is all right."

With that, he walked away from her and did not look back.

You'll find out what happens to Ryan and Victoria in *A Heart Divided* by Al Lacy, the exciting second volume of the "Battles of Destiny" series. Available at your local Christian bookstore.

OTHER COMPELLING STORIES BY AL LACY

Books in the Battles of Destiny series:

☞ *A Promise Unbroken*

Experience the heartache and victory of two couples battling jealousy and racial hatred amidst a war that would cripple America. From a prosperous Virginia plantation to a grim jail cell outside Lynchburg, follow the dramatic story of a love that could not be destroyed.

☞ *A Heart Divided*

Ryan McGraw—leader of the Confederate Sharpshooters—is nursed back to health by beautiful army nurse Dixie Quade. Their romance would survive the perils of war, but can it withstand the reappearance of a past love?

Books in the forthcoming Journeys of the Stranger series:

☞ *Legacy* (available April 1994)

Can John Stranger, a mysterious hero who brings truth, honor, and justice to the Old West, bring Clay Austin back to the right side of the law...and restore the code of honor shared by the woman he loves?

Available at your local Christian bookstore